Adobe Photoshop

2024 Release

Classroom in a Book®

The official training workbook from Adobe

Conrad Chavez

Cover Illustration: João Cunico, behance.net/joaocunico

Back cover: Arch image: Styve Reineck/Shutterstock

ISBN-13:   978-0-13-826252-5
ISBN-10:   0-13-826252-7

3 2024

WHERE ARE THE LESSON FILES?

Purchase of this Classroom in a Book in any format gives you access to the lesson files you'll need to complete the exercises in the book.

1 Go to peachpit.com/PhotoshopCIB2024.

2 Sign in or create a new account.

3 Click Submit.

Note: If you encounter problems registering your product or accessing the lesson files or web edition, go to peachpit.com/support for assistance.

4 Answer the questions as proof of purchase.

5 The lesson files can be accessed through the Registered Products tab on your Account page.

6 Click the Access Bonus Content link below the title of your product to proceed to the download page. Click the lesson file links to download them to your computer.

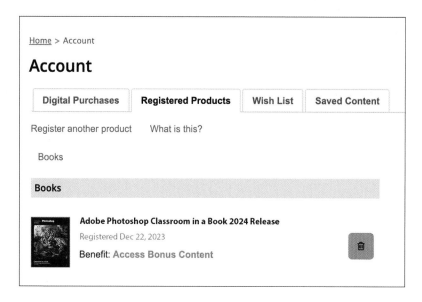

Note: If you purchased a digital product directly from peachpit.com, your product will already be registered. Look for the Access Bonus Content link on the Registered Products tab in your account.

CONTENTS

WHERE ARE THE LESSON FILES?   iii

GETTING STARTED   1

About Classroom in a Book.................................. 1

What's new in this edition.................................. 2

Prerequisites 2

Installing Adobe Photoshop, Adobe Bridge,
and Adobe Camera Raw 3

Installing fonts... 4

Starting Adobe Photoshop.................................. 4

Online content 4

Restoring default preferences 5

Additional resources 6

1 GETTING TO KNOW THE WORK AREA   8

Starting to work in Adobe Photoshop 10

Starting a new document 13

Adding an image 14

Touring the Photoshop work area 15

Using the tools 17

Combining elements using layers 22

Adding type 26

Adding a solid color layer 29

Painting a graphic element............................... 31

Undoing and redoing steps 34

Extending an image 36

2 BASIC PHOTO CORRECTIONS   **42**

Opening a file with Adobe Bridge 44

Evaluating an image for editing 46

Straightening and cropping the image 47

Correcting tone and color 51

Cleaning up with the Remove tool 53

Retouch a deleted area using Generative Fill 57

Sharpening the image 61

3 WORKING WITH SELECTIONS   **64**

About selecting and pixel selection tools 66

Getting started 67

Using cloud documents 67

Using the Magic Wand tool 70

Using the Quick Selection tool 71

Moving a selected area 72

Using the Object Selection tool 73

Manipulating selections 73

Selecting with the lasso tools 77

Rotating selected pixels 78

Selecting with the Magnetic Lasso tool 79

Selecting from a center point 80

Resizing and copying a selection 81

Cropping an image 86

4 LAYER BASICS   **88**

About layers 90

Getting started 90

Using the Layers panel 91

Rearranging layers 96

Applying a gradient to a layer 106

Applying a layer style 110

Adding an adjustment layer 114

Updating layer effects 116

Creating a border from a selection. 116

Flattening and saving files 118

5   QUICK FIXES   122

Getting started. 124

Improving a snapshot. 124

Adjusting facial features with Liquify 128

Blurring around a subject 130

Creating a panorama 134

Filling empty areas when cropping 138

Correcting image distortion. 141

Extending depth of field 144

Adjusting perspective in an image. 147

6   MASKS AND PATTERNS   154

Why masks are useful 156

Getting started 156

Using Select And Mask and Select Subject. 157

Manipulating an image with Puppet Warp. 168

Creating a pattern for the background. 170

7   TYPOGRAPHIC DESIGN   176

About type 178

Getting started 178

Creating a clipping mask from type. 179

Creating type on a path 185

Warping point type 188

Designing paragraphs of type. 190

Finishing up 193

8   VECTOR DRAWING TECHNIQUES   198

About bitmap images and vector graphics. 200

About paths and the Pen tool 201

Getting started with vector drawing. 201

Drawing a shape with the Pen tool 202

Drawing a path traced from a photo. 208

Converting a path to a selection and a layer mask..........212

Creating a logo with text and a custom shape 213

9 ADVANCED COMPOSITING   **222**

Getting started 224

Arranging layers 225

Using Smart Filters.......................................228

Painting a layer 234

Adding a background......................................236

Using the History panel to undo edits 237

Improving a low-resolution image.........................243

10 PAINTING WITH THE MIXER BRUSH   **246**

About the Mixer Brush 248

Getting started 248

Selecting brush settings 249

Mixing colors...252

Mixing colors with a photograph.........................255

Using brush presets to paint and mix colors 258

11 EDITING VIDEO   **266**

About video and animation in Photoshop 268

Using the Timeline panel.................................269

Getting started 270

Adding video 270

Adding audio...273

Changing clip durations in a video group.................274

Animating with keyframes 275

Adding transitions 279

Rendering the timeline as a finished video file 280

12 WORKING WITH CAMERA RAW   **286**

Getting started 288

About camera raw files...................................289

Processing files in Camera Raw...........................290

Retouching a portrait in Camera Raw.....................310

13 PREPARING FILES FOR THE WEB   **324**

Getting started 326

Creating placeholders with the Frame tool.................327

Using layer groups to create button graphics 332

Automating a multistep task 340

Designing with artboards 346

14 PRODUCING AND PRINTING CONSISTENT COLOR   **358**

Preparing files for printing 360

Getting started 361

Performing a "zoom test"..................................362

About color management...................................366

Setting up color management defaults 367

Identifying out-of-gamut colors 368

Proofing document colors on a monitor 369

Bringing colors into the output gamut.....................371

Converting an image to CMYK 373

Saving the image as Photoshop PDF.......................375

Printing to a desktop color printer.......................376

15 EXPLORING NEURAL FILTERS   **382**

Understanding Neural Filters..............................384

Getting started 384

Exploring the Neural Filters workspace 385

Restoring an antique portrait photo 386

Adding color and depth blur 387

Creating a more convincing composite 390

INDEX   **398**

GETTING STARTED

Adobe® Photoshop®, the benchmark for digital imaging excellence, provides professional image editing features enhanced by machine learning and cloud integration. Photoshop supports a wide range of workflows including print, web, and video. Photoshop gives you the digital editing tools you need to transform images more easily than ever before.

Photoshop works with other important tools that you'll use in this book. Adobe Camera Raw, included with Photoshop, helps you get the most quality out of camera raw images. Adobe Bridge is a digital asset manager that helps you browse and organize files you want to use with Photoshop and other Adobe Creative Cloud applications.

About Classroom in a Book

Adobe Photoshop Classroom in a Book® 2024 Release is part of the official training series for Adobe graphics and publishing software, developed with the support of Adobe product experts. The lessons are designed to let you learn at your own pace. If you're new to Adobe Photoshop, you'll learn the fundamental concepts and features you'll need to master the program. And if you've been using Adobe Photoshop for a while, you'll find that Classroom in a Book teaches many advanced features, including tips and techniques for using the latest version of the application and preparing images for the web.

Although each lesson provides step-by-step instructions for creating a specific project, there's room for exploration and experimentation. You can follow the book from start to finish or do only the lessons that match your interests.

What's new in this edition

This edition covers new features in Adobe Photoshop, such as the Remove tool, generative AI, and the Contextual Task Bar. This edition also covers the upgraded Gradients feature, adds coverage of frame animation, and includes many new and updated tips.

As in every edition, you'll learn best practices for organizing, managing, and showcasing your photos, as well as how to optimize images for print, web, and video.

Prerequisites

Before you begin to use *Adobe Photoshop Classroom in a Book 2024 Release*, you should have a working knowledge of your computer and its operating system. Make sure that you know how to use the mouse and standard menus and commands and how to open, save, and close files. If you need to review these techniques, see the documentation for your Microsoft® Windows® PC or Apple® Mac® computer.

● **Note:** The official version numbers of Adobe applications don't necessarily align with years because many existed before the year was part of the name. For example, Photoshop was released in 1990 as version 1, and the year did not appear in the name until Photoshop CC 2014, which is version 15.

To complete the lessons in this book, you'll need Adobe Photoshop 2024 Release and Adobe Bridge 2024 installed on your computer. The exact version number of the software is different than the year in the application name; this book was specifically tested using Photoshop version 25.0, Bridge version 14.0, and Camera Raw 16.0:

- To find the version of Photoshop that you are running, choose Help > System Info and look at the first line (Adobe Photoshop Version).
- To find the version of Bridge that you are running, choose Help > About Bridge (Windows) or Adobe Bridge > About Bridge (macOS) and look at the first line in the window that opens.
- To find the version of Camera Raw that you are running, look in the Camera Raw window title bar when Camera Raw is open.

If your versions of those applications are older, you may be able to get the versions matching this book by opening the Creative Cloud desktop application and clicking the Updates button. If newer versions don't appear in the Updates list, see if your computer meets the current system requirements because they may have changed.

If your versions are newer and don't match some of the steps in this book, you may be able to install a version matching this book; see "Installing a different version."

Installing Adobe Photoshop, Adobe Bridge, and Adobe Camera Raw

Before you begin using *Adobe Photoshop Classroom in a Book 2024 Release*, make sure that you've installed the required software. You must have an active license for Adobe Photoshop software, because it is not included with this book.

Note: For Windows, a 64-bit operating system is required. (All supported versions of macOS are already 64-bit.)

Your computer and its operating system software must meet Photoshop system requirements, which you can view at helpx.adobe.com/photoshop/system-requirements.html. In the system requirements, system memory (also called *random access memory* or *RAM*) is used by the operating system and applications. The graphics processing unit (GPU) needs its own memory (also called *graphics memory*, *video RAM*, or *VRAM*) for features such as GPU acceleration. If your computer has *discrete graphics* hardware (also called a *dedicated GPU* or *video card*), that hardware has a specific amount of its own graphics memory. If your computer has *integrated graphics* (more common, especially in laptop computers), it may not list a specific amount of graphics memory because system memory is shared with graphics hardware. Photoshop works with both discrete and integrated graphics.

Many of the lessons in this book use Adobe Bridge, and one lesson uses Adobe Camera Raw. You install Photoshop and Bridge on your computer using the Adobe Creative Cloud desktop application, available at adobe.com/creativecloud/desktop-app.html; follow the onscreen instructions. Adobe Camera Raw is automatically installed when you install Photoshop.

Installing a different version

If your version of Photoshop, Bridge, or Camera Raw is newer than those used in this edition of Classroom in a Book and works differently than in the lessons, you may be able to install a compatible version using the Creative Cloud desktop application:

Note: You can use the Creative Cloud desktop application to install the two most recent major versions of an application; for example, if the current version is 25, you can install version 25 or 24.

1 Start the Creative Cloud desktop application, and in the All Apps section, click the ... menu and choose Other Versions.

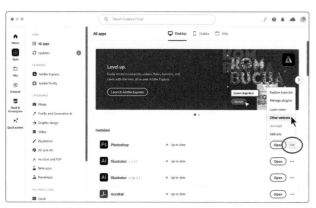

2　Find the versions of the software listed in "Prerequisites," and click Install for each of those versions.

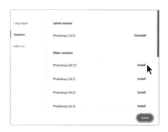

Adobe Camera Raw is not in the list because it's updated automatically. To install an older version of Camera Raw, download its installer from:

helpx.adobe.com/camera-raw/kb/camera-raw-plug-in-installer.html

Installing fonts

Some lessons in this book may suggest specific fonts. If a suggested font is not installed on your computer, you may be able to sync it to your computer using Adobe Fonts, which is part of a personal Creative Cloud subscription. (Adobe Fonts might not be included in some educational or organizational subscriptions.) To activate a font from Adobe Fonts and sync it to your computer while in Photoshop, choose Type > More from Adobe Fonts and follow the directions.

Starting Adobe Photoshop

You start Photoshop just as you do most software applications.

To start Adobe Photoshop in Windows: Click the Start button in the taskbar, and in the alphabetical list under A, click Adobe Photoshop 2024.

To start Adobe Photoshop on a Mac: Click the Adobe Photoshop 2024 icon in the Launchpad or Dock.

If you don't see Adobe Photoshop, type **Photoshop** into the search box in the taskbar (Windows) or in Spotlight search (macOS), and when the Adobe Photoshop 2024 application icon appears, select it, and press Enter or Return.

Online content

Your purchase of this Classroom in a Book includes the following online materials provided on your Account page on peachpit.com/adobepress.

Lesson files

To work through the projects in this book, you will need to download the lesson files by following the instructions on the next page.

Web Edition

The Web Edition is an online interactive version of the book providing an enhanced learning experience. Your Web Edition can be accessed from any device with a connection to the Internet, and it contains:

* The complete text of the book

* Hours of instructional video keyed to the text

* Interactive quizzes

Accessing the lesson files and Web Edition

You must register your purchase on peachpit.com to access the online content:

1 Go to peachpit.com/PhotoshopCIB2024.

2 Sign in or create a new account.

3 Click Submit.

4 Answer the question as proof of purchase.

5 The lesson files can be accessed from the Registered Products tab on your Account page. Click the Access Bonus Content link below the title of your product to proceed to the download page. Click the lesson file link(s) to download them to your computer.

The Web Edition can be accessed from the Digital Purchases tab on your Account page. Click the Launch link to access the product.

● **Note:** If you purchased a digital product directly from peachpit.com/ adobepress, your product will already be registered. Look for the Access Bonus Content link on the Registered Products tab in your account.

Restoring default preferences

Like many applications, Adobe Photoshop stores various general settings in a document called a *preferences file*. Each time you quit Photoshop, certain workspace settings (such as the last-used options for some tools and commands) are recorded in the preferences file. Any changes you make in the Preferences dialog box are also saved in the preferences file.

To ensure that what you see onscreen matches the images and instructions in this book, you should restore the default preferences as described at the beginning of each lesson. If you choose to not reset your preferences, be aware that the tools, panels, and other settings in Photoshop may not match those described in this book.

If you have changed the settings in the Edit > Color Settings dialog box, those settings are saved in a different location than the Preferences file, so use the following procedure to save them as a preset before you start work using this book. When you want to restore your color settings, you can simply select the preset you created.

▶ **Tip:** Color Settings can affect whether you see color profile alert messages when you open a document or paste content in Photoshop. One clue that color settings were altered is that profile alerts appear when they previously didn't, or they no longer appear when they used to.

To save your current color settings:

1 Start Adobe Photoshop.

2 Choose Edit > Color Settings.

3 Note what is selected in the Settings menu:

- If it is anything other than Custom, write down the name of the settings file, and click OK to close the dialog box. You do not need to perform steps 4–6 of this procedure.

- If Custom is selected in the Settings menu, click Save (*not* OK).

The Save dialog box opens. The default location is the Settings folder, which is where you want to save your file. The default filename extension is .csf (color settings file).

4 In the File Name field (Windows) or Save As field (macOS), type a descriptive name for your color settings, preserving the .csf file extension. Then click Save.

5 In the Color Settings Comment dialog box, type any descriptive text that will help you identify the color settings later, such as the date, specific settings, or your workgroup.

6 Click OK to close the Color Settings Comment dialog box, and again to close the Color Settings dialog box.

To restore your color settings:

1 Start Adobe Photoshop.

2 Choose Edit > Color Settings.

3 From the Settings menu in the Color Settings dialog box, choose the settings file you noted or saved in the previous procedure, and click OK.

Additional resources

Adobe Photoshop Classroom in a Book 2024 Release is not meant to replace documentation that comes with the program or to be a comprehensive reference for every feature. Only the commands and options used in the lessons are explained in this book. For comprehensive information about program features and tutorials, refer to these resources:

▶ **Tip:** If you find that the Discover panel (Edit > Search) is useful, consider memorizing its keyboard shortcut in Photoshop: Press Ctrl+F (Windows) or Command+F (macOS). To close the panel, press the shortcut again.

Home screen: In Photoshop, the Learn section of the Home screen offers tutorials.

Search command: Choose Edit > Search to open the Discover panel, which offers a wealth of tutorials, suggestions, and links before you even enter a search term. If you enter a term (such as **crop**) and press Enter or Return, the Discover panel can highlight relevant Photoshop tools and commands for you and provides links to more information.

Adobe Photoshop Help and Support: Choose Help > Photoshop Help to open the Discover panel with a list of online help resources including the User Guide and Support Community. You can also use your web browser to go to helpx.adobe.com/support/photoshop.html to find Help and Support content on Adobe.com.

Photoshop tutorials: Choose Help > Hands-On Tutorials to open the Discover panel with a list of guided lessons. Follow along in Photoshop with the provided sample documents. To find more tutorials online, go to helpx.adobe.com/photoshop/tutorials.html.

Photoshop blog: blog.adobe.com/en/topics/photoshop brings you tutorials, product news, and inspirational articles about using Photoshop.

Julieanne Kost's blog: jkost.com/blog/ is where veteran Adobe product evangelist Julieanne Kost posts useful tips and videos that introduce and provide valuable insights on the latest Photoshop features.

Adobe Support Community: community.adobe.com lets you tap into user forums where you can ask questions about Photoshop and other Adobe applications.

Adobe Photoshop product home page: Find product information at adobe.com/products/photoshop.html.

Plug-ins menu: To find add-on "plug-in" software modules to extend and add features to your Creative Cloud tools, in Photoshop choose Plugins > Browse Plugins.

Creative Cloud desktop application: Click Discover to see tutorials, online streaming video, inspirational examples of creative work, and other links and resources for Photoshop and other Adobe applications you have installed.

▶ **Tip:** You'll see the same Creative Cloud learning resources (and access to your work stored on Creative Cloud servers) when you use the Creative Cloud mobile app or when you're signed into creative.adobe.com.

Resources for educators: adobe.com/education and edex.adobe.com offer a treasure trove of information for instructors who teach classes on Adobe software. Find solutions for education at all levels, including free curricula that use an integrated approach to teaching Adobe software and can be used to prepare for the Adobe Certified Associate exams.

Adobe training partners

Adobe training partners offer instructor-led courses for Adobe software. A directory of Adobe training partners is available at trainingpartners.adobe.com.

1 GETTING TO KNOW THE WORK AREA

Lesson overview

In this lesson, you'll learn how to do the following:

- Open image files in Adobe Photoshop.

- Select and use tools in the Tools panel.

- Set options for a selected tool using the options bar.

- Use various methods to zoom in to and out from an image.

- Select, rearrange, and use panels.

- Choose commands in panel and context menus.

- Open and use a panel in the panel dock.

- Undo actions to correct mistakes or to make different choices.

 This lesson will take about an hour to complete. To get the lesson files used in this chapter, download them from the web page for this book at peachpit.com/PhotoshopCIB2024. For more information, see "Accessing the lesson files and Web Edition" in the Getting Started section at the beginning of this book.

PROJECT: HISTORY COURSE PROMOTIONAL IMAGE

As you work with Adobe Photoshop, you'll discover that you can often accomplish the same task in several ways. To make the best use of the extensive editing capabilities in Photoshop, you must first learn to navigate the work area.

Starting to work in Adobe Photoshop

The Adobe Photoshop work area includes menus, toolbars, and panels that give you quick access to tools and options for editing and adding elements to your image.

In Photoshop, you primarily work with bitmapped digital images: continuous-tone images that have been converted into a series of small squares, or picture elements, called *pixels*. You can also work with *vector graphics*, which are drawings made of smooth lines that retain their crispness when scaled. And you can add text, which is a form of vector graphics. You can create original artwork in Photoshop, or you can import and combine images from many sources, such as:

- Photographs from a digital camera or mobile phone
- Stock photography, such as images from the Adobe Stock service
- Scans of photographs, transparencies, negatives, graphics, or other documents
- Digital video clips
- Artwork created in drawing or painting programs

You'll learn about type in more detail in Lesson 7, and you'll learn about vector graphics in Lesson 8.

Starting Photoshop

● **Note:** Typically, you won't need to reset defaults when you're working on your own projects. However, you'll reset the preferences before working on most lessons in this book to ensure that what you see onscreen matches the descriptions in the lessons. For more information, see "Restoring default preferences" on page 5.

To begin, you'll start Adobe Photoshop and reset the default preferences.

1 Click the Adobe Photoshop 2024 icon in your Start menu (Windows) or the Launchpad or Dock (macOS), and then simultaneously hold down Ctrl+Alt+Shift (Windows) or Command+Option+Shift (macOS) to reset the default settings.

If you don't see Adobe Photoshop 2024, type **Photoshop** into the search box in the taskbar (Windows) or in Spotlight (macOS), and when the Adobe Photoshop 2024 application icon appears, select it, and press Enter or Return.

2 When prompted, click Yes to confirm that you want to delete the Adobe Photoshop Settings file.

Using the Home screen

After starting Photoshop, the first thing you see is the Home screen, which gives you a number of ways to get started, as shown in the following illustration.

A. Switch to Photoshop workspace
B. Create new document
C. Open document
D. Home screen content and recently opened local documents
E. Learn with tutorials
F. Cloud Documents you created on Windows, macOS, or iPad
G. Cloud Documents shared with you
H. Your photos in the Lightroom cloud
I. Deleted Cloud Documents
J. Cloud storage sync status
K. Search, Help, and Learn
L. What's New in Photoshop
M. Visit your Creative Cloud account in a web browser

On the left you see a list of view options:

- **Home** helps you use and learn about the current version and includes a tour. After you open at least one local or cloud document, a Recent section of previously opened documents appears at the bottom of the Home screen.

- **Learn** presents links to tutorials that open in Photoshop, where the Learn panel leads you through a lesson's steps that you follow using Photoshop itself.

- **Your Files** lists Photoshop Cloud Documents, including those you created on devices such as an iPad. You'll learn more about Cloud Documents in Lesson 3, "Working with Selections." Your Files does not list documents stored locally.

- **Shared with You** lists Cloud Documents that others have invited you to see by using the File > Invite command.

- **Lightroom Photos** lists images synced to your Creative Cloud account's Lightroom online storage. This does not include Lightroom Classic local storage.

- **Deleted** lists Cloud Documents you've deleted, in case you change your mind and want to recover them (similar to the Recycle Bin or Trash on your computer desktop). This list includes Cloud Documents only, not files you deleted from Lightroom Photos or from your computer's local storage.

Tip: To skip past the Home screen and go straight to the Photoshop application workspace, click the Photoshop icon in the upper-left corner.

Tip: To manage files in the Deleted list, click the ellipsis (…) button next to a file, and choose Restore or Permanently Delete.

Tip: If you want to change how dark or light the Photoshop workspace appears, open the Preferences dialog box, select the Interface panel, and select a different Color Theme.

When you click the Search icon in the upper-right corner and enter text, Photoshop looks for matching content in the Learn tutorials about Photoshop and in Adobe Stock images. When a document is open, the Search icon can find specific commands and tools in Photoshop. In the Home screen, the Search icon can find content in your cloud-synced Lightroom images; for example, enter **bird** to find your Lightroom cloud photos that contain birds.

The Home screen automatically hides when you open a document, which is what you're going to do next. You can return to the Home screen by clicking the Home icon in the upper-left corner of the application window.

Open a document

You'll use the traditional Open command to view a Photoshop document.

Tip: If you drag and drop a compatible file anywhere on the Home screen, Photoshop will open it.

1 Choose File > Open. If a dialog box appears that says Open from Creative Cloud at the top, click On Your Computer at the bottom of the dialog box.

2 Navigate to the Lessons/Lesson01 folder that you copied to your hard drive from the peachpit.com website. (If you haven't downloaded the files, see "Accessing the lesson files and Web Edition" on page 4.)

3 Select the 01End.psd file, and click Open. Click OK if the Embedded Profile Mismatch dialog box appears, and click No if a message about updating text layers appears.

The 01End.psd file opens in its own window, in the default Photoshop workspace. You'll learn more about the workspace later in this lesson.

The end files in this book show you what you are creating in each project. In this project, you'll create a preview image for a streaming video presentation. If you want, you can leave this file open to refer to, because you're about to build it.

4 If you don't want to leave the file open, choose File > Close. Do not close Photoshop, and don't save changes to the document.

Starting a new document

You'll begin by creating the document you'll work on in this lesson. How you start a document depends on the final delivery requirements of your project. For example, a document that will be printed usually has different requirements for color and resolution than a document that will be posted to a website or included in a video.

This document will promote a streaming video presentation on web pages, in streaming video applications, and on TV screens. It needs to be about the same size and shape as an HDTV video frame. You'll design it at HDTV pixel dimensions (1920 pixels wide by 1080 pixels tall). It can later be scaled down to the smaller sizes used for video preview thumbnails on web pages and video apps.

Fortunately, Photoshop offers new document presets that help you more quickly create a new document for common image sizes.

1 Choose File > New. (You can also click the New File button on the Home screen.)

2 In the New Document dialog box, click Film & Video.

Although you aren't creating a video in this lesson, the Film & Video presets give you a head start in creating a document at the appropriate pixel dimensions and frame aspect ratio (proportions) for common document types.

When you click a New Document preset, the settings change in the Preset Details panel on the right. In this way you can inspect the settings used by any preset, and you can customize the New Document settings.

▶ **Tip:** What do you do if you're not sure if the final document will be printed or displayed on screen? Create a high-resolution, full-color source document from which you can derive copies optimized for different media.

▶ **Tip:** You don't have to start by selecting a preset. Instead, you can enter the settings you want in the Preset Details options.

▶ **Tip:** If you frequently enter the same custom settings, you can save them as your own New Document preset. In the first row under Preset Details, name your preset and click the Save button (⬇) next to the name.

A. Preset categories   **B.** HDTV 1080p preset   **C.** Presets in current category   **D.** Preset Details

3 Click the preset HDTV 1080p, and then click Create.

Photoshop creates a new, blank, untitled document. It also includes guides, displayed in cyan. For this New Document preset, the guides are intended to help remind you to keep important video content away from frame edges, because some TVs (typically older ones) slightly crop the image. In your own projects, you can add guides to help align items in a design; you'll do this in later lessons.

4   Choose File > Save As, name the file **01Working.psd**, and click OK or Save.

Adding an image

With the new document created, you can now start adding to it. You'll import an image that will be the basis of the design.

▶ **Tip:** You can also add an image using drag-and-drop: Drag it from the desktop or another application, and drop it inside a Photoshop document window. This is the same as using the Place Embedded command.

1   Choose File > Place Embedded, and in the Lesson01 folder, select the file Arch.jpg and click Place.

The image appears on the canvas, a bounding box with handles appears around the image, and the image was added as a new layer in the Layers panel. (You'll learn more about layers in Lesson 4.) Adding the image is not complete as long as the bounding box is active. Its handles give you an opportunity to *transform* (move, resize, or rotate) the image as you import it, and in this case, you want to take advantage of that right now and then finish the import.

▶ **Tip:** The Place Embedded command copies the imported file into the Photoshop document. The Place Linked command adds the imported file as a placeholder linked to the external file, instead of copying the entire file into the Photoshop document, so that the document file size doesn't grow as much. Place Linked is similar to how web pages, page layout, and video editing applications add external graphics by linking to them.

2   Drag any handle on the bounding box so that the image covers the entire width of the canvas and so that the building is centered vertically within the canvas. You can also reposition the image by dragging anywhere within it.

Notice that parts of the layer that extend beyond the canvas are not visible, but the bounding box handles indicate that those parts still exist. If you reposition or scale down the layer, areas beyond the canvas can become visible again.

3 In the options bar, click the check mark button (✔) to finish (commit) adding the image. The bounding box disappears.

● **Note:** Committing changes by pressing Enter or Return doesn't work when there's an active text cursor on a text layer so that Enter and Return can type a paragraph break character. Instead, commit type changes by clicking the check mark in the options bar or by clicking the canvas away from the type layer.

Some features in Photoshop happen in a special mode, such as the transformation bounding box you just used. Committing your changes exits that mode and returns you to the general Photoshop feature set. If you get tired of moving the mouse up to the options bar to click that check mark button, you can also commit changes by pressing the Enter or Return key.

Touring the Photoshop work area

As you work in Photoshop, you'll often have two kinds of questions:

- What is the state of the document or the selected item? (For example, what is the view magnification of the document? Or what is the font size of selected text?)

- What are the options for editing the document or selected item?

The following parts of the Photoshop workspace answer those questions:

Tools panel. This panel provides tools for creating and editing document elements.

Options bar. This panel offers options that customize the selected tool, so the options bar changes depending on which tool is selected in the Tools panel.

Document tab. When documents are open, one or more document windows also appear, which you can identify by the tabs across the top of the document window, similar to a web browser. The text in the tab displays information that can include the filename, magnification level, selected layer, and bit depth per channel.

Panels. Panels contain options for various tasks, objects, and attributes. For example, the Layers panel lists document layers and indicates which one is selected, and the Swatches panel lists color swatches that you can create, organize, and apply.

Properties panel. This panel offers options for the selected element and can contain categories that consolidate options offered by multiple panels. For example, when a type layer is selected, the Properties panel can display Transform, Character, and Paragraph options at the same time, so instead of looking at the options bar and two other panels, you can simply look in the Properties panel. When nothing is selected, the Properties panel displays options for the entire document.

Contextual Task Bar. Suggests features to use with the selection. The Contextual Task Bar changes depending on what's selected and can help you become aware of options that are normally out of view in menu commands or panels.

▶ **Tip:** The options bar, Properties panel, and Contextual Task Bar may seem similar but are different in important ways. The options bar is only about the selected tool, the Properties panel is about the selected layer(s), and the Contextual Task Bar also offers to help perform tasks for the selected layer.

▶ **Tip:** If you see an asterisk (*) at the end of a document tab, the current document state is not saved. After you save the document, the asterisk disappears.

Document Status Bar. This displays information about the document. You can change what information it displays by clicking the arrow next to it. By default, the document Status Bar displays the document dimensions and resolution.

Search, Help, and Learn. This lets you enter a search term, which brings you a list of tools, commands, and tutorials. It's great for learning more about Photoshop or finding out where to find a tool or feature.

Workspaces menu. This menu offers different preset arrangements of panels.

Components such as the options bar, Properties panel, and Contextual Task Bar are constantly useful to refer to, so it's recommended that you keep them visible.

The Photoshop workspace is similar to those in Adobe Illustrator® and Adobe InDesign®, so learning how to use the tools and panels in one application makes it easier to learn and use the other applications. As in other applications, Photoshop features are distributed among tools, menu commands, and panels.

Each lesson will introduce you to more Photoshop features so that you can build a solid foundation for exploring other parts of Photoshop on your own.

● **Note:** This illustration shows the macOS version of Photoshop. The arrangement is similar in Windows, but operating system styles may vary.

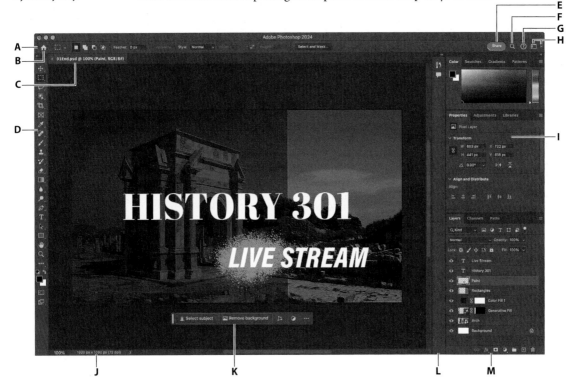

A. Options bar	**E.** Share button (for online review)	**J.** Document Status Bar
B. Switch to Home screen	**F.** Search, Help, and Learn	**K.** Contextual Task Bar
C. Document tab	**G.** Tutorials	**L.** Panel stack collapsed
D. Tools panel	**H.** Workspaces menu	**M.** Panel stack expanded
	I. Properties panel	

Getting information and finding tools and options

There are so many tools, panels, and commands in Photoshop that it can be a challenge to get information about a selection or to find the options you need. To make Photoshop easier to use, keep the right information visible and know where to look.

Essential panels. If you work on a smaller screen and need to close panels to free up space to work, try to keep open the Layers panel, the options bar, the Properties panel, and the Contextual Task Bar. Together, they show you much of what you need to know most of the time and make it less necessary to open additional panels. You can show or hide any panel using the Window menu.

All in one: The Properties panel. We recommend keeping the Properties panel visible because it gives you information about the currently selected layer (such as layer dimensions or the currently applied font) and consolidates editing options so that you can leave many other panels closed. For example, for a type layer, it shows layer dimensions, paragraph options, and character options in one place.

For more information: The Info panel. For some workflows, the Info panel (Window > Info) is useful to keep visible. It displays information such as the color values under the pointer and the dimensions of a marquee selection, and if you customize it, it can be another place to monitor information displayed in the Status Bar. (The Status Bar can display only one type of information at a time.)

Just a click away. Menu commands can be inconvenient if you have to move the pointer a long way to reach them, especially on a large display. Remember that right-clicking (Windows) or Control-clicking (macOS) pops up a contextual menu under the pointer, typically listing commands useful for the item under the pointer.

If you think a feature exists but you can't find it in any of the panels or on the menus, choose Edit > Search.

▶ **Tip:** In macOS, you can enable right-click in System Settings > Mouse options. If you're using a trackpad, the Trackpad options provide more ways to open a context menu; look in the Secondary Click options for settings such as two-finger tap or bottom-right corner tap.

Using the tools

Photoshop tools are available in the Tools panel, the narrow strip along the left side of the application window. Generally, you select a tool when you want to create or edit by interacting directly with the image (by clicking and dragging the pointer). You'll start by using the Zoom tool. If you haven't already used a similar tool in other applications, the Zoom tool lets you change the view magnification interactively. But before you do that, you'll first find out the current magnification.

Tip: The zoom percentage also appears in the document tab.

1 Examine the Status Bar near the bottom-left corner at the bottom of the document window, and notice the percentage displayed in the box to the left of the Status Bar. This represents the current view magnification, or zoom level.

Zoom level   Status Bar

100%   1920 px x 1080 px (72 ppi)

Tip: If the bottom of the Tools panel is cut off by the bottom of your screen, click the double arrows at the top of the Tools panel to display it as two shorter columns.

Now you'll select a tool.

2 Move the pointer over the Tools panel, and hover it (hold without clicking) over the magnifying-glass icon until a tool tip appears. The tool tip displays the tool's name (Zoom tool), keyboard shortcut (Z), a Learn More link, and a button that plays a short tutorial video.

Zoom tool [Z]

Zoom in and out on an image. Learn more

Watch quick video

3 Click the Zoom tool icon (Q) in the Tools panel to select it.

Tip: To select the Zoom tool using a keyboard shortcut, press the Z key. Tool shortcuts are single keys (do not press modifier keys such as Ctrl or Command). If a tool has a keyboard shortcut, you'll see it in the pop-up tool tip.

4 Move the pointer over the document window. The pointer now looks like a tiny magnifying glass with a plus sign in the center of the glass (⊕).

5 Click anywhere in the document window.

Each time you click, the Zoom tool magnifies by another level. If you want to know the current magnification percentage, look at the Status Bar or document tab.

6 Hold down the Alt key (Windows) or Option key (macOS) so that the Zoom tool pointer appears with a minus sign in the center of the magnifying glass (⊖), and then click anywhere in the image. Then release the Alt or Option key.

Now the view zooms out to a lower preset increment so you can see more of the image but in less detail. You can also drag the Zoom tool.

About view magnifications

How do you know if an image is at the correct size for web pages, video, and print? The answer is different depending on the final delivery medium.

What 100% zoom percentage means. At 100% magnification in Photoshop, each image pixel is shown on one screen pixel, providing an accurate view of the image at the pixel level. However, 100% magnification does not represent how large the image will be reproduced when printed, because 100% isn't related to print resolution. How large 100% looks varies across displays with different DPI resolutions.

Previewing size for a web page or video frame. To preview image dimensions for on-screen media, first try 100% magnification. If 100% magnification in Photoshop displays an image at half the width and height that it appears in a web browser, your computer is probably using an HiDPI (Windows) or Retina (macOS) display. On these displays, try viewing web graphics in Photoshop at 200% magnification to match the size displayed in a web browser.

This happens because Retina/HiDPI displays typically have twice (2x) the pixel density (in dots per inch, or DPI) of older 1x displays, so pixels on those displays are half as wide and tall as on 1x displays. If a website is not specifically coded to handle images at 2x resolution on HiDPI/Retina displays, web browsers typically apply 2x scaling to graphics to keep them from looking half as large as they should.

Previewing printed dimensions. To show an image on screen at the size that it will print, choose the View > Actual Size command. Actual Size detects the DPI resolution of the display, using that and the document resolution (in pixels per inch, or PPI) to calculate its print size in inches or centimeters.

Print Size. Although the View > Print Size command sounds like it should preview print dimensions, it's an older command that doesn't detect the resolution of the display. It can still be useful for previewing for arbitrary resolutions, but manually setting it up to do that is outside the scope of this book.

● **Note:** Don't use the Actual Size command to preview image dimensions for a web page or mobile app. Actual Size is designed to calculate print dimensions only.

● **Note:** You'll learn more about the difference between dots per inch (DPI) and pixels per inch (PPI) in Lesson 2.

7 Position the pointer anywhere on the canvas, and drag the Zoom tool to the right. The image enlarges from where you started dragging. Drag the Zoom tool to the left to zoom out.

This continuous magnification is called Scrubby Zoom and happens when the Scrubby Zoom setting is enabled in the options bar for the Zoom tool. When the setting is disabled, dragging the Zoom tool first creates a rectangle that indicates the canvas area that will fill the document window.

● **Note:** In this book, any time a step tells you to *drag*, hold down the mouse button as you move the pointer. When you move the pointer without pressing the mouse button, that simply repositions the pointer on the screen.

8 Click Fit Screen in the options bar to see the entire image again.

▶ Tip: On the View menu you can choose common magnification levels and the Zoom In, Zoom Out, and Fit on Screen commands.

As you work through the lessons in this book, feel free to use any combination of the different ways you changed magnification with the Zoom tool, such as clicking, holding down a modifier key while clicking, dragging left or right, and clicking a button in the options bar. You can also zoom using gestures, such as dragging the Zoom tool or pinching with two fingers on a trackpad, and you can enter a magnification percentage in the Status Bar. You also learned how to customize how a tool works by using options bar settings and modifier keys.

Zooming and scrolling with the Navigator panel

The Navigator panel (choose Window > Navigator to open it) is another speedy way to make large changes in the zoom level, especially when the exact percentage of magnification is unimportant. It's also a great way to inspect a magnified image, because the thumbnail shows you exactly what part of the image appears in the document window.

The slider under the image thumbnail in the Navigator panel enlarges the image when you drag to the right (toward the large mountain icon) and reduces it when you drag to the left.

The red rectangular outline represents the area of the image that appears in the document window. When you zoom in far enough that the document window shows only part of the image, you can drag the red outline around the thumbnail area to see other areas of the image. This is also an excellent way to verify which part of an image you're working on when you work at very high zoom levels.

Using the Tools panel

Tools are central to Photoshop, so you'll benefit from using the Tools panel efficiently.

Two-column mode. If the Tools panel is too tall for your display, click the double arrows at the top of the Tools panel to switch it to two-column mode.

Single-key shortcuts. Most tools have a single-key shortcut. For example, you can switch to the Move tool by pressing the V key. Note that single-key shortcuts don't work when you're entering text.

Identifying tools. If you see a tool and want to know its name and single-key shortcut, hover the pointer over it in the Tools panel.

Hidden tools. To save space on your screen, some visible tools hide other tools under them. If hidden tools exist under a visible tool, you see a small triangle in the lower-right corner of a tool space. To select a hidden tool, hold down the mouse button on the visible tool, and in the tool menu that pops out, select the tool you want. That tool becomes the visible tool. There are also two shortcuts for cycling through hidden tools:

- Alt-click (Windows) or Option-click (Mac) the visible tool until the tool you want becomes the visible tool.

- Add the Shift key to the single-key shortcut. For example, to cycle through the lasso selection tools, press Shift-L repeatedly.

Customizable. If you want to arrange the tools differently, hold down the mouse button on the Tools panel ellipsis button (•••) and choose Edit Toolbar.

Include a custom toolbar in a saved workspace. If you create a custom workspace (see "About workspaces" on page 31), one option is to include the Toolbar. For example, in Lesson 10 you switch to the Painting workspace, which changes the Tools panel to put all the brush tools up front, hiding others. When you switch back to the Essentials (Default) workspace, the default Tools panel returns.

Combining elements using layers

There are more elements to add to this project. Next you'll create the colored rectangles. You'll start by creating a new pixel layer for the rectangle.

Creating a new layer

● **Note:** If no layers are selected in the Layers panel, a new layer appears at the top of the layer stack.

Although you could create the colored rectangles directly on the Arch layer, that would permanently replace some of its original pixels. Instead, you'll add the rectangles on a separate layer so you can edit them without altering the Arch layer. For the orange rectangle, you want its layer to be visible in front of the Arch layer. A new layer is added in front of the selected layer, so first you'll select the Arch layer.

1 In the Layers panel, click the Arch layer to select it.

2 In the Layers panel, click the Create a New Layer button (⊞).

3 In the Layers panel, double-click the layer name, change it to **Rectangles**, and press Enter or Return.

The new layer is now ready for you to fill with color. But first, make sure you're working in the correct unit of measure.

A. Layer name   *B. Create a New Layer*

Setting the unit of measure

▶ **Tip:** When rulers are displayed (View > Rulers), you can change the unit of measure by right-clicking (Windows) or Control-clicking (macOS) a ruler.

You can change the unit of measure you use to work in Photoshop. This graphic will be displayed on screens, so you'll work in pixels.

1 Choose Edit > Preferences > Units & Rulers (Windows) or Photoshop > Settings > Units & Rulers (macOS).

2 In the Rulers menu under Units, make sure Pixels is selected, and click OK.

● **Note:** In macOS 12 or earlier, the Settings command is called Preferences.

▶ **Tip:** If you can't remember where to find a preference setting, look for it using the Search Preferences field in the upper-right corner of the Preferences dialog box, in the title bar.

Selecting pixels

The 01End file shows that the orange rectangle covers only a narrow vertical strip along the left edge of the canvas. How will you restrict the color to that area? You'll mark pixels for editing by creating a *selection*. This selection will be a simple rectangle. You'll learn how to quickly create more complex selections (such as outlines of people) in Lessons 2, 3, and 6.

1 In the Tools panel, click the Rectangular Marquee tool to select it.

2 Position the pointer just beyond the upper-left corner of the canvas, and then drag it down and to the right to create a dashed line selection marquee; release the mouse button when the rectangular marquee snaps to the bottom of the canvas and the first vertical cyan guide. At that point, the indicator next to the pointer should report a width (W) of 96 pixels and a height (H) of 1080 pixels.

▶ **Tip:** If you hover the pointer over the Rectangular Marquee tool, a tool tip offers a Learn More link, and a button plays a short tutorial video.

A selection can exist only within the canvas, so even though you may have started dragging outside the canvas edges, the final selection is within the canvas edges.

▶ **Tip:** If you want to know the dimensions of a selection after releasing the mouse button, open the Info panel (Window > Info), which displays width (W) and height (H) values for the current selection.

Fill a selection with color

Now you'll complete the rectangle by applying a color fill to the selection.

1 In the Layers panel, make sure the Rectangles layer is selected so that the color you're about to create will be applied to that layer.

2 In the Contextual Task Bar, click the Fill Selection button, and choose Fill Color.

The Fill Selection button is a shortcut for the Edit > Fill command.

3 Create an orange color. We used the hexadecimal (hex) RGB value **ff7f00**, which you can enter into the # field near the bottom of the Color Picker dialog box. Hex color values are commonly used for web and mobile design.

4 Click OK to close the Color Picker dialog box, and then click OK to close the Fill dialog box. The orange color fills the rectangular selection.

▶ **Tip:** If the selected pixels already had color, pressing the Delete key would remove the color.

5 Choose Select > Deselect, because you no longer need the selection. The selection marquee disappears.

Create the blue rectangle

You'll create the blue rectangle the same way, with different pixel dimensions.

1 With the Rectangular Marquee tool, position the pointer just beyond the upper-right corner of the canvas, and then drag it down and to the left; release the mouse button when the transformation values next to the pointer report a width (W) of 660 pixels and a height (H) of 1080 pixels.

This time you'll open the Fill command using the actual menu command.

2 With the selection active and the Rectangles layer selected, choose Edit > Fill.

3 Click the Contents menu and choose Color, and then create a vivid blue color. We used the hexadecimal RGB value **0053b2**.

4 Click OK to close the Color Picker dialog box, and then click OK to close the Fill dialog box. The blue color fills the rectangular selection.

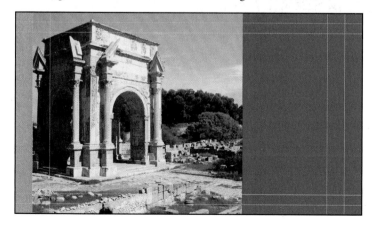

> **Tip:** If the selected pixels already had color, pressing the Delete key would remove the color.

5 Choose Select > Deselect, and choose File > Save. Click OK in the Photoshop Format Options dialog box.

In the 01End file, you'll notice that the colors are not solid; the image shows through them. *Blending modes* are used to control how colors in the Rectangles layer combine with colors in underlying layers.

Note: A layer's blending mode is separate from its opacity value, which you see next to the blending mode menu in the Layers panel. You can apply one or both.

6   In the Layers panel, make sure the Rectangles layer is selected, and choose Color from the blending modes menu.

The Color blending mode combines the hue and saturation values of the Rectangles layer with the luminance of the layers under it. You'll learn more about blending modes in Lesson 4. Feel free to try other blending modes.

Adding type

You'll need to add two lines of type to this graphic. Photoshop offers high-quality typographic tools; you'll learn more about them in Lesson 7. Type exists on its own layer. You'll set up the type specifications for the first type layer you'll add.

Note: If a lesson in this book uses a font that isn't installed on your system, you may be able to install it from Adobe Fonts as part of your Creative Cloud subscription: In Photoshop, choose Type > More from Adobe Fonts. (Some educational or organizational Creative Cloud plans might not include Adobe Fonts.)

1   In the Tools panel, select the Horizontal Type tool (**T**).

The buttons and menus in the options bar now relate to the Type tool.

2   In the options bar, select a font from the first pop-up menu. We used Abril Fatface, which is available from Adobe Fonts, but you can select a different font.

3   Specify **210 pt** for the font size.

Font   Style   Size   Left align text   Color
                                      Center text   swatch
                                      Right align text

You can specify 210 points by typing directly in the font-size text box and pressing Enter or Return or by *scrubbing* the font-size menu label (see the tip in the margin). Scrubbing works with most labels for values in Photoshop panels. You can make the value change faster by holding down the Shift key as you drag.

Tip: To scrub a value, position the pointer over its label and drag horizontally.

4 In the options bar, click the Center Text button.

5 In the options bar, click the color swatch, specify solid white, and click OK.

6 Click the Horizontal Type tool slightly below the center of the canvas.

Tip: You can also change font size in the Character panel, and in the Contextual Task Bar when a type layer is selected.

Tip: If you want to select just some of the text in a layer, drag the Horizontal Type tool over a range of characters.

A new type layer appears both on the canvas and in the Layers panel, with "Lorem Ipsum…" placeholder text selected so that you can preview the current settings. In the 01End file, this text is all capital letters, but instead of typing it that way, you can apply a type option.

7 If the Properties panel is not visible, click its tab or choose Window > Properties, scroll it down to the Type Options section, and click the first option, All Caps.

8 With the type still selected, type **History 301**. Because you applied the All Caps option, you don't need to use the Shift or Caps Lock keys.

Tip: The Properties panel shows type options because a type layer is selected in the Layers panel. You can also apply detailed type settings using the Character panel (Window > Character) and the Paragraph panel (Window > Paragraph).

9 In the options bar, click the check mark button (✔) to commit editing the text.

▶ **Tip:** As you drag the Move tool, magenta lines called *Smart Guides* may appear. They help align the edges and centers of dragged content to other objects and guides. If they are getting in your way, you can disable them by deselecting the View > Show > Smart Guides command or by holding down the Control key as you drag.

10 If the type layer is not centered properly, drag it with the Move tool to center it.

Now add the other line of text.

11 Choose Select > Deselect Layers so that the options you set next don't affect the existing type layer.

12 Make sure the Horizontal Type tool is selected, and then in the options bar, select a font. We used Acumin Pro Condensed Black Italic (also available from Adobe Fonts), but you can select a different font.

13 In the options bar, specify **165 pt** for the font size, and in the options bar, click the Right Align Text button.

14 With the Horizontal Type tool, position the pointer at the inner vertical guide near the right edge of the canvas, click about two-thirds of the distance from the existing line of type and the bottom of the canvas, and type **Live Stream**. It should appear in all capital letters because the All Caps setting you applied in step 7 should still be in effect (if not, apply it).

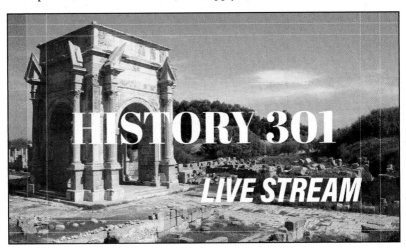

▶ **Tip:** Another way to deselect a layer is clicking away from the layer, but before you click, move the pointer far enough that it's changed to a black arrow *without* the four-headed move arrows next to it.

15 In the options bar, click the check mark button (✔) to commit editing the text.

Great job so far! But there's a little more to do. The white type is difficult to read against the lighter tones of the image, and that's why the 01End file shows a dark green color across the image. You'll add that next.

Adding a solid color layer

You could fill a layer with green the same way you did earlier to create the rectangles, but now you'll quickly add a layer of solid color using a different method that lets you easily edit the color later.

Tip: To edit a Solid Color fill layer later, simply double-click the layer's thumbnail in the Layers panel.

1 In the Layers panel, select the Arch layer so the next layer is created above it.

2 Click the Create New Fill or Adjustment Layer button at the bottom of the Layers panel, and choose Solid Color.

3 In the Color Picker, specify a dark green color; we used the hex RGB value **0c3303**. Click OK.

Layer blending mode   Layer opacity percentage

4 In the Layers panel, with the new Color Fill 1 layer selection, choose Hard Light from the blending mode menu. To lower the effect a little, next to the blending mode menu, change the layer Opacity value to 90%.

5 If the cyan guides are showing, choose View > Show > Guides to deselect it, hiding the guides. You won't need them for the rest of the lesson.

Using panels

Photoshop presents many important features in panels. If you can't find the panel you want, you can open it by choosing its name from the Window menu. To save space, less commonly used panels are hidden by default, and other panels are organized by grouping and docking.

Grouped panels. When panels are *grouped*, you see only the frontmost panel in the group. Panels behind it are indicated by a row of tabs across the top of the group, similar to tabbed documents or web pages. To bring forward a panel in a group, click its tab.

Docked panels. When panels are *docked*, they're joined at one or more edges, for example, side by side or as a vertical column.

To add a panel to others, drag its tab over another panel or group, and release the mouse button when a blue line appears around the destination panel (to group) or along a panel edge (to dock). To move them, drag the bar across the top of the panels. To remove a panel from a panel group or docked panels, drag its tab away; now it's a *floating* panel. To resize a panel, drag an edge.

Docking to the application frame. To dock panels or a panel group to an edge of the Photoshop application frame, drag a panel tab or tab bar over the left, right, or bottom edge of the application frame, and release the mouse button when a blue line appears along that edge. Panel groups and the Tools panel can dock to the left and right edges, and the options bar can dock to the top edge.

Collapsing and expanding panels. To keep a panel available but free up space, collapse it by double-clicking its tab; expand it the same way. You can collapse or expand panels horizontally: Click the double arrows in the bar across the top of a panel. You can drag the side of collapsed panels inward to collapse it to icons only. In the default Essentials workspace, the inner docked panel group is collapsed to icons, and the outer group is fully expanded.

You can hide and show all panels by pressing the Tab key. When hidden this way, reveal panels docked to the left or right edge by positioning the pointer at that edge.

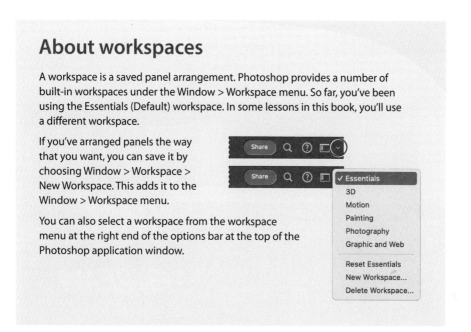
Painting a graphic element

The design for the 01End file includes a splash of color to help emphasize the word "Live." You'll create this by painting it with the Brush tool. First you'll set up the color.

Sampling a color

Photoshop maintains a *foreground color* and *background color*. Most of the time you'll pay attention to the foreground color, which is often the default color and is used to load a brush. The background color is used when a secondary color is needed. For example, it can be a second color for multi-color effects such as gradients, or the default color that's revealed when you erase on the Background layer.

By default, the foreground color is black, and the background color is white. You can change the foreground and background colors by clicking their icons in the Tools panel. If you want to use a color that's already in the document, you can simply sample it with the Eyedropper tool, which loads it as the foreground color. You'll use that method to create a color based on the blue already in this document.

Set default foreground and background colors

Switch foreground and background colors

Set foreground color

Set background color

Tip: You can reset the foreground and background colors using the keyboard: To reset to default colors, press D. To exchange them, press X.

1 Select the Eyedropper tool (⌖) in the Tools panel.

2 With the Eyedropper tool, click a lighter blue area to sample a blue color, and then in the Color Picker brighten it so that it contrasts with the green and blue area under the word "Live." We used the hex RGB value **4099ff**.

The foreground color changes in the Tools panel and the Color panel. Anything you paint will be this color until you change the foreground color again.

Painting with a brush

With the foreground color set, you can now paint. But first you'll create and name a layer to paint on, in the appropriate position in the layer stacking order.

1 In the Layers panel select the Rectangles layer, and then hold down Alt (Windows) or Option (macOS) as you click the Create a New Layer button (⊞).

That modifier key lets you name a layer as you create it, saving a step.

2 In the New Layer dialog box, for Name enter **Paint**, and click OK.

3 Select the Brush tool (🖌) in the Tools panel.

4 Choose Window > Brushes to open the Brushes panel. It may expand from a collapsed panel stack.

▶ **Tip:** The Brushes panel stores brush presets. To make detailed changes to the current brush, use the Brush Settings panel (Window > Brush Settings). You'll learn more about brushes in Lesson 10.

The Brushes panel contains brush presets, some of which are organized into groups (folders). Photoshop offers many types of brushes, from basic round and flat brushes to highly textured effects brushes. You'll use a brush that creates spattered paint.

5 In the Brushes panel, expand the Special Effects Brushes group, and select the first brush, Kyle's Spatter Brushes - Spatter Bot Tilt.

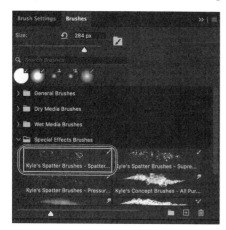

6 Drag the Brush tool across the word "Live" to paint a few strokes, building up the spatter effect. The brush strokes may not match the size or shape of the spot in the 01End file, but you'll soon redo it, so don't be concerned about it for now.

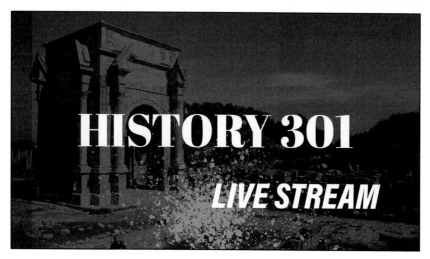

The brush strokes appear behind the word "Live." That's because you're painting on the Paint layer, which is behind the Live text layer.

▶ **Tip:** To rearrange the layer stacking order, simply drag layers up and down in the Layers panel.

Undoing and redoing steps

The Undo command is one of the greatest things about a computer: You can easily back out of a mistake you make. Photoshop offers three Undo/Redo commands, making it easier to experiment and do before/after comparisons. In this case, you'll undo the brush strokes you made so that you can do them over.

▶ **Tip:** The keyboard shortcut for Edit > Undo is Ctrl+Z (Windows) or Command+Z (macOS). For Edit > Redo, it's Ctrl+Shift+Z (Windows) or Command+Shift+Z (macOS).

1 Choose Edit > Undo Brush Tool, or press to undo your last step.

If you painted multiple brush strokes, you may have to repeat step 1 until they're all undone. If you need to repeat step 1, stop when the Undo command says Undo New Layer, because you don't want to undo that step.

▶ **Tip:** To see the steps you can undo and redo, look at the History panel (Window > History).

If you want to restore steps you undid, you can choose the command Edit > Redo, but you don't need to do that for this lesson. The Edit > Redo command is available until you perform a new step, because that starts a different history from that point, replacing all existing Redo steps.

Now you'll paint another brush stroke after adjusting the brush size. Although you could do this using the Brush Settings panel where all brush settings are available, for quick access you'll use the Brush tool options bar.

▶ **Tip:** Another shortcut for opening the Brush Presets picker is to right-click (Windows) or Control-click (macOS) the canvas when the Brush tool is selected.

2 With the Brush tool selected, in the options bar click the arrow next to the Brush Presets picker, set the Size to **80**, and click away from the brush picker to close it.

3 With the Paint layer selected, position the pointer over the Live text, and drag in a circular pattern to build up the brush stroke as a large spot behind the word.

Now you'll quickly compare the layer state before and after the last step.

4 Choose Edit > Toggle Last State, look at the canvas, and then choose Edit > Toggle Last State again. Your painting step was undone and redone.

If you think you'll often use this, consider developing the habit of pressing the keyboard shortcut for the Toggle Last State command, because that's easier than repeatedly choosing its menu command with the mouse: Press Ctrl+Alt+Z (Windows) or Command+Option+Z (macOS).

5 Save the document.

About presets panels

As you work on more projects with Photoshop, you may find that you use certain graphics elements repeatedly, such as color swatches. Presets panels let you save your favorites for quick access and organize them. Presets panels include the Swatches, Gradients, Patterns, and Shapes panels.

To apply a preset, drag a preset from the panel, and drop it on a layer on the canvas. Or, select a layer, and then click a preset in a presets panel. The Shapes panel is an exception because it doesn't contain attributes, it contains graphics; so you drag one onto the canvas where it becomes a new layer.

A. *Panel menu*
B. *Search field*
C. *Recently used presets*
D. *Presets list*
E. *Create a New Group button*
F. *Create a New Preset button*
G. *Delete Preset button*

Presets panels have common features.

Customizable. Options for viewing and managing presets, including some of the following options, are available on a presets panel menu.

Searchable. The first item in a presets panel is a search field so that you can search preset names.

Recents. The row under the search field lists recent presets you've applied, which is convenient if you want to continue applying presets you recently used.

List or thumbnail. You can display presets as a list with names, or as thumbnail icons, using thumbnail and list commands in the panel menu. When you see a preset displayed as a thumbnail, you can find out its name by hovering the mouse pointer over it.

Groups. You can organize presets into groups (folders) by dragging them in and out of groups in the panel. To create a new group, click the Create a New Group button at the bottom of a presets panel.

Import/export. A presets panel menu includes commands for importing and exporting presets, so that you can back them up separately, share them, or copy them to other computers.

Extending an image

The document now looks similar to the 01End lesson file. But there's one big difference: The photo of the arch is too far to the left. The composition would be more visually balanced if the Arch layer was moved closer to the center.

1 Select the Move tool, and in the options bar, deselect Auto-Select.

Auto-Select is often useful because it lets you select a layer by clicking it on the canvas. But that isn't useful for this step, because you want to move the Arch layer which is behind other layers. If Auto-Select is enabled, the Move tool will select one of the layers in front of the Arch layer. That's why you deselected Auto-Select. But when Auto-Select is disabled, you must manually select a layer.

2 In the Layers panel, select the Arch layer.

3 Position the Move tool over the canvas, and drag the Arch layer until it's centered within the green area.

This looks better, except that when the arch is centered, the image does not extend to the left enough to cover the canvas. You can have Photoshop create content that fills that area using Generative Fill, an AI-powered feature (see the sidebar "About Generative Fill" in this lesson). That will be easier if you hide all other layers first.

4 Hold down the Alt (Windows) or Option (macOS) key as you click the eye icon for the Arch layer in the Layers panel to hide all layers except Arch. Now you need to tell Photoshop which area to fill with generated content.

5 Select the Rectangular Marquee tool, and drag to create a selection marquee that covers all of the empty area between the left edge of the canvas and the left edge of the Arch layer; overlap the Arch layer slightly to ensure there won't be a gap.

Note: Generative Fill can create almost any type of image. Adobe requires you to agree to the Generative Fill User Guidelines so that you agree to use the feature to generate images that are within the guidelines, and not images that are harmful, deceptive, or illegal.

6   In the Contextual Task Bar, click Generative Fill. Its options change. If a message appears asking you to read and agree to the Generative Fill User Guidelines, click Agree when you're ready.

An empty text field appears in the Contextual Task Bar. It's there so that you can type a description of what you want to generate, but to simply fill in the selection with consistent content you can leave it blank and continue.

7   Make sure the Arch layer is selected in the Layers panel, and then in the Contextual Task Bar, click Generate.

When it finishes, you'll see three new things:

Note: When using Generative Fill, consider how the image will be used. As a graphic design illustration, it may not be important that the generated content doesn't exactly match the actual site. But if this image was intended to be used for news or reference (such as for historical research), it should not include content that never actually existed.

- On the canvas, the empty selection is replaced with new content.

- In the Layers panel, a new Generative Fill layer was created above the Arch layer. This contains the new content so that it doesn't alter the original layer.

- In the Properties panel, a Variations section offers alternatives you can click to try. The selected variation is the one you see on the canvas.

8   In the Layers panel, right-click (Windows) or Option-click (macOS) the eye icon for the Generative Fill layer, and choose Hide/Show All Other Layers.

Now you can see how the content looks in the context of the total composition.

9   In the Properties panel, click each variation and select the one you like the most.

Congratulations! You've completed the graphic for the live stream by learning the basics of combining images, text, painted brush strokes, and other layers to create a composite Photoshop document.

10 Close the document; if you are alerted to unsaved changes, click Save. If you left the 01End file open, close it without saving changes.

About Generative Fill and Adobe Firefly

You may be aware that artificial intelligence (AI) image generation has advanced rapidly in recent years, able to render photorealistic images and convincing artistic styles from a text description. Adobe Firefly is a generative AI technology that Adobe has incorporated into several applications, including the Generative Fill feature and the Remove tool in Photoshop. Generative Fill is useful not just for creating new images, but also for repairing, extending, and enhancing your own images. There are some guidelines and restrictions for using Generative AI; for more information, see www.adobe.com/legal/licenses-terms/adobe-gen-ai-user-guidelines.html.

Creating with confidence

Generative imagery is created by training software models using large numbers of images. Some AI services may train using found images without securing appropriate usage rights. Rights issues may lead to legal liability, so some companies and organizations may avoid using work created by services that can't provide information on training image rights. Adobe Firefly generative AI is designed to be "commercial safe" in part because it's trained using images where usage rights are known, such as images from the Adobe Stock library and in the public domain. (Note: *Public domain* has a specific legal definition and is not the same as a copyrighted image being publicly viewable online.) For more information, see helpx.adobe.com/firefly/faq.html#training-data.

Another issue is being able to determine whether an image is original or contains generative AI content. Adobe is part of an industry-wide effort called the Content Authenticity Initiative (contentauthenticity.org). This includes an effort to create an open, global standard for sharing metadata (image information) that can include creator attribution, generative AI transparency (letting people know that generative AI was used for at least part of the image) and is tamper-evident (so you can know if the metadata was altered). Adobe is developing a Content Credentials feature to support this. For more information and links about how Content Credentials work and how they relate to Photoshop, see helpx.adobe.com/creative-cloud/help/content-credentials.html.

Will Adobe use your images to train generative AI? You can control this in Photoshop. In the Preferences dialog box, view the Product Improvement panel and enable or disable the option "I give Adobe permission to use my images and associated data to train Adobe's generative AI models." The option can be edited only when the "Yes, I'd like to participate" option is enabled.

Generative Credits

It takes a lot of cloud computing power to run generative AI solutions, so Adobe came up with a system to manage server usage called Generative Credits. Creative Cloud members receive a certain number of Generative Credits every month. The number of credits you get depends on the Creative Cloud plan used by you or your school or organization. If you run out of Generative Credits before the end of a month, you can continue to use Generative Fill, but it may run more slowly because your jobs will have a lower priority. If you need to restore performance priority, it's possible to purchase more credits. For more information, see helpx.adobe.com/firefly/using/generative-credits-faq.html.

At the time of the release of Photoshop 2024 (version 25), Adobe is continuing to work out how to best provide generative AI services, so the quality and resolution of the results, and aspects such as Generative Credits policies, may change or improve over time.

Review questions

1 Describe at least two types of images you can open or add to a document.

2 How do you select tools in Photoshop?

3 Describe two ways to zoom in to or out from an image.

4 How would you reverse the most recent change you made?

5 What are some ways to make panels use less space on your screen?

Review answers

1 You can use a photograph from a digital camera. You can also use a scanned image of a photographic print, a transparency or negative film frame, or a graphic. You can use images downloaded from the internet such as photography from Adobe Stock, or images uploaded to your Cloud Documents or your Lightroom photos.

2 To select a tool in Photoshop, click its icon in the Tools panel, or press the tool's keyboard shortcut. A selected tool remains active until you select a different tool. To select a hidden tool, either use a keyboard shortcut to toggle through the tools or click and hold the tool in the Tools panel to open a pop-up menu of the hidden tools.

3 Choose commands from the View menu to zoom in on or out from an image or to fit it onscreen, or use the zoom tools and click or drag over an image to enlarge or reduce the view. You can also use keyboard shortcuts or the Navigator panel to control the display of an image.

4 Choose Edit > Undo or Edit > Toggle Last State, or press its keyboard shortcut. (Another correct answer is to choose an earlier document state in the History panel, although that was not shown in this lesson.)

5 You can use any combination of grouping and docking panels together, collapsing them, or hiding them.

2 BASIC PHOTO CORRECTIONS

Lesson overview

In this lesson, you'll learn how to do the following:

- Understand image resolution and size.

- View and open files using Adobe Bridge.

- Straighten and crop an image.

- Adjust the tonal range of an image.

- Delete unwanted or distracting items using the Remove tool.

- Replace a large deleted area using Generative Fill.

- Apply the Smart Sharpen filter to finish retouching photos.

This lesson will take about an hour to complete. To get the lesson files used in this chapter, download them from the web page for this book at peachpit.com/PhotoshopCIB2024. For more information, see "Accessing the lesson files and Web Edition" in the Getting Started section at the beginning of this book.

As you work on this lesson, you'll preserve the start files. If you need to restore the start files, download them from your Account page.

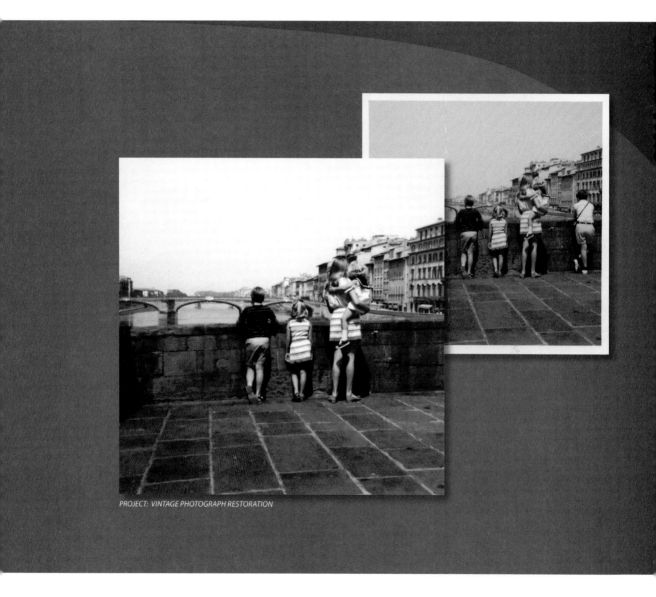
PROJECT: VINTAGE PHOTOGRAPH RESTORATION

Photoshop includes a variety of tools and commands
for improving the quality of a photographic image.
This lesson steps you through the process of cropping,
resizing, and retouching a vintage photograph.

Note: In this lesson, you retouch an image using Photoshop. For some images, such as those captured in camera raw format, it may be more efficient to edit in Adobe Camera Raw, which is installed with Photoshop. You'll learn about the tools Camera Raw has to offer in Lesson 12, "Working with Camera Raw."

Note: If Bridge isn't installed, the File > Browse in Bridge command in Photoshop will start the Creative Cloud desktop app, which will download and install Bridge. After installation completes, you can start Bridge.

Note: If Bridge asks you if you want to import preferences from a previous version of Bridge, select Don't Show Again, and click No.

Opening a file with Adobe Bridge

For each lesson in this book, you can perform the steps using a specific folder of files. You may make copies of these files and save them under different names or locations, or you may work from the original files and then download them from the peachpit.com website again if you want a fresh start.

In this lesson, you'll retouch a scan of a damaged and discolored vintage photograph so it can be shared online, or printed 7 × 7 inches at 300 ppi.

In Lesson 1, you used the Open command to open a file. You'll start this lesson by comparing the original scan to the finished image in Adobe Bridge, a visual file browser that integrates with Photoshop and other Creative Cloud applications.

1 Start Photoshop, and then simultaneously hold down Ctrl+Alt+Shift (Windows) or Command+Option+Shift (macOS) to reset the default settings.

2 When prompted, click Yes to confirm that you want to delete the Adobe Photoshop Settings file.

3 Choose File > Browse In Bridge. If you're prompted to enable the Photoshop extension in Bridge, click Yes or OK.

Adobe Bridge opens, displaying a collection of panels, menus, and buttons.

4 Select the Folders tab in the upper-left corner, and then browse to the Lessons folder you downloaded to your computer so that the lessons in the Lessons folder appear in the Content panel.

5 With the Lessons folder still selected in the Folders panel, choose File > Add To Favorites.

The Favorites panel lets you quickly access files, folders, applications, and other assets that you frequently use.

Tip: In Bridge, if the Favorites panel list and a folder you want to add to Favorites are both visible, you can drag the folder and drop it in the Favorites panel. You can even drag and drop to add a folder from your computer desktop to the Favorites panel.

6   Click the Favorites tab to open the panel, and click the Lessons folder to open it. Then, in the Content panel, double-click the Lesson02 folder.

Thumbnail previews of the folder contents appear in the Content panel.

7   Compare the 02Start.tif and 02End.psd files. To enlarge the thumbnails in the Content panel, drag the thumbnail slider at the bottom of the Bridge window to the right.

Tip: In Bridge, you can see a larger preview of a selected item by using the Preview panel (choose Window > Preview). If that's not big enough, you can resize the Preview panel. Or, press the spacebar to see a full-screen preview of the selected item.

In the 02Start.tif file, notice that the image is tilted, the colors are relatively dull, and the image has a green color cast and a distracting crease. You'll fix these problems in this lesson, and a few others.

8   Double-click the 02Start.tif thumbnail to open the file in Photoshop. Click OK if you see the Embedded Profile Mismatch dialog box, and close any messages that appear about new features.

9   In Photoshop, choose File > Save As. Choose Photoshop from the Format menu, and name the file **02Working.psd**. Then click Save.

Note: If Photoshop displays a dialog box about the difference between saving to Cloud Documents and On Your Computer, click Save On Your Computer. You can also select Don't Show Again, but that setting will deselect after you reset Photoshop preferences.

Evaluating an image for editing

You can simply jump in and start editing, but it's often useful to take a moment to look over the image to understand what kind of editing an image needs. As you gain experience with more Photoshop features, evaluating an image before editing can help you plan what work needs to be done, and in what order.

In the era when only film photography existed, it was common to make a test print and mark it up to indicate changes to make in a darkroom for the final version. Today, in a Photoshop document, you can add comments by using the Notes tool, add comments online with File > Share for Review, or add layers (that you can hide) to scribble or type on. You'll learn about those features later in the book.

The tasks you do, and the order, will vary depending on the project. In a typical workflow, correcting tone and color are early steps, and the last steps include adjusting the pixel dimensions and sharpening for the final delivery medium. If an image will be used in different media, such as to be printed, shared online, and shown in a video, first edit to create a full-resolution high-quality source image. Then, for specific uses, save or export copies adjusted for each medium's requirements.

This image needs straightening, tone and color correction, and some retouching. It's a faded print that was digitized by a family that would like to be able to reprint it 7 inches wide at 300 ppi. First, set up the Status Bar to show document dimensions. This will help you see if the document is meeting the print size requirement.

1   If the image dimensions aren't already displayed in the status area at the bottom of the application window, click the arrow there and choose Document Dimensions from the pop-up menu that appears.

The Status Bar says this image is 2160 × 2160 pixels at 240 ppi. This image is intended to be printed, so it will be better to set the unit of measure to inches.

▶ **Tip:** Another way to change the unit of measure is to right-click (Windows) or Control-click (macOS) the rulers, and then choose a unit from the context menu that appears.

2   Choose View > Rulers to enable the Rulers command and display the rulers.

3   Double-click the rulers; this opens the Units & Rulers pane in the Preferences dialog box. Choose Inches from the Rulers Menu in the Units section, and click OK.

You changed the unit of measure for the document, which affects the rulers and units in many panels and in the Status Bar. The Status Bar now shows that the document is 9 × 9 inches at 240 ppi. (2160 pixels divided by 240 pixels per inch equals 9 inches.)

Tip: Changing the unit of measure changes the units shown in the Status Bar, in the rulers, in panels, and in the Units/Rulers setting in the Photoshop Preferences dialog box's Units & Rulers pane.

Straightening and cropping the image

You'll start by using the Crop tool, which can also straighten an image.

1 In the Tools panel, select the Crop tool (⌗.). Crop handles appear.

2 In the options bar, choose W × H × Resolution from the Select A Preset Aspect Ratio or Crop Size menu. (Ratio is the default value.) A crop overlay appears.

3 In the options bar, type **7 in** into both the width and height fields, and enter **300** in the px/in field (Resolution).

Filling in the Resolution field will cause the Crop tool to *resample* the image, deleting original pixels (or making up new ones) so that after applying the crop, the image will have exactly the number of pixels needed to print 7 × 7 inches at 300 ppi.

Tip: If the Crop tool is selected but the crop handles aren't visible, press the Enter or Return key. If they still aren't visible, click the View menu and make sure the Extras command is enabled.

Tip: When you crop an image for the web or screens, in the options bar enter the required width and height in pixels (such as "800 px"), and leave the px/in resolution field empty. Inch units and px/in resolution are useful only for print.

Next, you'll straighten the image.

Understanding image size and resolution

Resolution is a term that has different meanings depending on the medium. For video and electronic displays, resolution means *pixel dimensions*: the width and height of an image in *pixels*, the small squares that describe an image. For example, the resolution of a 4K video frame is 3840 × 2160 pixels. For print, resolution means *pixel density*, such as 300 pixels per inch (ppi).

Pixels in a photographic image

In Photoshop, the most common ways to change image pixel dimensions are the Crop tool and the Image > Image Size command. To change pixel density (ppi), when using the Crop tool, enter a value in the Resolution field; or when using Image > Image Size, enable the Resample option.

How do you know how many pixels are in an image?

Multiply the width and height of an image, in pixels. For example, in this lesson you crop an image to 2100 × 2100 pixels, which equals 4,410,000 pixels or 4.41 *megapixels* (one million pixels equals one megapixel). Pixel dimensions affect file size and upload/download time.

How do you know an image's resolution in pixels per inch?

Divide an image's width or height in pixels by its number of inches. For example, if the 2100 × 2100 pixels pixel image in this lesson is set to 7 inches wide, then each dimension is 2100 pixels divided by 7 inches, or 300 pixels per inch.

How much resolution is enough?

The requirements of a delivery medium determine how much resolution an image needs. For example, in video, if an image must fill every pixel of a 4K frame, it must be 3840 × 2160 pixels. For a print job, an image must have enough pixels to print at the required size with the required pixel density. For example, if an image must fill a space 7 inches wide and the production requirement for resolution is 300 ppi, then the image must be at least 2100 pixels wide (7 inches times 300 ppi).

How does physical reproduction size affect resolution?

Changing an image's reproduction size alters its *effective resolution*, because the same number of pixels now cover a smaller or larger area. For example, if you print this lesson's 7-inch wide image at 14 inches wide (double its original width), then its 2100 pixels divided by 14 inches equals 150 ppi.

Its effective resolution was halved because the same number of pixels is spread across twice the width. For this reason, when preparing images for print, knowing that they need to be 300 ppi is not enough. You also need to know at what size in inches each image needs to be 300 ppi.

Viewing distance influences the pixel density our eyes actually perceive, and this affects resolution requirements too. The traditional 300 ppi guideline for print is based on a viewing distance of roughly arm's length, like when you read a book. A very large photo print intended to be seen from several feet away can be printed at lower than 300 ppi, because beyond a certain viewing distance, your eyes see the pixels as dense enough to have a high effective resolution. For the same reason, a 50 ppi image can appear perfectly sharp on a highway billboard because it's seen from hundreds of feet away.

Does image resolution always have to match the resolution of the printer or display?

Because of the way display and output technologies work, an image file might not need to match the resolution of the hardware that reproduces the image. For example, some commercial printing plate-setters and photo-quality inkjet printers have a device resolution of 2400 dots per inch (dpi) or more, but the appropriate image resolution to send to those devices may be only 200 to 360 ppi for photos. This is because the 2400 dpi dots printed by the hardware are grouped into larger halftone cells or dot patterns that build tones and colors. Similarly, a 500-ppi smartphone display may not necessarily require 500-ppi images. Whatever your medium, ask your production team or output service provider to verify the pixel dimensions or ppi value they require in the final images you deliver.

What's considered high resolution?

For images reproduced on screens, one way to currently define *high resolution* is when an image has enough pixels to fill every pixel on a HiDPI (Windows/Android) or Retina (Apple) display. These displays generally have twice the pixel density of older displays.

For print, an image might be considered high resolution when its ppi value is around 240–360 ppi at its final reproduction size, because at that pixel density, it can reproduce enough detail to take advantage of the device resolutions of printing presses and professional photo printers.

Does changing resolution affect the storage size of a file?

Only when the pixel dimensions change. For example, this lesson's image has final pixel dimensions of 2100 × 2100 pixels set to 7 × 7 inches at 300 ppi. If you change either the size in inches or the ppi value (resolution) but keep the pixel dimensions at 2100 × 2100 pixels, the file size does not change. But if you change the size in inches without changing the ppi value (or vice versa), the pixel dimensions must change (this is called *resampling*), which changes the file size. For example, if this lesson's image is changed to 72 ppi while maintaining 7 × 7 inches, the pixel dimensions must change to 504 × 504 pixels, and the file size decreases accordingly.

It's important to remember that file size is determined by more than just the pixel dimensions. The file size of an image can also go up or down depending on its file type, bit depth, number of channels and layers, its compression method (if compressed), and more.

Tip: If you want the document to keep the pixels outside the crop area, deselect Delete Cropped Pixels in the options bar. That will let you reveal previously cropped areas by enlarging the Crop tool rectangle, which is useful if you change your mind later.

4   Click the Straighten icon in the options bar. The pointer changes to the Straighten tool.

5   Position the pointer at the top-left corner of the image (where the sky ends), hold down the mouse button and drag to create a straight line following the top edge, and then release.

Tip: If you need to see crop edges more clearly, it's OK to change the view magnification while the crop rectangle is active.

Photoshop rotates the image using the angle at which you dragged the Straighten tool. In general, when you see something in an image that should be perfectly vertical or horizontal, such as the edge of a building, drag the Straighten tool along that.

A *crop shield* is now visible outside the crop handles; it helps focus your attention on the cropped area and shows you what areas will be trimmed when the crop is applied. Next, you'll crop out the white border and scale the image.

Tip: The Crop tool will continue to create a 7 × 7 inch, 300 ppi crop as long as those are the current options bar settings. If you want to crop with total freedom, click the Clear button in the Crop tool options bar.

6   Drag the corners of the crop rectangle inward to crop out the white border. If you need to adjust the position of the photo inside the crop, position the pointer within the crop rectangle and drag the photo.

7   Press Enter or Return to apply the crop.

The image was cropped, straightened, and resampled by the Crop tool options. The Status Bar should now show that the image is 7 × 7 in at 300 ppi.

8   Choose File > Save to save your work. Click OK if you see the Photoshop Format Options dialog box.

Correcting tone and color

● **Note:** The color and tone edits in this lesson are relatively basic; it's possible to do them all using only Levels or Curves. For example, you can use the color balance eyedroppers and set the tonal range in both. Typically, the reason to use Curves is for a more precise or complex adjustment.

You'll use Curves and Levels adjustment layers to remove the color cast and adjust the color and tone in the image. The Curves or Levels options may look complex, but don't be intimidated. You'll work with them more in later lessons; for now, you'll take advantage of their tools to quickly brighten and adjust the tone of the image.

1   In the Adjustments panel, scroll down to the Single Adjustments category. If it's collapsed, click the arrow to expand it, and click Curves. This adds a Curves adjustment layer; its controls appear in the Properties panel.

2   Select the White Point tool on the left side of the Properties panel.

▶ **Tip:** On your own, experiment with the presets categories at the top of the Adjustments panel. They're useful for quick fixes, and you can learn how they're done by inspecting the layer group each preset adds to the document.

The White Point tool defines what color value should be made a neutral white. Once defined, all other colors and tones shift accordingly. This is a quick way to remove a color cast and correct image brightness. To properly set the white point, click an area of the image that should be the brightest neutral area of the image that contains detail—not a blown-out area like the sun or a lamp and not a specular highlight such as a reflection of sunlight on chrome.

3   Click a white stripe on the girl's dress to use it as the sample for white balancing.

 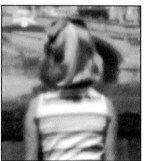

▶ **Tip:** If you want to know the color values of the pixels that the pointer is positioned over, they're displayed in the Info panel (Window > Info).

The White Point tool shifts color balance and brightness based on how different the sampled color is from neutral white; clicking another area may produce a different correction. The image looks sunny again, removing the color shift introduced by age-related print fading.

▶ **Tip:** Settings for an adjustment layer are always in the Properties panel. The more you use adjustment layers (they're used three times in this lesson), the more you'll want the Properties panel to be open all the time in your Photoshop workspace.

▶ **Tip:** If you're not sure what adjustments to make, try selecting a preset from the Presets menu near the top of the Properties panel. You'll see both how a preset changes the image, and what changes in the Properties panel created that look. This might help you decide how you want to change the settings.

Now you'll use a Levels adjustment layer to refine the tonal range of the image.

4   In the Adjustments panel (if needed, click its tab to make it visible), in the Single Adjustments category click Levels (⬛) to add a Levels adjustment layer.

For both Curves and Levels, the Properties panel displays a *histogram*—a graph displaying the distribution of tonal values in the image, from black on the left to white on the right. For Levels, the left triangle under the histogram represents the black point (the tonal level you want to set as the darkest in the image), the right triangle represents the white point (the tonal level you want to set as the lightest in the image), and the middle triangle represents the midtones.

5   Drag the left triangle (black point) under the histogram to the right, where significant shadow tones start to appear. Our value was **15**. All tones less than 15 become black.

6   Drag the middle triangle to the right to adjust the midtones. Our value was **.90**.

● **Note:** Flattening also removes content preserved beyond the visible edge of the canvas. For example, if you used the Crop tool with the Delete Cropped Pixels option disabled, flattening removes the hidden pixels that the Crop tool preserved.

Now you'll *flatten* the image, which merges all layers into one Background layer. It's common to avoid flattening until you no longer need the flexibility of adjusting edits made using separate layers; many advanced Photoshop users flatten only the copy that's handed off to a client. If you're just getting started with Photoshop, flattening makes it easier to work during the next phase, retouching.

7   Choose Layer > Flatten Image.

The appearance of the image did not change, and the Layers panel now shows only the Background layer.

Cleaning up with the Remove tool

The next task is to repair the crease in the photo. You'll use the Remove tool to do this and to address other similar image problems. The Remove tool quickly removes blemishes and other imperfections and makes a repair look consistent in content, tone, and color compared to the rest of the image.

1   Zoom into the top half of the image to clearly see the vertical crease in the sky.

2   In the Tools panel, click and hold the mouse button on the Spot Healing Brush tool (🩹) to reveal the other retouching tools in its tool group, and select the Remove tool (🩹).

3   In the options bar, set a brush Size of about **25** px, and make sure Remove After Each Stroke is selected.

4   Position the Remove tool at the top of the crease in the image, and then drag down along the crease in the sky, stopping just before the bridge. If it's difficult to control one very long stroke, you can drag multiple smaller strokes. Each stroke you drag appears magenta at first, and then when you release the mouse, the Remove tool repairs the image under that stroke.

5   Continue removing the rest of the crease by dragging the Remove tool down along the crease over the far and near bridges.

▶ **Tip:** If you digitize many photo prints by placing multiple prints on a scanner, try opening a scan and choosing File > Automate > Crop And Straighten Photos. When a scan contains multiple photos, that command can automatically separate them into individual documents, as long as there is empty space between each print.

As owner of Gawain Weaver Art Conservation, Gawain Weaver has conserved and restored original works by artists ranging from Eadweard Muybridge to Man Ray and from Ansel Adams to Cindy Sherman. He teaches workshops internationally as well as online on the care and identification of photographs.

Find out more at gawainweaver.com.

Real-world photo restoration

The tools in Photoshop make restoration of old or damaged photographs seem like magic, giving virtually anyone the power to scan, retouch, print, and frame their photo collections.

However, when dealing with works by famous artists, museums, galleries, and collectors need to preserve original objects to the greatest degree possible despite deterioration or accidental damage. Professional art conservators are called upon to clean dust and soiling from print surfaces, remove discoloration and staining, repair tears, stabilize prints to prevent future damage, and even paint in missing areas of a work.

Carleton E. Watkins, Nevada Fall, 700 FT, Yosemite Valley, CA, mammoth albumen print, 15⅝" × 20¾".
This print was removed from its mount to remove the stains and then remounted.

"Photograph conservation is both a science and an art," says Weaver. "We must apply what we know about the chemistry of the photograph, its mount, and any varnishes or other coatings in order to safely clean, preserve, and enhance the image. Since we cannot quickly 'undo' a step in a conservation treatment, we must always proceed with great caution and a healthy respect for the fragility of the photographic object, whether it's a 160-year-old salt print of Notre Dame or gelatin silver print of Half Dome from the 1970s."

Many of the manual tools of an art conservator have analogous digital versions in Photoshop:

 An art conservator might wash a photograph to remove the discolored components of the paper, or even use a mild bleaching process known as light-bleaching to oxidize and remove the colored components of a stain or overall discoloration. In Photoshop, you can use a Curves adjustment layer to remove the color cast from an image.

 A conservator working on a fine-art photograph might use special paints and fine brushes to manually "in-paint" damaged areas of a photograph. Likewise, you can use the Spot Healing Brush tool in Photoshop to spot out specks of dust or dirt on a scanned image.

 A conservator might use Japanese papers and wheat-starch paste to carefully repair and rebuild torn paper before finalizing the repair with some skillful in-painting. In Photoshop, you can remove a crease or repair a tear in a scanned image with a few clicks of the Clone Stamp tool.

A fixative was applied to the artist's signature with a small brush to protect it when the mount was washed.

"Although our work has always been first and foremost about the preservation and restoration of the original photographic object, there are instances, especially with family photographs, where the use of Photoshop is more appropriate," says Weaver. "More dramatic results can be achieved in far less time. After digitization, the original print can be safely stored away, while the digital version can be copied or printed for many family members. Often, we first clean or unfold family photographs to safely reveal as much of the original image as possible, and then we repair the remaining discoloration, stains, and tears on the computer after digitization."

AFTER

6 If you chose to paint multiple strokes, you may find that the Remove tool becomes less effective at removing the crease on the bridge. Painting just part of the crease on the bridge may make the Remove tool think that the unpainted rest of the crease is a feature of the bridge to be preserved. If that happens, then in the options bar, deselect Remove After Each Stroke. Now, when you drag multiple strokes, the Remove tool won't apply the repair until you press Enter or Return, which you should do only after you finish painting over the entire crease. Enabling Remove After Each Stroke lets the Remove tool see all strokes as part of the same single item to remove.

● **Note:** If the Remove tool doesn't work well with a certain image or if it runs slowly on your computer, for small repairs you can try the Spot Healing Brush or Healing Brush tool. The Healing Brush tool can retouch using a different area of the image as the source, which you define.

7 If you disabled Remove After Each Stroke, enable it again after you finish erasing all of the crease.

8 Zoom in to see the white hair in the upper right area of the image. Then use the Remove tool to paint over the hair.

9 Look in the sky for bits of dust or dirt, and retouch them with the Remove tool.

The boy at the right end of the bridge is not part of the same family, so you'll remove him from the photo.

10 In the options bar, set the brush Size to 100.

11 Zoom out if necessary to see the entire boy, and then paint over the boy with the Remove tool, making sure to include the boy's shadow.

How good the result looks can vary depending on the image and the area you covered with the Remove tool. If you'd like a better result, you have some options:

- Drag the Remove tool again to paint over the imperfections it created, because in many cases that refines and improves the result.

- Undo and try the Remove tool again, painting the area slightly differently.

- Undo and try a different method such as Generative Fill. You'll do that next, so now you'll undo removing the boy so you can start over.

12 Choose Edit > Undo Remove Tool to restore the boy.

13 Save your work so far.

Retouch a deleted area using Generative Fill

The Remove tool and Generative Fill are newer features based on recent advances in machine learning, so they're more likely to produce great-looking repairs more quickly than older tools. Generative Fill can solve a much wider range of image problems than the Remove tool. For example, you can use Generative Fill to create new objects and scenes. In this lesson, Generative Fill can remove the boy more effectively than the Remove tool, by offering more flexible options.

Before you can remove the boy, you must first create a selection around him to tell Photoshop what area you want to replace. The Object Selection tool can automatically detect objects, so you don't have to manually draw an outline.

▶ **Tip:** Like other selection tools, you can add to the results of Object Selection by holding down Shift as you drag tool around areas that were missed. To exclude unwanted areas, Alt-drag (Windows) or Option-drag (macOS) the tool. Or, to draw a more precise initial selection, choose Lasso from the Mode menu in the options bar.

1 In the Tools panel, select the Object Selection tool (▧), and hover it over each person in the photo, without clicking. Each person highlights when hovered.

As the Object Selection tool automatically detects an object, clicking the highlighted area selects it. The automatic highlight may not include the entire subject; in this case the automatic highlight around the boy might not include all of his shadow. To help ensure a more complete selection, you'll drag the tool instead.

2 Drag the Object Selection tool to draw a rectangle around the boy, and then release the mouse.

The resulting selection includes the entire boy and his shadow. The Contextual Task Bar appears below the selection.

3 In the Contextual Task Bar, click the Generative Fill button. If a message appears asking you to read and agree to the Generative Fill User Guidelines, click Agree when you're ready.

▶ **Tip:** The Photo Restoration filter can reduce the amount of manual retouching that's needed. Choose Filter > Neural Filters, enable Photo Restoration, and adjust options. For black-and-white photos, Neural Filters also include a Colorize filter. Neural Filters take advantage of machine learning; you'll learn more about them in Lesson 15, "Exploring Neural Filters."

The Contextual Task Bar changes to display a field where you can enter text, followed by a Generate button. If you wanted to fill the selection with something specific, you could describe it by typing into the text field. In this case, you simply want to fill the selection with something consistent with the background, so you don't need to type anything before you continue.

4 Click Generate.

A progress bar appears, which may take longer on older computers. When it's done, the boy is replaced by new content that's consistent with the background. If it isn't a good fit, you're not stuck with what it gave you.

- In the Layers panel, the result is a separate new layer named Generative Fill. If you click the layer's eyeball icon to hide it, the original content is visible again. This separate layer makes it possible for you to use just a portion of the results, or to restore the original content at any time.

- When Generative Fill is selected in the Layers panel, the Properties panel shows options that let you change the result. In the Variations section are three versions of the results. The highlighted variation is the one you currently see.

Tip: When you hover the pointer over an item in the Variations list for Generative Layer properties, an ellipsis menu (…) appears. Clicking on it lets you rate or delete each variation. Rating helps improve the software.

5   In the Properties panel, click each of the other variations, and select the one you think is the best, based on how well the background buildings and bridge wall are filled in. If you don't like any variation, click the Generate button to create more, until you like one well enough to select it.

Tip: If you don't like how the Object Selection tool keeps highlighting as you move the pointer over the image, switch to another tool such as the Move tool or Hand tool.

In the past, convincingly repairing such a large area used to require extensive, time-consuming manual retouching. Generative Fill gives you multiple variations in seconds.

Manual retouching with the healing and cloning tools

Some retouching tasks are specialized or simple enough that you might want to use the more traditional Photoshop healing and cloning tools instead of Generative Fill and the Remove tool.

The easiest tools to use are those you can simply click, or click and drag, to repair an area. These include the Spot Healing Brush tool (✏) and the Remove tool (✏). Both fill in the repair area using content from around the area where you click or drag. The Remove tool uses newer technology that can produce better results when repairing larger or more complex areas.

Sometimes it works better to tell Photoshop to use a specific area as a source for filling in the area you're retouching. You can do that with the Clone Stamp tool (▲) and Healing Brush tool (✏). The Clone Stamp tool retouches by exactly copying pixels you sample from another area. The Healing Brush tool tries to blend sampled content into the area you're repairing. To use these tools, first click while holding down the Alt (Windows) or Option (macOS) to sample an area, and then click or drag the tool to apply the sampled pixels to the area you want to retouch. For both tools, the Window > Clone Source panel offers more options that don't fit in the options bar.

The Patch tool (⬤) is similar to the Spot Healing brush tool, but instead of setting the source by Alt/Option-clicking to sample a small area, you drag the Patch tool to select a region of any size or shape.

The Content-Aware Move tool (✂) is useful for moving or copying a selection to another area of an image and blending it into the new area. You can use the Content-Aware Move tool to extend content such as grass or a building, by selecting the Extend setting in the Mode menu in the options bar.

Also, remember that you can find the location of and step-by-step instructions for any Photoshop tool by choosing Edit > Search. As with all tools, you can customize how they work by using the options bar to change settings for the current tool.

Sharpening the image

Typically, sharpening is one of the last editing steps. Photoshop offers many ways to sharpen, from basic to advanced. You'll use the Smart Sharpen filter because it produces good results while also being relatively easy to use.

1 Choose Layer > Flatten Image. Merging layers is necessary so that the upcoming sharpening step affects the entire image, not just the selected layer.

2 Choose Filter > Sharpen > Smart Sharpen.

3 In the Smart Sharpen dialog box, make sure that Preview is selected so you can see the effect of settings you adjust in the document window.

▶ **Tip:** For a before/after comparison of your changes, toggle the Preview option. It displays the result in the document window, not just in the dialog box. You'll find the Preview option in many dialog boxes in Photoshop.

You can drag inside the preview window in the dialog box to see different parts of the image, or you can click the magnification buttons below the thumbnail.

4 Make sure Lens Blur is chosen in the Remove menu.

You can choose to remove Lens Blur, Gaussian Blur, or Motion Blur in the Smart Sharpen dialog box. Lens Blur is good for general sharpening. Gaussian Blur is similar to the older Unsharp Mask filter. Motion Blur helps reduce streaks from the camera or subject moving in one direction when the photo was taken.

5 Drag the Amount (of sharpening) slider to about **100**%.

6 Drag the Radius slider to about **3**.

The Radius value determines the number of pixels surrounding the edge pixels that affect the sharpening. If an image starts out relatively sharp, a typical Radius value is 1 pixel. In this image the finest details are not sharp, so a higher Radius value helps.

▶ **Tip:** Images with coarse details or slight blur may benefit from a larger Radius setting. Images showing very fine details and no blur may benefit from a smaller Radius value.

7 When you're satisfied with the results, click OK to apply the Smart Sharpen filter.

8 Choose File > Save, and then close the project file.

Your image is ready to share or print!

Extra credit

Creatively converting a color image to black and white

You can control how a color image converts to black and white to get the look you want. The lightness of colors is not the same. For example, at maximum saturation, yellow is much lighter than blue. When you convert using the Black & White adjustment layer, you can control the lightness of different colors. For example, if the original sky is light blue, lowering the Blue value in the Black & White adjustment layer darkens the sky in the black-and-white version. This technique started in film photography, where a photographer would attach a color filter to the front of the lens to change the lightness of the sky, foliage, or portrait skin relative to the other original colors in the image.

1 Choose File > Open, navigate to the Autumn.jpg file in the Lesson02 folder, and click Open.

2 In the Adjustments panel, scroll down to the Single Adjustments category, and click the Black & White button. A new Black & White adjustment layer appears in the Layers panel, and the options for it appear in the Properties panel.

3 In the Properties panel, adjust the color sliders to change the lightness of different colors until you create the tonal relationships you want.

You can experiment with options from the Preset menu, such as Darker or Infrared. Or, select the on-image adjustment tool (✋) in the upper-left corner of the Properties panel, position it in the image over a color you want to adjust, and drag horizontally. The tool moves the sliders associated with the original color of the image where you started dragging; for example, dragging on the yellow leaves adjusts the lightness of all yellow areas.

4 If you want to colorize the entire photo with a single hue, select Tint in the Properties panel, click the color swatch, and select a tint color. You can continue to adjust the color sliders.

Review questions

1 What does *resolution* mean?

2 What are some ways to use the Crop tool to improve an image?

3 How can you adjust the tone and color of an image in Photoshop?

4 How can you instantly create a precise selection of an irregularly shaped object?

5 What tools can you use to remove blemishes in an image?

6 What are some ways Generative Fill can help retouch an image?

Review answers

1 For media such as print, the term *resolution* refers to the number of pixels per unit of physical width or height in an image, such as pixels per inch (ppi). Printer resolution may be expressed in dots per inch (dpi), because device dots do not always correspond to image pixels. For media measured in pixels, such as web and video, resolution typically refers to pixel dimensions (height and width), not pixels per inch.

2 You can use the Crop tool to trim, straighten, resize, and change the resolution of an image.

3 You can adjust the tone and color of an image in Photoshop using the Curves and Levels adjustment layers.

4 The Object Selection Tool recognizes objects in an image. You can click a highlighted object you want to select, or drag around it, and the resulting selection will follow the outline of the object.

5 In this lesson, you used the Remove tool and Generative Fill. Many other healing/cloning/patching tools are also available in Photoshop.

6 Generative Fill can be effective at filling large deleted areas in a convincing way, either by matching the background or generating new objects. It also generates variations so that you can choose from alternative solutions.

3 WORKING WITH SELECTIONS

Lesson overview

In this lesson, you'll learn how to do the following:

- Make specific areas of an image active using selection tools.

- Reposition a selection marquee.

- Move, rotate, and duplicate the contents of a selection.

- Use keyboard-mouse combinations that save time and hand motions.

- Deselect a selection.

- Adjust the position of a selected area using the arrow keys.

- Add to and subtract from a selection.

- Use multiple selection tools to make a complex selection.

- Save your work as a Photoshop cloud document you can easily open in Photoshop on other devices, and for online collaboration.

This lesson will take about an hour to complete. To get the lesson files used in this chapter, download them from the web page for this book at peachpit.com/PhotoshopCIB2024. For more information, see "Accessing the lesson files and Web Edition" in the Getting Started section at the beginning of this book. The lesson steps that use Adobe Cloud Documents require Internet access.

As you work on this lesson, you'll preserve the start files. If you need to restore the start files, download them from your Account page.

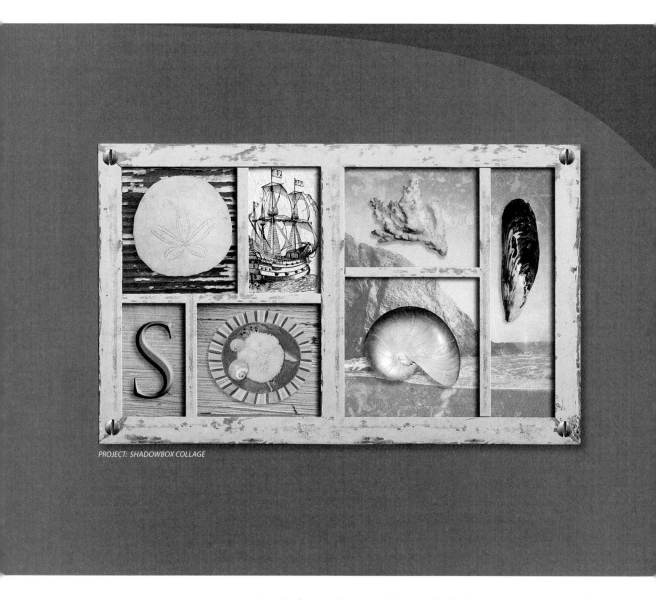

PROJECT: SHADOWBOX COLLAGE

Learning how to select areas of an image is of primary importance—you must first select what you want to affect. As long as a selection is active, only the area within the selection can be edited.

About selecting and pixel selection tools

Tip: The concept of selecting the content you want to change is common across many image-editing applications. As soon as you understand how selections work in one application, you can use that knowledge in other similar applications.

When you want to edit just an area of a pixel layer, you use a two-step process. First, *select* (mark) the area you want to change, using one of the selection tools. Then use another tool, filter, or other feature to make the changes, such as moving the selected pixels to another location or applying a filter. When a selection is active on a pixel layer, changes you make apply only to the selected area; other areas are unaffected. Similar pixel selection tools are grouped in the Tools panel:

Content- and edge-based selections. The Object Selection tool (▣) uses machine learning to identify subjects that you select with a simple click or drag; this is a quick and easy way to select people, animals, and other non-geometric shapes (you used the Object Selection tool in Lesson 2). The Quick Selection tool (◔) quickly expands the area you drag by looking for distinct regions of content in the image.

Color-based selections. The Magic Wand tool (✒) selects parts of an image based on similarity in pixel color. It's useful for selecting odd-shaped areas that share a specific range of colors or tones.

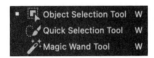

Note: This lesson focuses on tools and techniques for manual and semi-automated selection. This lesson doesn't cover the fully automated selection commands such as Edit > Sky Replacement (which you'll use in Lesson 5, "Quick Fixes") and Select > Subject (which you'll use in Lesson 6, "Masks and Patterns").

Geometric selections. The Rectangular Marquee tool (⬚) selects a rectangular area. The Elliptical Marquee tool (◯) selects an elliptical area. The Single Row Marquee tool (⋯) and Single Column Marquee tool (⑊) select either a 1-pixel-high row or a 1-pixel-wide column, respectively.

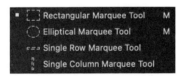

Freehand selections. The Lasso tool (◯) traces a freehand selection around an area. The Polygonal Lasso tool (▷) lays down straight-line segments around an area. The Magnetic Lasso tool (▷) automatically follows edges, typically giving the best results when high contrast exists between the area you want to select and its surroundings.

Getting started

First, you'll look at the image you will create as you explore the selection tools in Photoshop.

1 Start Photoshop, and then simultaneously hold down Ctrl+Alt+Shift (Windows) or Command+Option+Shift (macOS) to restore the default preferences. (See "Restoring default preferences" on page 5.)

2 When prompted, click Yes to confirm that you want to delete the Adobe Photoshop Settings file.

3 Choose File > Browse In Bridge to open Adobe Bridge.

4 In the Favorites panel, click the Lessons folder. Then double-click the Lesson03 folder in the Content panel to see its contents.

5 Study the 03End.psd file. Move the thumbnail slider to the right if you want to see the image in more detail.

The project is a shadow box that includes a piece of coral, a sand dollar, a mussel, a nautilus, and a plate of small shells. The challenge in this lesson is to arrange these elements, which were scanned together on the single page you see in the 03Start.psd file.

Note: If Bridge isn't installed, the File > Browse In Bridge command in Photoshop will start the Creative Cloud desktop app, which will download and install Bridge. After installation completes, you can start Bridge.

Note: If Bridge asks you if you want to import preferences from a previous version of Bridge, click No.

Using cloud documents

Photoshop document sizes can become large, especially for high-resolution images that use many layers. When you work with documents stored online, large file sizes upload and download more slowly; on a limited data plan you may reach the data limit more quickly. Adobe cloud documents help you edit online documents efficiently by using file formats optimized for networks. For example, editing a Photoshop file as a cloud document means only the parts affected by an edit are transmitted, instead of the entire file. If you use Photoshop on both a computer and an Apple iPad and you save an image as a cloud document, you'll find it in the Photoshop Home screen on both devices, always updated with your latest changes.

Tip: Using cloud documents can be more efficient than putting a Photoshop file on a cloud-based file sharing service. A cloud document transfers only the parts of a file that change, and you can open it in one click on the Photoshop Home screen.

Using cloud documents is easy; the only thing you have to do is save it to cloud documents. After you do this, your Photoshop document filename will have a .psdc filename extension to indicate that it's now a cloud document, and you will now find it listed in the cloud documents section in the Photoshop Home screen. The conversion to the PSDC format is automatic, so you don't have to think about it.

1 In Bridge, double-click the 03Start.psd thumbnail to open the image file in Photoshop. Close any messages that appear about new features. You've opened the document from your local storage.

2 Choose File > Save As, and click Save to Creative Cloud. If you see the standard Save As dialog box, first click the Save To Cloud Documents button.

▶ **Tip:** You can also find your cloud documents in the Creative Cloud app (mobile or desktop) and website, in the Your Files tab in the Cloud Documents panel. The list may also contain cloud documents from other Adobe applications.

3 Rename the file **03WorkingCloud**, and click Save. The file is uploaded to Cloud Documents. In the document window tab, you can see a cloud icon before the filename, and the filename now ends in .psdc.

● **Note:** Adobe cloud documents are not the same as Creative Cloud Libraries.

4 Close the document.

Now you'll open the cloud document. Again, this will be slightly different than opening a document from local storage.

1 In the Photoshop Home screen, select Your Files on the left side. It lists cloud documents you uploaded using your Adobe ID. You can also select Home, where the Recent list shows local and cloud documents you recently opened.

Tip: You can organize your cloud documents in folders on the server. When viewing Your Files on the Photoshop Home screen, click the folder icon near the top to create a new folder.

Tip: If you want to manage or delete a cloud document, click the document's ellipsis (…) button in the Your Files list on the Photoshop Home screen, and choose Rename, Delete, Make Available Offline Always, or Move.

2 Click 03WorkingCloud, the file you just saved. This downloads the file to your computer and opens it in Photoshop.

If you're editing a Photoshop Cloud (PSDC) Document, how can you provide that file to a client who requires a PSD file? By saving the cloud document to your own local storage. Again, the conversion is automatic, so it's easy and seamless.

1 Choose File > Save As. If you see the Save to Creative Cloud dialog box, click On Your Computer at the bottom to see the conventional Save As dialog box. Notice that the filename extension is now .psd, because you are saving this document to your local storage, not Cloud Documents.

2 Name the document **03Working.psd**, and save it into the Lesson03 folder. Now you have your own local PSD format copy that you can distribute and back up traditionally (without cloud services).

For this lesson, you can continue with your local copy (03Working.psd), or you can close the local PSD copy and instead open and work with your cloud documents copy (03WorkingCloud.psdc).

Note: You can't find a cloud document on your computer by looking through folders on your desktop; you see cloud documents in the Home screen in Photoshop. A cloud document is stored on Adobe servers and cached only to your local storage. If you need a local copy of a cloud document, choose File > Save As and save it to your computer as described to the left.

Using the Magic Wand tool

The Magic Wand tool selects pixels of a specific color range. It's most useful when the color or tone of the area you want to select is distinct from its background.

The Tolerance option sets the range of tonal levels the Magic Wand tool selects, starting from the pixel you click. The default tolerance value of 32 selects the color you click plus 32 lighter and 32 darker tones of that color. If the Magic Wand tool doesn't select the entire area you expect, try increasing the Tolerance value. If the tool selects too much, try decreasing the Tolerance value.

1 Select the Zoom tool in the Tools panel, and then zoom in so that you can see the entire sand dollar in detail.

2 Select the Magic Wand tool (✏️), hidden under the Object Selection tool (▪️).

3 In the options bar, confirm that the Tolerance value is **32**. This value determines the range of colors the wand selects.

4 Click the Magic Wand tool on the red background outside the sand dollar.

Tip: If a Magic Wand tool selection picks up too many similar colors outside the area you want to select, try enabling the Contiguous option in the options bar.

The Magic Wand tool perfectly selected the red background, because all of the background colors are similar enough to the pixel you clicked (within the 32 levels specified in the Tolerance setting). But it's the shell we want, so let's start over.

5 Choose Select > Deselect.

6 Position the Magic Wand tool over the sand dollar, and click.

Look carefully at the animated selection marquee that appears over the sand dollar. If this was a perfect selection, the selection marquee would tightly follow the outer edge of the sand dollar. But notice that some interior areas of the sand dollar show selection marquees, because their colors differ from the color you clicked by more than 32 levels (the Tolerance setting). The current selection doesn't include all interior colors.

When you want to select a subject that is mostly the same color and value, against a relatively solid background, you can often solve this by increasing the Tolerance value. But the more complex the subject or background, the more likely a wide Tolerance value will also select unwanted parts of the background. In that case, it's usually better to use a different selection tool, such as the Quick Selection tool. You'll do that next, but first let's deselect the current selection.

7 Choose Select > Deselect.

Using the Quick Selection tool

To use the Quick Selection tool you simply click or drag it within a subject, and the tool looks for the subject's edges. You can add or subtract areas of the selection until you have exactly the area you want. This works better than the Magic Wand tool because the Quick Selection tool is more aware of image content, instead of relying on color similarity alone. Let's see if the Quick Selection tool does a better job selecting the sand dollar.

▶ **Tip:** Notice that the Quick Selection tool looks for a subject outward from where you click or drag the tool, and the Object Selection tool looks for a subject inside the area you drag with that tool.

1 Select the Quick Selection tool (◉◢) in the Tools panel. It's grouped with the Object Selection tool (▣) and Magic Wand tool (✦).

2 Select Enhance Edge in the options bar.

Selecting Enhance Edge should improve the quality of the selection, with edges that are truer to the object. If you're using a slower or older computer, you might notice a slight delay when using Enhance Edge.

3 Click or drag within the sand dollar (do not cross over into the background).

The Quick Selection tool looks at what content is probably connected to the area where you clicked or dragged and finds the full edge automatically, selecting the entire sand dollar. The sand dollar is simple enough that the Quick Selection tool can isolate it instantly. When the Quick Selection tool doesn't complete the selection initially, click or drag over areas you want to add to the selection.

Leave the selection active so that you can use it in the next exercise.

▶ **Tip:** If the Quick Selection tool includes areas outside the subject, you can remove unwanted areas from the selection by clicking or dragging over them while holding down the Alt (Windows) or Option (macOS) key. That's the shortcut for selecting the Subtract From Selection icon in the options bar.

Moving a selected area

Once you've made a selection, any changes you make apply exclusively to the pixels within the selection. The rest of the image is not affected by those changes.

To move the selected area to another part of the composition, you use the Move tool. This image has only one layer, so the pixels you move will replace the pixels beneath them. This change is not permanent until you deselect the moved pixels, so you can try different locations for the selection you're moving before you commit it.

▶ **Tip:** If you deselect an area by accident, you may be able to restore the selection by choosing Edit > Undo or Select > Reselect.

1 If the sand dollar is not still selected, repeat the previous exercise to select it.

2 Zoom out so you can see both the shadow box and the sand dollar.

3 Select the Move tool (✥). Notice that the sand dollar remains selected.

4 Drag the selected area (the sand dollar) to the upper-left area of the frame, which is labeled "A." Position it over the silhouette in the frame, leaving the lower-left part of the silhouette showing as a shadow.

5 Choose Select > Deselect, and then choose File > Save.

There's more than one way to deselect a selection. You can choose Select > Deselect, press Ctrl+D (Windows) or Command+D (macOS), or click outside the selection with any selection tool (not the Move tool).

Adding to and subtracting from pixel selections

If a pixel selection isn't quite right, you can edit it, even with a different selection tool. When a selection tool is active, its options bar displays icons that change how your next action affects the existing selection. The options are New (■), Add (▣), Subtract (▣), and Intersect (▣). New replaces the current selection, Add extends the current selection, Subtract removes from the current selection, and Intersect keeps the area in common between the current selection and your next selection tool action.

The Quick Selection tool works like a brush, so its options are New (◔), Add (◔), and Subtract (◔).

For adding and subtracting, you can hold down modifier keys instead of clicking a button. Hold down Shift to add, and hold down Alt (Windows) or Option (macOS) to subtract. For example, if you want to use the Lasso tool to remove a few pixels from a pixel selection, hold down the Alt or Option key as you drag the tool.

Using the Object Selection tool

To use the Object Selection tool, all you have to do is draw a rough selection around the object you want to select, and the Object Selection tool identifies the object and creates a tight selection for it. For an object that has a complicated outline, such as the coral, the Object Selection tool will typically be much faster than trying to draw that irregular outline by hand.

1   Select the Object Selection tool (⬚), which is grouped with the Quick Selection tool (◔) and Magic Wand tool (🪄).

2   Drag a selection around the piece of coral. It doesn't have to be precise or centered. What's important is that it's a relatively tight selection with a small amount of space between the coral and the edges of the selection marquee. You're simply showing Photoshop which object you want to select.

Note: A colored highlight may appear over an object when you hover over it with the Object Selection tool. The highlight indicates that it's automatically identifying a potential selection. If the area you want to select is highlighted, just click.

The Object Selection tool analyzes the area inside the rectangular selection, finds the object, and creates a selection marquee along its complicated edge.

3   Select the Move tool (✛), and drag the coral to the area of the shadow box labeled "B," positioning it so that a shadow appears to the left of and below the coral.

4   Choose Select > Deselect, and then save your work.

Tip: If the Object Selection tool creates a selection that's too tight, choose Select > Modify > Expand and enter a pixel value; usually 1 to 3 is enough. As with other selection tools, you can add missed bits to the selection (by Shift-dragging the tool around the missed parts). Or subtract from the selection by holding down Alt (Windows) or Option (macOS) as you drag the tool around the area to remove.

Manipulating selections

You can move selections, reposition them as you create them, and even duplicate them. In this section, you'll learn several ways to manipulate selections. Most of these methods work with any selection; you'll use them here with the Elliptical Marquee tool, which lets you select ovals or perfect circles.

One of the most useful things you may learn about in this section are the modifier keys that can save you time and steps.

Repositioning a selection marquee while creating it

Selecting ellipses and rectangles can be tricky. Sometimes the selection will be off-center or the ratio of width to height won't match what you need. In this exercise, you'll learn techniques such as two important keyboard-mouse combinations that can make your Photoshop work much easier.

As you perform this exercise, be careful to follow the directions about keeping the mouse button or specific keys pressed. If you accidentally release the mouse button at the wrong time, simply start the exercise again from step 1.

1 Select the Zoom tool (Q), and click or drag it until the plate of shells at the bottom of the document window is at least 100% magnification (use 200% if the entire plate of shells still fits in the document window).

2 Select the Elliptical Marquee tool (◯), hidden under the Rectangular Marquee tool (▢).

Note: You don't have to include every pixel in the plate of shells, but the selection should be the shape of the plate and should contain the shells comfortably.

3 Move the pointer over the plate of shells, and drag diagonally across the oval plate to create a selection, but *do not release the mouse button*. It's OK if your selection does not match the plate shape yet.

If you accidentally release the mouse button, draw the selection again. In most cases—including this one—the new selection replaces the previous one.

4 Still holding down the mouse button, hold down the spacebar, and continue to drag the selection. Instead of resizing the selection, now you're moving it. Position the selection so that it more closely aligns with the plate.

Tip: The technique of holding down the spacebar to reposition as you draw also works with other drawing tools in Photoshop, such as the shape tools and the Pen tool.

5 Carefully release the spacebar (but not the mouse button) and continue to drag, trying to make the size and shape of the selection match the oval plate of shells as closely as possible. If necessary, hold down the spacebar again, and drag to move the selection marquee into position around the plate of shells.

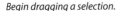

Begin dragging a selection.   *Press the spacebar to move it.*   *Complete the selection.*

6 When the selection border is positioned appropriately, release the mouse button.

Tip: If you want to resize a selection after releasing the mouse button, choose Select > Transform Selection.

7 Choose View > Fit On Screen or use the slider in the Navigator panel to reduce the zoom view so that you can see all of the objects in the document window.

Leave the Elliptical Marquee tool and the selection active for the next exercise.

Moving selected pixels with a keyboard shortcut

Now you'll use a modifier key to move the selected pixels onto the shadow box. The shortcut temporarily switches the active tool to the Move tool, so you don't need to select it from the Tools panel.

1 If the plate of shells is not still selected, repeat the previous exercise to select it.

2 With the Elliptical Marquee tool (◯) selected in the Tools panel, press Ctrl (Windows) or Command (macOS), and hover the pointer within the selection. Continue to hold down the key for the next step.

The pointer icon now includes a pair of scissors (▶✂), indicating that the selection will be cut from its current location.

3 While continuing to hold down the Ctrl or Command key, drag the plate of shells onto the area of the shadow box labeled "C." (You'll use another technique to nudge the oval plate into the exact position in a minute.)

● **Note:** In step 2, if you try to move the pixels but Photoshop displays an alert saying "Could not use the Move tool because the layer is locked," make sure you start dragging by positioning the pointer inside the selection.

4 Release the mouse button and the key, but don't deselect the plate of shells.

Moving a selection with the arrow keys

You can make minor adjustments to the position of selected pixels by using the arrow keys. You can nudge the selection in increments of 1 pixel or 10 pixels.

▶ **Tip:** If a selection becomes deselected accidentally, choose Select > Reselect.

When a selection tool is active in the Tools panel, the arrow keys nudge the selection border, but not the contents. When the Move tool is active, the arrow keys move both the selection border and its contents.

You'll use the arrow keys to nudge the plate of shells. Before you begin, make sure that the plate of shells is still selected in the document window.

1 Select the Move tool (✛), and press the Up Arrow key (🔼) on your keyboard a few times to move the oval upward.

Notice that each time you press the arrow key, the plate of shells moves 1 pixel. Experiment by pressing the other arrow keys to see how they affect the selection.

Softening the edges of a selection

To smooth the hard edges of a selection, you can apply anti-aliasing or feathering or use the Select and Mask option.

Anti-aliasing smooths the jagged edges of a selection by softening the color transition between edge pixels and background pixels. Since only the edge pixels change, detail loss is minimal. Anti-aliasing is useful when you cut, copy, and paste selections to create composite images.

Anti-aliasing is available for the Lasso, Polygonal Lasso, Magnetic Lasso, Elliptical Marquee, and Magic Wand tools. (Select the tool to display its options in the options bar.) To apply anti-aliasing, you must select the option before making the selection. Once a selection is made, you cannot add anti-aliasing to it.

Feathering blurs edges by building a transition at the boundary between the selection and its surrounding pixels. This can blur detail at the edge of the selection.

You can define feathering for the marquee and lasso tools as you use them, or you can add feathering to an existing selection. Feathering effects become apparent when you move, cut, or copy the selection.

- To feather a selection edge using the Select and Mask option, make a selection, and then click Select and Mask in the options bar to open its dialog box. In there you can smooth the outline, feather it, or contract or expand it.

- To anti-alias a selection edge, select a lasso tool, or the Elliptical Marquee or Magic Wand tool, and select Anti-alias in the options bar.

- To define a feathered edge for a selection you're about to draw, select any of the lasso or marquee tools. Enter a Feather value in the options bar. This value defines the width of the feathered edge and can range from 1 to 250 pixels.

- To define a feathered edge for an existing selection, choose Select > Modify > Feather. Enter a value for the Feather Radius, and click OK.

2   Hold down the Shift key as you press an arrow key.

When you hold down the Shift key, the selected pixels move 10 pixels every time you press an arrow key.

▶ **Tip:** Selection edges, guidelines, and other visible items that aren't actual objects are called *extras*, so another way to hide the selection edges is to deselect the View > Extras command or press its keyboard shortcut, Ctrl+H (Windows) or Command+H (macOS).

Sometimes the selection marquee can distract you as you make adjustments. You can hide the edges of a selection temporarily without actually deselecting and then display the selection border once you've completed the adjustments.

3   Choose View > Show > Selection Edges to deselect the command, hiding the selection border around the plate of shells.

4   Use the arrow keys to nudge the plate of shells until it's positioned over the silhouette so that there's a shadow on the left and bottom of the plate. Then choose View > Show > Selection Edges to reveal the selection border again.

Hidden selection edges.   Visible selection edges.

5   Choose Select > Deselect, or press Ctrl+D (Windows) or Command+D (macOS).

6   Choose File > Save to save your work so far.

Selecting with the lasso tools

Photoshop includes three lasso tools: the Lasso tool, the Polygonal Lasso tool, and the Magnetic Lasso tool. You can use the Lasso tool to make selections that require both freehand and straight lines, using keyboard shortcuts to move back and forth between the Lasso tool and the Polygonal Lasso tool. You'll use the Lasso tool to select the mussel. It takes a bit of practice to alternate between straight-line and freehand selections—if you make a mistake while you're selecting the mussel, simply deselect and start again.

1   If the window magnification is below 100%, select the Zoom tool (⌕), and click or drag to zoom in to at least 100%.

2   Select the Lasso tool (⌒). Starting at the lower-left section of the mussel, drag around the rounded end of the mussel, tracing the shape as accurately as possible. *Do not release the mouse button.*

3   When you reach a corner or straight part of the edge, press the Alt (Windows) or Option (macOS) key, and then release the mouse button so that the lasso pointer changes to the polygonal lasso shape (⋈). *Do not release the Alt or Option key.*

4   Begin clicking along the end of the mussel to place anchor points, following the contours of the mussel. Be sure to hold down the Alt or Option key throughout this process. This lets you create perfectly straight segments along the selection.

▶ **Tip:** Because the lasso tools are manual, they can be the most time-consuming way to create a selection. They are typically most useful for selecting simple shapes or adjusting an existing selection.

▶ **Tip:** Go slowly until you become comfortable with the Lasso tool. If you make a mistake or accidentally release the mouse button during steps 2–8, choose Edit > Undo, and start again at step 2.

Drag with the Lasso tool.   Click with the Polygonal Lasso tool.

The selection border automatically stretches like a rubber band between anchor points.

5   When you reach the tip of the mussel, hold down the mouse button as you release the Alt or Option key. The pointer again appears as the lasso icon.

6   Carefully drag around the tip of the mussel, holding down the mouse button.

7   When you finish tracing the tip and reach the straight segments along the lower side of the mussel, first press Alt or Option again, and then release the mouse button. Click along the straight segments of the lower side of the mussel as needed. Continue to trace the straight and curved mussel edges until you arrive back at the starting point of your selection at the left end of the mussel.

● **Note:** To make sure that the selection is the shape you want when you use the Lasso tool, end the selection by dragging across the starting point of the selection. If you start and stop the selection at different points, Photoshop draws a straight line between the start and end points of the selection.

8   Click the starting point of the selection, and then release Alt or Option. The mussel is now entirely selected. Leave the mussel selected for the next exercise.

Rotating selected pixels

Now you'll rotate the mussel.

Before you begin, make sure that the mussel is still selected.

1   Choose View > Fit On Screen to resize the document window to fit on your screen.

2   Press Ctrl (Windows) or Command (macOS) as you drag the selected mussel to the section of the shadow box labeled "D."

The pointer changes to the Move tool icon when you press Ctrl (Windows) or Command (macOS).

3   Choose Edit > Transform > Rotate.

The mussel and selection marquee are enclosed in a bounding box.

▶ **Tip:** You can constrain rotation to common angles such as 90 degrees by holding down the Shift key as you drag the bounding box.

4   Move the pointer outside the bounding box so that it becomes a curved, two-headed arrow (↱). Drag to rotate the mussel to a 90-degree angle. You can verify the angle in the transformation values display next to the pointer, or in the Rotate box in the options bar. Press Enter or Return to commit the transformation.

5 If necessary, select the Move tool (✥), and drag to reposition the mussel, leaving a shadow to match the others. When you're satisfied, choose Select > Deselect.

6 Choose File > Save.

Selecting with the Magnetic Lasso tool

You can use the Magnetic Lasso tool to make freehand selections of areas with high-contrast edges. When you draw with the Magnetic Lasso tool, the selection border automatically snaps to the edge between areas of contrast. You can also control the selection path by occasionally clicking the mouse to place anchor points in the selection border.

You'll use the Magnetic Lasso tool to select the nautilus so that you can move it to the shadow box.

1 Select the Zoom tool (🔍), and click or drag to zoom in on the nautilus.

2 Select the Magnetic Lasso tool (🧲), hidden under the Lasso tool (🔗).

3 Click once along the left edge of the nautilus, and then move the Magnetic Lasso tool along the edge to trace its outline.

▶ **Tip:** In low-contrast areas, you may want to click to place your own fastening points. You can add as many as you need. To remove the most recent fastening point, press Delete, and then move the mouse back to the remaining fastening point and continue selecting.

Even if you don't hold down the mouse button, the tool snaps to the edge of the nautilus and automatically adds fastening points.

4 When you reach the left side of the nautilus again, double-click to return the Magnetic Lasso tool to the starting point, closing the selection. Or you can move the Magnetic Lasso tool over the starting point and click once.

5 Double-click the Hand tool (🖑) to fit the entire image in the window.

6 Select the Move tool (✛), and drag the nautilus onto its silhouette in the section of the frame labeled "E," leaving a shadow below it and on the left side.

7 Choose Select > Deselect, and then choose File > Save.

Selecting from a center point

In some cases, it's easier to make elliptical or rectangular selections by drawing a selection from an object's center point. You'll use this technique to select the head of the screw for the shadow box corners.

1 Select the Zoom tool (🔍), and zoom in on the screw to a magnification of about 300%. Make sure that the entire screw head is visible in your document window.

2 Select the Elliptical Marquee tool (⬭) in the Tools panel.

3 Move the pointer to the approximate center of the screw.

4 Click and begin dragging. Then, without releasing the mouse button, press Alt (Windows) or Option (macOS) as you continue dragging the selection to the outer edge of the screw.

The selection is centered over its starting point.

▶ **Tip:** To select a perfect circle, press Shift as you drag. Hold down Shift while dragging the Rectangular Marquee tool to select a perfect square.

5   When you have the entire screw head selected, release the mouse button first, and then release Alt or Option (and the Shift key if you used it). Do not deselect, because you'll use this selection in the next exercise.

6   If necessary, reposition the selection border using one of the methods you learned earlier. If you accidentally released the Alt or Option key before you released the mouse button, select the screw again.

Resizing and copying a selection

Now you'll move the screw to the lower-right corner of the wooden shadow box and then duplicate it for the other corners.

Resizing the contents of a selection

You'll start by moving the screw, but it's too large for the space. You'll need to resize it as well.

Before you begin, make sure that the screw is still selected. If it's not, reselect it by completing the previous exercise.

1   Choose View > Fit On Screen so that the entire image fits within the document window.

2   Select the Move tool (✛) in the Tools panel.

3   Position the pointer within the screw selection.

The pointer becomes an arrow with a pair of scissors (▶✄), indicating that dragging the selection will cut it from its current location and move it to the new location.

4   Drag the screw onto the lower-right corner of the shadow box.

▶ **Tip:** If the screw won't move or resize smoothly, as if it gets "stuck," hold down the Control key to temporarily disable snapping to magenta Smart Guides as you drag. Or permanently disable them by deselecting the View > Show > Smart Guides command.

5   Choose Edit > Transform > Scale. A bounding box appears around the selection.

6   Drag one of the corner points inward to reduce the screw to about 40% of its original size or until it is small enough to sit on the shadow box frame.

As you resize the object, the selection marquee resizes, too. Both resize proportionally by default.

7   Press Enter or Return to commit the change and remove the transformation bounding box.

8   Use the Move tool to reposition the screw after resizing it so that it is centered in the corner of the shadow box frame.

▶ **Tip:** If you don't want to maintain original proportions while resizing, press the Shift key as you drag a corner handle of a transformation bounding box.

9   Leaving the screw selected, choose File > Save to save your work.

Moving and duplicating a selection simultaneously

You can move and duplicate a selection at the same time. You'll copy the screw for the other three corners of the frame. If the screw is no longer selected, reselect it now, using the techniques you learned earlier.

1   With the Move tool (✛) selected, press Alt (Windows) or Option (macOS) as you position the pointer inside the screw selection.

The pointer changes, displaying the usual black arrow and an additional white arrow, which indicates that a duplicate will be made when you move the selection.

2   Continue holding down the Alt or Option key as you drag a duplicate of the screw straight up to the top-right corner of the frame. Release the mouse button and the Alt or Option key, but don't deselect the duplicate image.

3   Hold down Alt+Shift (Windows) or Option+Shift (macOS), and drag a new copy of the screw straight left to the upper-left corner of the frame.

Pressing the Shift key as you move a selection constrains the movement horizontally or vertically in 45-degree increments.

4 Repeat step 3 to drag a fourth screw to the lower-left corner of the frame.

5 When you're satisfied with the position of the fourth screw, choose Select > Deselect, and then choose File > Save.

Copying selected pixels

You can use the Move tool to copy selected pixels as you drag them within or between images, or you can copy and move selections using commands on the Edit menu. The Move tool uses less memory, because it doesn't use the clipboard.

Photoshop has several copy and paste commands on the Edit menu:

- **Copy** takes the selected area on the active layer and puts it on the clipboard.
- **Copy Merged** creates a merged copy of all the visible layers in the selected area.
- **Paste** inserts the clipboard contents at the center of the image. If you paste into another image, the pasted content becomes a new layer.

On the Edit > Paste Special submenu, Photoshop also provides specialized pasting commands to give you more options in certain situations:

- **Paste without Formatting** pastes text without the formatting it may have been copied with, such as font and size. It helps ensure that text pasted from another document or application matches the formatting of a Photoshop text layer.
- **Paste in Place** pastes clipboard content at the location it had in the original image, instead of at the center of the document.
- **Paste Into** pastes clipboard content inside the active selection in the same or a different image. The source selection is pasted onto a new layer, and the area outside the selection is converted into a layer mask.
- **Paste Outside** is the same as Paste Into except that Photoshop pastes the content outside the active selection and converts the area inside the selection to a layer mask.

If two documents have different pixel dimensions, content you paste between them may appear to change size. This is because content maintains its pixel dimensions when pasted into a document with different pixel dimensions. You can resize a pasted selection, but the image quality of the selection may decrease if enlarged.

Other ways to select pixels

When the outline of a subject is too difficult or time-consuming to make a selection by clicking or dragging a selection tool (such as the Lasso tool), it may be faster to select in other ways. You can accomplish more challenging selections by combining multiple selection methods.

Selecting by tone or color

Color Range command. With the Select > Color Range command, you can specify a range of colors to select. Some range presets are built into the Select menu, such as Skin Tones, Highlights, and Shadows. You can also click the image to sample a color to use as the starting point for the color range, similar to clicking the Magic Wand tool but with the ability to refine the range.

Thumbnail previews. In the Layers or Channels panel, Ctrl-click (Windows) or Command-click (macOS) a thumbnail preview to select based on pixel values. For example, in the Layers panel this technique selects all non-transparent pixels. In the Channels panel, this technique creates a selection based on luminance (brightness), used in advanced techniques such as creating a luminance mask. Ctrl/Command-clicking the composite channel selects composite luminance, and Ctrl/Command-clicking one channel (such as the Blue channel of an RGB image) selects that channel's luminance.

Selecting with machine learning

Using advanced machine learning, the Select > Subject and Select > Sky commands can select a main subject or the sky, respectively, and the Object Selection tool recognizes individual items in a picture.

Selecting by painting, with Quick Mask mode

If you think it would be easier to select an area by painting with a brush, click the QuickMask icon in the Tools panel (or press the Q key) to enter Quick Mask mode, select a brush tool, and start painting. In the Layers panel, the layer becomes red while in QuickMask mode. When you're done, click the Quick Mask icon (or press Q) again to exit the mode. The area you painted becomes a pixel selection.

Selecting by what's in focus

If you want to edit only the in-focus part of an image, choose Select > Focus Area. Use the options to refine which parts you want Focus Area to consider to be in focus. When you click OK, the area you defined as in focus becomes a selection.

Creating a refined selection with Select and Mask

For selections with fuzzy edges such as hair, try the specialized tools and options in the Select and Mask workspace. You'll learn more about Select and Mask in Lesson 6.

Selecting different kinds of content

This lesson focuses on selecting the pixels you want to edit. In Photoshop you will also work with non-pixel items, so it's useful to know how to select them too:

Pixels. An area of selected pixels is also called a *marquee* selection, which appears as an animated "marching ants" border. You can select pixels by using tools in the marquee and lasso tool groups, the Object Selection, Quick Selection, and Magic Wand tools, and by using commands on the Select menu. You can also use the methods in the sidebar "Other ways to select pixels" in this lesson.

List items in panels. Some features affect only what's selected in a panel list, such as in the Layers and Paths panels. For example, many Photoshop commands, and many settings in the Properties panel, affect only the layer selected in the Layers panel.

Type. You can select a type layer in the Layers panel. To select characters on that type layer, use a text tool. You'll learn more about working with text in Lesson 7.

Paths. When you work with paths, they're vector objects (not pixels), so you select them in the Paths panel, select subpaths using the Path Selection Tool, and select path points and segments with the Direct Selection tool. Shape layers are paths you can export and print, and you select shape layers in the Layers panel. You'll learn more about paths and shape layers in Lesson 8.

Using different kinds of selections together

For some features, you might need to use a specific kind of selection or multiple kinds of selection simultaneously. For example, to apply a filter to an entire layer, first select that layer in the Layers panel list; and to apply that filter only to a specific area on that layer, also select an area of pixels.

Marquee selecting pixels on the layer selected in the Layers panel.

Converting between pixel selections and paths

It can be useful to convert between different kinds of selections. For example, sometimes it's faster to draw the intended area using a shape tool or Pen tool instead of with a lasso selection tool and then convert the path into a pixel selection. You can convert either way using the Paths panel:

A. Load Path as a Selection button
B. Make Work Path from Selection button

- To convert a path to a pixel selection, click the Load Path as a Selection button.

- To convert a pixel selection to a path, click the Make Work Path from Selection button.

Cropping an image

Now that your composition is in place, you'll crop the image to a final size. You can use either the Crop tool or the Crop command to crop an image.

1 Select the Crop tool (⌐), or press C to switch from the current tool to the Crop tool. Photoshop displays a crop boundary around the entire image.

2 In the options bar, make sure Ratio is selected in the Preset pop-up menu and that there are no ratio values specified. (If there are, click Clear.) Then confirm that Delete Cropped Pixels is selected.

When Ratio is selected but no ratio values are specified, you can freely crop the image to any proportions.

▶ **Tip:** To crop an image with its original proportions intact, choose Original Ratio from the Preset pop-up menu in the options bar.

3 Drag the crop handles so that the shadow box is in the highlighted area, omitting the backgrounds from the original objects at the bottom of the image. Crop the frame so that there's an even area of white around it.

4 When you're satisfied with the position of the crop area, click the Commit Current Crop Operation button (✓) in the options bar.

5 Choose File > Save to save your work.

You've used several different selection tools to move all the seashells into place. The shadow box is complete!

Review questions

1 Once you've made a selection, what area of the image can be edited?

2 How do you add to and subtract from a selection when using a tool such as the Quick Selection or Lasso tool?

3 How can you move a selection while you're creating it?

4 What is the difference between the Quick Selection tool and the Object Selection tool?

5 How does the Magic Wand tool determine which areas of an image to select? What is tolerance, and how does it affect a selection?

Review answers

1 When a selection is active, edits apply only within that selection.

2 To add to a selection, click the Add To Selection button in the options bar, and then click the area you want to add. To subtract from a selection, click the Subtract From Selection button in the options bar, and then click the area you want to subtract. You can also add to a selection by pressing Shift as you drag or click; to subtract, press Alt (Windows) or Option (macOS) as you drag or click.

3 To reposition a selection as you're creating it, keep holding down the mouse button as you also hold down the spacebar and drag.

4 The Quick Selection tool attempts to detect content edges, while the Object Selection tool attempts to recognize subjects (such as people) and objects in the image.

5 The Magic Wand tool selects adjacent pixels based on their similarity in color. The Tolerance value determines how many color tones the Magic Wand tool will select. The higher the tolerance setting, the more tones are selected.

4 LAYER BASICS

Lesson overview

In this lesson, you'll learn how to do the following:

- Organize artwork on layers.

- Create, view, hide, and select layers.

- Rearrange layers to change the stacking order of artwork.

- Apply blending modes to layers.

- Resize and rotate layers.

- Apply a gradient to a layer.

- Apply a filter to a layer.

- Add text and layer effects to a layer.

- Add an adjustment layer.

- Save a copy of the file with the layers flattened.

 This lesson will take less than an hour to complete. To get the lesson files used in this chapter, download them from the web page for this book at peachpit.com/PhotoshopCIB2024. For more information, see "Accessing the lesson files and Web Edition" in the Getting Started section at the beginning of this book.

As you work on this lesson, you'll preserve the start files. If you need to restore the start files, download them from your Account page.

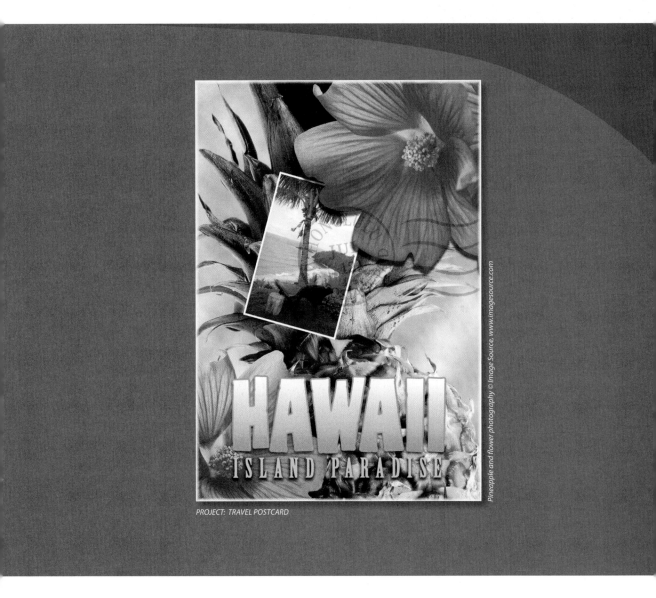

PROJECT: TRAVEL POSTCARD

In Photoshop, you can organize different parts of an image using layers. Each layer can then be edited as discrete artwork, giving you tremendous flexibility as you compose and revise an image.

About layers

Note: Some file formats, such as JPEG and GIF, don't support layers. To save those images with layers, you must save them in Photoshop or TIFF format. Also, some color modes (on the Image > Mode submenu), such as Bitmap and Indexed Color, don't support layers. The lesson files in this lesson are Photoshop documents in RGB color mode.

Every Photoshop file contains one or more *layers*. All new layers in an image are transparent until you add text or artwork. Working with layers is analogous to placing portions of a drawing on clear sheets of film, such as those viewed with an overhead projector: Individual sheets may be edited, repositioned, and deleted without affecting the other sheets. When the sheets are stacked, the entire composition is visible.

Many of the lesson files for this book have a *background layer*, a layer behind all others that is always completely opaque. Photoshop documents intended for print, digital camera images, and scanned images typically have a background layer. Photoshop documents created for mobile devices and websites might not have a background layer; for example, website graphics may need transparent areas that won't block a web page's background or other elements. To learn more about the background layer, see "About the background layer" on page 92.

Getting started

You'll start the lesson by viewing an image of the final composition.

1 Start Photoshop, and then simultaneously hold down Ctrl+Alt+Shift (Windows) or Command+Option+Shift (macOS) to restore the default preferences. (See "Restoring default preferences" on page 5.)

2 When prompted, click Yes to delete the Adobe Photoshop Settings file.

Note: If Bridge isn't installed, you'll be prompted to install it. For more information, see page 3.

3 Choose File > Browse In Bridge to open Adobe Bridge.

4 In the Favorites panel, click the Lessons folder. Then double-click the Lesson04 folder in the Content panel to see its contents.

5 Study the 04End.psd file. Move the thumbnail slider to the right if you want to see the image in more detail.

This layered composite represents a postcard. You will assemble it in this lesson as you learn how to create, edit, and manage layers.

Note: If Photoshop displays a dialog box telling you about the difference between saving to Cloud Documents and On Your Computer, click Save On Your Computer. You can also select Don't Show Again, but that setting will deselect after you reset Photoshop preferences.

6 Double-click the 04Start.psd file to open it in Photoshop. Close any messages that appear about new features.

7 Choose File > Save As, rename the file **04Working.psd**, and click Save. Click OK if you see the Photoshop Format Options dialog box.

Saving another version of the start file frees you to make changes without worrying about overwriting the original.

Using the Layers panel

The Layers panel lists all the layers in an image, displaying the layer names and thumbnail previews of the content on each layer. You can use the Layers panel to hide, view, reposition, delete, rename, and merge layers. The layer thumbnails are automatically updated as you edit the layers.

1 If the Layers panel is not visible in the work area, choose Window > Layers.

The Layers panel lists five layers for the 04Working.psd file (from top to bottom): Postage, HAWAII, Flower, Pineapple, and Background.

2 Select the Background layer to make it active (if it's not already selected). Notice the layer thumbnail and the icons shown for the Background layer:

▶ **Tip:** Use the context menu to hide or resize the layer thumbnail (the small preview picture next to the layer name). Right-click (Windows) or Control-click (macOS) a thumbnail in the Layers panel to open the context menu, and then choose a thumbnail size.

- The lock icon (🔒) indicates that the layer is protected from layer changes. That's why the options above the layer list are unavailable. However, it's still possible to edit the layer content itself, such as painting on it.

- The eye icon (👁) indicates that the layer is visible in the document window. If you click the eye, the document window no longer displays that layer.

The first task for this project is to add a photo of the beach to the postcard. First, you'll open the beach image in Photoshop.

3 In Photoshop, choose File > Open, navigate to the Lesson04 folder, and then double-click the Beach.psd file to open it.

The Layers panel changes to display the layer information for the active Beach.psd file. Notice that only one layer appears in the Beach.psd image: Layer 1. It's not a Background layer, so it can use layer features such as transparency.

About the background layer

If you see a layer named Background at the bottom of the Layers panel and it displays a lock icon, it's a *background layer*, which does not act like other layers. You can't change a background layer's position in the stacking order, and it's always opaque (no transparent areas). When you flatten the layers of a Photoshop document, the document contains only a background layer.

You can convert a background layer to a regular layer or create a document without a background layer. When a Photoshop document has no background layer, any pixels that don't contain content can be transparent. That makes it possible for the content in a Photoshop document to have a non-rectangular shape when placed over another background in Photoshop or in other applications.

To convert a background layer into a regular layer:

Click the lock icon next to the Background layer name. It changes to a default layer name. (Or, double-click the Background layer, set options, and click OK.)

To convert a regular layer into a background layer:

1 Select a layer in the Layers panel.

2 Choose Layer > New > Background From Layer.

Renaming and copying a layer

To add content, drag and drop one or more files or Photoshop layers into a Photoshop document window. You can drag layers from a source document window, drag them from the Layers panel, or drag a compatible file from the desktop. Each item you drop into a Photoshop document is added as a separate layer.

You'll drag the Beach.psd image onto the 04Working.psd file. Before you begin, make sure that both the 04Working.psd and Beach.psd files are open and that the Beach.psd file is selected.

First, you'll give Layer 1 a more descriptive name.

1   In the Layers panel, double-click the name Layer 1, type **Beach**, and then press Enter or Return. Keep the layer selected.

2   Choose Window > Arrange > 2-Up Vertical. Photoshop displays both of the open image files. Select the Beach.psd image so that it is the active file.

3   Select the Move tool (✛), and use it to drag the Beach.psd image onto the 04Working.psd document window.

▶ **Tip:** Dragging many layers to another document can be easier if you combine them into a layer group first. Select them in the Layers panel, and then choose Layer > Group Layers. Now you have only one thing to drag: the layer group (which uses a folder icon).

● **Note:** When you rename a layer, make sure you double-click the layer name text. If you double-click outside the name, other layer options may appear instead.

▶ **Tip:** If you hold down Shift as you drag an image from one file into another, the dragged image automatically centers itself in the target image window.

▶ **Tip:** You can also transfer layers between documents by copying and pasting: Select layers in the Layers panel, choose Edit > Copy, switch to another document, and choose Edit > Paste.

Tip: Need images for a project like this one? In Photoshop, choose File > Search Adobe Stock to download low-resolution placeholder images from the Adobe Stock online photo library. If you license the images, Photoshop replaces the placeholders with high-resolution images.

The Beach layer now appears in the 04Working.psd file document window and its Layers panel, between the Background and Pineapple layers. Photoshop always adds new layers directly above the selected layer; you selected the Background layer earlier.

4 Close the Beach.psd file without saving changes to it.

Viewing individual layers

Tip: To center a layer that's already added, drag it near the center of the document, and magenta Smart Guides appear when a layer is snapped to the horizontal and vertical document center.

The 04Working.psd file now contains six layers. Some of the layers are visible, and some are hidden. The eye icon (👁) next to a layer thumbnail in the Layers panel indicates that the layer is visible.

1 Click the eye icon (👁) next to the Pineapple layer to hide the image of the pineapple.

You can hide or show a layer by clicking this icon or clicking in its column, also called the Show/Hide Visibility column.

2   Click again in the Show/Hide Visibility column to display the pineapple.

Adding a border using the Stroke layer style

Now you'll add a white border around the Beach layer to create the impression that it's an old photograph.

1   Select the Beach layer. (To select the layer, click the layer name in the Layers panel.)

The layer is highlighted, indicating that it is active. Changes you make in the document window affect the active layer.

2   To make the opaque areas on this layer more obvious, hide all layers except the Beach layer: Press Alt (Windows) or Option (macOS) as you click the eye icon (👁) next to the Beach layer.

The white background and other objects in the image disappear, leaving only the beach image against a checkerboard background. The checkerboard indicates transparent areas of the active layer.

3   Choose Layer > Layer Style > Stroke.

The Layer Style dialog box opens. Now you'll select the options for the white stroke around the beach image.

▶ **Tip:** When the Preview option is enabled in a dialog box such as Layer Style, you can watch the selected layer change as you adjust the options.

4 Specify the following settings:

- Size: **5** px
- Position: Inside
- Blend Mode: Normal
- Opacity: **100**%
- Color: White (Click the Color box, and select white in the Color Picker.)

● **Note:** Layer styles apply to the opaque pixels of a layer only. For example, the Stroke layer style draws its line around the opaque pixels of the Beach layer and doesn't change the transparent pixels.

5 Click OK to commit the effect to the layer.

Rearranging layers

The order in which the layers of an image are organized is called the *stacking order*. Stacking order determines how the image is viewed—you can change the order to make certain parts of the image appear in front of or behind other layers.

You'll rearrange the layers so that the beach image is in front of another image that is currently hidden in the file.

1 Make the Postage, HAWAII, Flower, Pineapple, and Background layers visible by clicking the Show/Hide Visibility column next to their layer names.

▶ **Tip:** When you want to hide or show a continuous series of layers, you can also drag through their eye icons in the Show/Hide Visibility column, instead of clicking each eye icon separately.

The beach image is almost entirely blocked by images on other layers.

2 In the Layers panel, drag the Beach layer up so that it is positioned between the Pineapple and Flower layers—as you drag, a blue line indicates where it will be dropped—and then release the mouse button.

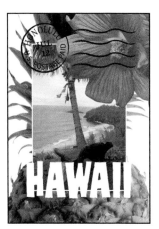

The Beach layer moves up one level in the stacking order, and the beach image appears on top of the pineapple and background images but under the postmark, flower, and the word "HAWAII."

▶ **Tip:** You can also control the stacking order of layered images by selecting them in the Layers panel, choosing Layer > Arrange, and then choosing Bring To Front, Bring Forward, Send Backward, or Send To Back.

Changing the opacity of a layer

You can reduce the opacity of any layer to reveal the layers below it. In this case, the postmark is too dark on the flower. You'll edit the opacity of the Postage layer to let the flower and other images show through.

1 Select the Postage layer, and then click the arrow next to the Opacity field to display the Opacity slider. Drag the slider to 25%. You can also type **25** in the Opacity box or scrub the Opacity label.

The Postage layer becomes partially transparent so you can better see the layers underneath. Notice that the change in opacity affects only the content of the Postage layer. The Pineapple, Beach, Flower, and HAWAII layers remain opaque.

2 Choose File > Save to save your work.

Duplicating a layer and changing the blending mode

You can apply different blending modes to a layer. *Blending modes* affect how the color pixels on one layer blend with pixels on the layers behind it (see the "Blending modes" sidebar on page 100). First you'll use blending modes to increase the intensity of the image on the Pineapple layer so that it doesn't look so dull. Then you'll change the blending mode on the Postage layer. (Currently, the blending mode for both layers is Normal.)

1 Click the eye icons next to the HAWAII, Flower, and Beach layers to hide them.

▶ **Tip:** If you prefer using the menu bar, Duplicate Layer is also available by choosing Layer > Duplicate Layer.

2 Right-click or Control-click the Pineapple layer name, and choose Duplicate Layer from the context menu. (Make sure you click the layer name; other areas may display a different context menu.) Click OK in the Duplicate Layer dialog box.

A layer called "Pineapple copy" appears above the Pineapple layer in the Layers panel.

3 With the Pineapple copy layer selected, choose Overlay from the Blending Modes menu in the Layers panel.

The Overlay blending mode blends the Pineapple copy layer with the Pineapple layer beneath it to create a vibrant, more colorful pineapple with deeper shadows and brighter highlights.

4 Select the Postage layer, and choose Multiply from the Blending Modes menu.

The Multiply blending mode multiplies the color values of its layer with those of the underlying layers. In this example, areas of the postmark that are over the pineapple are darkened using the tonal values of the pineapple.

Each blending mode uses different math to combine a layer with the layers behind it. Overlay tends to increase contrast; Multiply tends to darken its layer.

5 Choose File > Save to save your work.

Tip: Notice that the image changes as you move the mouse over the options in the Blending Modes menu. This is a quick way to preview which one will do what you want.

Tip: If the effect of a blending mode is too strong, reduce the Opacity of that layer.

Tip: As the list of layers becomes longer, it can be difficult to locate the layer you want. You can use the filter field at the top of the Layers panel to limit the layer list by attributes such as layer kind, layer name, effect, and more.

Tip: In the Layers panel list, you can display the selected layers only and hide the rest: Choose Select > Isolate Layers. When you do this, the filter switch in the Layers panel turns red to let you know that some layers are hidden in the list.

Blending modes

Blending modes affect how the color pixels on a layer blend with pixels on the layers behind them. The default blending mode, Normal, hides pixels beneath the top layer unless the top layer is partially or completely transparent. Each of the other blending modes lets you control the way the pixels in the layers interact with each other.

Often, the best way to see how a blending mode affects your image is simply to try it. You can easily experiment with various blending modes in the Layers panel, watching the image change as you move the mouse over the options in the Blending Modes menu. As you experiment, keep in mind how different groups of blending modes affect an image:

- To darken underlying layers, try Darken, Multiply, Color Burn, Linear Burn, or Darker Color.
- To lighten underlying layers, try Lighten, Screen, Color Dodge, Linear Dodge, or Lighter Color.
- To increase the contrast between layers, try Overlay, Soft Light, Hard Light, Vivid Light, Linear Light, Pin Light, or Hard Mix.
- To change the color values of the image, try Hue, Saturation, Color, or Luminosity.
- To create an inversion effect, try Difference or Exclusion.

The following blending modes tend to be used more often and are good ways to start experimenting:

- **Multiply** does what the name implies: It multiplies the selected layer's color values with the color values of underlying layers.

Multiply

- **Lighten** uses the lightest color value it finds after comparing pixels on the selected layer to underlying layers.

- **Overlay** increases contrast in underlying layers, especially in light and dark areas. The difference is smaller the closer the selected layer's color value is to middle gray, which applies no change to underlying layers.

Lighten

- **Luminosity** replaces the luminance of underlying pixels, using the selected layer.

Overlay   *Luminosity*   *Difference*

- **Difference** subtracts darker colors from lighter ones. It's a great way to visually identify the differences between two nearly identical images on separate layers.

When you apply different blending modes to multiple layers, you can change the effect by applying the blending modes in a different order in the layer stack. Also, applying a blending mode to a layer group gives you a different result than applying the same blending mode to each layer in the group.

Resizing and rotating layers

Changing the position, size, and angle of layers gives you many creative possibilities. In Photoshop, these kinds of edits are called *transformations*. You performed transformations in Lesson 3 with selections, and they also apply to layers.

1 Click the Visibility column on the Beach layer to make the layer visible.

2 Select the Beach layer in the Layers panel, and choose Edit > Free Transform.

A Transform bounding box appears around the beach image. The bounding box has square handles on each corner and each side.

First, you'll resize and angle the layer.

3 Drag the lower-right corner handle inward to scale down the beach photo by about 50%. (Watch the Width and Height percentages in the options bar.)

4 With the bounding box still active, position the pointer just outside the bounding box until the pointer becomes a curved double arrow. Drag clockwise to rotate the beach image approximately 15 degrees. You can also enter **15** in the Set Rotation box in the options bar.

▶ **Tip:** The Edit > Free Transform command is so useful that you may want to memorize its keyboard shortcut: Ctrl+T (Windows) or Command+T (macOS).

A. *Width value*
B. *Height value*
C. *Set Rotation box*

5 Click the Commit Transform button (✔) in the options bar.

6 Make the Flower layer visible. Then select the Move tool (✛), and drag the beach photo so that its corner is tucked neatly beneath the flower, as in the illustration after step 7.

▶ **Tip:** You can also commit a transformation by clicking far outside the transform bounding box. Just make sure you aren't clicking somewhere that will alter a setting or layer accidentally.

7 Choose File > Save.

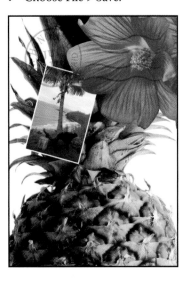

Using a filter to create artwork

Next, you'll create a new layer with no artwork on it yet. (Adding empty layers to a file is like adding blank sheets of clear film to a stack of images.) You'll use this layer to add realistic-looking clouds to the sky with a Photoshop filter.

1 In the Layers panel, select the Background layer to make it active, and then click the Create A New Layer button (⊞) at the bottom of the Layers panel.

A new layer, named Layer 1, appears between the Background and Pineapple layers. The layer has no content, so it has no effect on the image.

Note: You can also create a new layer by choosing Layer > New > Layer or by choosing New Layer from the Layers panel menu.

2 Double-click the name Layer 1, type **Clouds**, and press Enter or Return to rename the layer.

3   In the Tools panel, click the foreground color swatch, select a sky blue color from the Color Picker, and click OK. We selected a color with the following values: R=48, G=138, B=174. The Background Color remains white.

▶ **Tip:** If you expect to use a certain color frequently in multiple documents, add it to your Creative Cloud Libraries. Create a color in the Color panel, and then in the Libraries panel, click the Add Elements button (+) and choose Foreground Color. Now that color is available to any Photoshop document that you open.

4   With the Clouds layer still active, choose Filter > Render > Clouds.

Realistic-looking clouds appear behind the image.

5   Choose File > Save.

Dragging to add a new layer

You can add a layer to an image by dragging an image file from Bridge or from the desktop in Explorer (Windows) or the Finder (macOS). You'll add another flower to the postcard now.

▶ **Tip:** If you're adding artwork from a Creative Cloud library, you can simply drag and drop it from the Libraries panel into a Photoshop document. You can also do this with Adobe Stock images stored in your Creative Cloud Libraries.

1   If Photoshop fills your monitor, reduce the size of the Photoshop window:

*   On Windows, click the Restore button (⧉) in the upper-right corner, and then drag any corner of the Photoshop window to make it smaller.

*   On a Mac, click the green Maximize/Restore button (●) in the upper-left corner of the document window, or drag any corner of the Photoshop window to make it smaller.

2   In Photoshop, select the Pineapple copy layer in the Layers panel to make it the active layer.

3 In Explorer (Windows) or the Finder (macOS), navigate to the Lessons folder you downloaded from the peachpit.com/adobepress website. Then navigate to the Lesson04 folder, and position that window so you can see its contents next to the Photoshop window.

4 Select Flower2.psd, and drag it from Explorer or the Finder onto your image.

Tip: You can drag images from a Bridge window to Photoshop as easily as you can drag from the Windows or Mac desktop.

Note: If you don't see the Commit Transform button in the options bar, the Photoshop application window may be too narrow. Either resize the window to be wider or press the Enter or Return keyboard shortcut for committing an edit.

The Flower2 layer appears in the Layers panel, above the Pineapple copy layer.

5 Now that you are done importing, you can make the Photoshop application window larger again if it will give you more room to work comfortably.

6 Position the Flower2 layer in the lower-left corner of the postcard so that about half of the top flower is visible.

7 Click the Commit Transform button (✓) in the options bar to accept the layer. Its layer icon indicates that Photoshop placed the image as a Smart Object, which is a layer you can edit without making permanent changes. You'll work more extensively with Smart Objects in Lesson 5, "Quick Fixes."

Adding text

Now you're ready to create some type using the Horizontal Type tool, which places the text on its own type layer. You'll then edit the text and apply a special effect.

1 Make the HAWAII layer visible. You'll add text just below this layer and apply special effects to both layers.

2 Choose Select > Deselect Layers to ensure that no layers are selected.

3 In the Tools panel, select the Horizontal Type tool (**T**). Then choose Window > Character to open the Character panel. Do the following in the Character panel:

- Select a condensed font (we used Birch Std, which you can add from Adobe Fonts; if you use a different font, adjust other settings accordingly).

- Select a font style (we used Regular).

- Select a large font size (we used 36 points).

- Select a large tracking value (**VA**) (we used 250).

- Click the color swatch, select a shade of grassy green in the Color Picker, and click OK to close the Color Picker.

- If the font does not have a bold variant, click the Faux Bold button (**T**).

- Click the All Caps button (**TT**).

- Select Crisp from the Anti-aliasing menu (ᵃa).

4 In the options bar or Paragraph panel, click the Center Text icon (≣).

5 Click just below the "W" in the word "HAWAII," and type **Island Paradise**, replacing the selected placeholder text that appears. Then click the Commit Any Current Edits button (✔) in the options bar.

▶ **Tip:** If a font has a bold variant, always choose that instead of applying the Faux Bold option. True bold fonts are precisely crafted to be typographically consistent and well designed; Faux Bold is computer generated.

As you type, the text expands out from the center because you selected centered text alignment. The Layers panel now includes a layer named Island Paradise with a "T" thumbnail, indicating that it is a type layer. This layer is at the top of the layer stack because no layers were selected when it was created.

6   If the text is slightly off center relative to the "HAWAII" text, select the Move tool
    (✛), and drag to reposition the "Island Paradise" text layer as needed.

Applying a gradient to a layer

You'll apply a gradient to the "HAWAII" layer to make it more colorful. The general
workflow for adding a gradient is to set the gradient type and initial colors, apply the
gradient, and then adjust if needed.

1   Select the HAWAII layer in the Layers panel to make it active.

Note: Make sure
you click the thumbnail,
rather than the layer
name, or you'll see a
different context menu.

2   Right-click or Control-click the thumbnail in the HAWAII layer, and choose
    Select Pixels.

Note: Though the
layer contains the word
"HAWAII," it is no longer
an editable type layer.
The text was rasterized
(converted to pixels).

All non-transparent pixels on the HAWAII layer (the white lettering) are selected.
Now that you've selected the area to fill, you'll apply a gradient.

3   In the Tools panel, select the Gradient tool (▮).

4   In the options bar, make sure that the Linear Gradient (▮) style is selected.

5 Click the Foreground Color swatch in the Tools panel, select a bright shade of orange in the Color Picker, and click OK. The Background Color should still be white.

6 Click the Gradients panel tab to bring it forward, or if it isn't visible, choose Window > Gradients to open it.

7 In the Gradients panel, expand the Basics group, and click the Foreground to Background gradient preset (the first one in the Basics group). This preset uses the foreground and background colors you set in step 5. (You can also drag the gradient preset swatch and drop it on a layer.)

▶ **Tip:** To list the gradient options by name rather than by sample, click the menu button in the Gradient Picker, and choose either Small List or Large List. Or, hover the pointer over a thumbnail until a tool tip appears, showing the gradient name.

The gradient is applied within the selected pixels, starting with orange at the bottom and gradually blending to white at the top. In the Layers panel, a new Gradient Fill 1 layer was created above the HAWAII layer, appearing in the list indented with an arrow because it's added as a clipping mask attached to the HAWAII layer. (You'll learn more about clipping masks in Lesson 6.) A gradient is not always applied as a Gradient Fill clipping mask; how a gradient is applied depends on what's selected.

▶ **Tip:** Two more ways to apply a gradient: Drag a preset from the Gradients panel and drop it on the non-transparent pixels of a layer on the canvas, or drag the Gradient tool across the canvas.

You see gradient controls appear on the canvas over the "HAWAII" text, because the Gradient tool is selected and a Gradient Fill layer is selected in the Layers panel. A white bar indicates the gradient distance. The bar distance matches the height of the "HAWAII" text because the gradient length was based on the pixel selection you created in step 2. You can drag the controls to adjust those gradient settings.

For more information about creating and editing gradients, see the sidebar "About gradients," later in this lesson.

8 Save the work you've done so far.

About gradients

Gradients can add interest and dimension to your designs; recent versions of Photoshop have greatly expanded their power and flexibility. With many options for creating and editing gradients, knowing a few basic ideas will save you a lot of time.

The key features for working with gradients are the Gradients panel, the Properties panel, the Gradient tool, and the options bar when the Gradient tool is selected. You don't always need all of them, but it's important to know how they work together.

Setting up a new gradient

To set the type of gradient and its options before applying it, use the options bar when the Gradient tool is selected. Of the five gradient types, the most commonly used are the Linear Gradient and the Radial Gradient.

A. *Gradient presets*
B. *Linear gradient type*
C. *Radial gradient type*

To set a gradient's colors before creating it, set the Foreground and Background colors in the Tools panel, and then in the Gradients panel, select the Foreground to Background gradient preset (it's in the Basic presets group). In the Gradients panel, you manage and apply presets in the same way as in the other preset panels (Swatches, Shapes, and Patterns).

Applying a gradient to a layer

Applying a gradient to a layer is as simple as dragging a gradient preset swatch from the Gradients panel and dropping it on a non-Background layer on the canvas or in the Layers panel. How Photoshop applies the gradient depends on the layer type:

- For a pixel layer, such as brush strokes or a photo, a gradient is applied as a Gradient Fill layer clipping mask, which displays that layer only on the pixel layer's non-transparent pixels. To edit it, double-click that Gradient Fill layer. (For more about clipping masks, see page 115.)

- For a shape layer, such as a vector circle or polygon, a gradient is applied as a Gradient Fill (not a Gradient Fill layer). To edit it, select the layer and edit the Fill option in the Appearance section of the Properties panel, or in the options bar when a shape or pen tool is selected.

- For a type layer, a gradient is applied as a Gradient Overlay layer effect. To edit it, in the Layers panel double-click Gradient Overlay in the layer where it's applied.

A. *Gradient applied to layer as Gradient Fill clipping mask*
B. *Shape with gradient applied as Gradient Fill*
C. *Type layer with gradient applied as Gradient Overlay*
D. *Gradient Fill layer*

Adding a new Gradient Fill layer

When you want to create a gradient as an entire adjustable layer of its own,
add a new Gradient Fill layer by doing one of the following:

* With no layers selected, drag the Gradient tool to set the distance and angle of the gradient.
* Choose Layer > New Fill Layer > Gradient.

Editing a gradient using on-canvas controls

When a Gradient Fill is selected in the Layers panel and the Gradient tool is also selected, gradient controls
appear on the canvas. A white bar indicates the gradient distance. You can adjust the gradient distance and
angle by dragging the circular handles (color stops) at the ends of the bar. You can add a new circular color handle along the gradient by positioning the pointer near (not on) the gradient bar, and when the pointer appears
as an arrow with a plus sign (▷₊), click. Color handles are circular, a diamond-shaped midpoint stop appears
when a color stop is selected. You can change any color stop by double-clicking its circular handle, and you can
change the position of a color or midpoint stop by dragging it.

A. Gradient tool
B. Color stops
C. Midpoint stop
D. Gradient Fill layer
selected
E. Gradient Presets, Style,
Angle, and more
F. Gradient proxy and
color stops
G. Opacity proxy and
opacity stops

Editing a gradient using the Properties panel

When a Gradient Fill layer is selected in the Layers panel, the Properties panel displays a Gradient Controls
section where you can make detailed adjustments. For example, you can change the gradient Style and Angle,
and you can use the gradient proxy to edit color stops along the gradient. You can also vary opacity along the
gradient by editing and adding opacity stops in Opacity Controls.

Similar gradient options are also available in the Gradient Fill dialog box that opens when you double-click a
Gradient Fill layer in the Layers panel.

Applying a layer style

You can enhance a layer by adding a shadow, stroke, satin sheen, or other special effect from a collection of automated and editable layer styles. These styles are easy to apply, and they link directly to the layer you specify.

Like layers, layer styles can be hidden by clicking their eye icons (◉) in the Layers panel. Layer styles are nondestructive, so you can edit or remove them at any time.

Earlier, you used a layer style to add a stroke to the beach photo. Now, you'll add drop shadows to the text to make it stand out.

▶ **Tip:** You can also open the Layer Style dialog box by clicking the Add A Layer Style button at the bottom of the Layers panel and then choosing Drop Shadow or another layer style from the pop-up menu.

1 In the Layers panel, select the Island Paradise layer, and then choose Layer > Layer Style > Drop Shadow.

2 In the Layer Style dialog box, make sure that the Preview option is selected, and then, if necessary, move the dialog box so that you can see the "Island Paradise" text in the image window. A drop shadow is now applied.

3 In the Structure area, select Use Global Light, and then specify the following settings:

- Blend Mode: Multiply

- Opacity: **75**%

- Angle: **78** degrees

- Distance: **5** px

- Spread: **30**%

- Size: **10** px

▶ **Tip:** You can also change Global Light settings by choosing Layer > Layer Style > Global Light.

When Use Global Light is selected, a *global* (shared) lighting angle is available in many layer effects that use shading. If you set a lighting angle in one of these effects, every other effect with Use Global Light selected inherits the same angle setting.

Angle determines the lighting angle at which the effect is applied to the layer. Distance determines the offset distance for a shadow or satin effect. Spread determines how gradually the shadow fades toward the edges. Size determines how far the shadow extends.

Because the Preview option is selected, as you make changes Photoshop updates the drop shadow preview in the document window.

4 Click OK to accept the settings and close the Layer Style dialog box.

In the Layers panel, the layer style appears nested in the Island Paradise layer. An Effects heading is listed first, and under that, the layer styles applied to the layer appear. An eye icon (👁) appears next to the effect category and next to each effect. To turn off an effect, click its eye icon. Click the visibility column again to restore the effect. To hide all layer styles for that layer, click the eye icon next to Effects. To collapse the list of effects, click the arrow to the right of the layer name.

5 Make sure that eye icons appear for both items nested in the Island Paradise layer.

6 Press Alt (Windows) or Option (macOS), and in the Layers panel, drag the Effects listing or the fx symbol (fx) for the Island Paradise layer onto the HAWAII layer.

The Drop Shadow layer style is applied to the HAWAII layer, copying the settings you applied to the Island Paradise layer. Now you'll add a green stroke around the word "HAWAII."

▶ **Tip:** If you expect to use a layer style frequently in multiple documents, add it to your Creative Cloud Libraries. First create or open a library. In the document, select a layer that uses the style, click the Add Content button (**+**) at the bottom of the Libraries panel, and then click Layer Style. Now you can apply that style to any open Photoshop document.

7 Select the HAWAII layer in the Layers panel, click the Add A Layer Style button (*fx*) at the bottom of the panel, and then choose Stroke from the pop-up menu.

8 In the Structure area of the Layer Style dialog box, specify the following settings:

- Size: **4** px

- Position: Outside

- Blend Mode: Normal

- Opacity: **100**%

▶ **Tip:** Here's a quick way to match the color of the "Island Paradise" text. When the Color Picker is open for the Stroke Color, position the pointer outside the Color Picker dialog box so that it changes into an eyedropper icon. Click the "Island Paradise" text to sample its green color, loading it into the Color Picker.

- Color: Green (Select a shade that goes well with the one you used for the "Island Paradise" text.)

9 Click OK to apply the stroke.

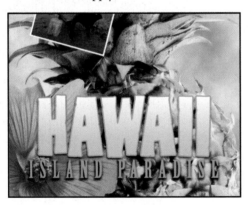

Now you'll add a drop shadow and a satin sheen to the flower.

10 Select the Flower layer, and choose Layer > Layer Style > Drop Shadow. Then change the following settings in the Structure area:

- Opacity: **60**%

- Distance: **13** px

- Spread: **9**%

- Make sure Use Global Light is selected and that the Blend Mode is Multiply. Do not click OK.

▶ **Tip:** As the Layers panel list of layers and effects becomes longer, you may want to give the Layers panel more room by hiding unneeded panels in the same stack. For example, if the Gradients panel is still visible, collapse it by double-clicking its panel tab.

11 With the Layer Style dialog box still open, click the word "Satin" on the left to select it and display its options. Then make sure Invert is selected, and apply the following settings:

- Color (next to Blend Mode): Choose a color that enhances the flower color, such as a fuchsia hue

- Opacity: **20**%

- Distance: **22** px

The Satin layer effect applies interior shading to create a satiny finish. The contour controls the shape of the effect; Invert flips the contour curve.

Note: Be sure to click the word "Satin." If you click only the check box, Photoshop applies the layer style with its default settings, but you won't see the options.

▶ **Tip:** You just added two different layer styles to the same layer, but you can also add multiple instances of the same layer style. For example, you can add multiple strokes to one layer. This works for any layer effect that has a [+] button next to its name in the Layer Styles dialog box.

12 Click OK to apply both layer styles. In the Layers panel you can see the two layer styles applied to the Flower layer, and you can use the eye icons to see what the Flower layer looks like with and without the layer styles applied.

Before applying layer styles.

The flower with the drop shadow and satin layer styles applied.

Adding an adjustment layer

You can add adjustment layers to apply color and tonal adjustments without permanently changing the pixel values in the image. For example, if you add a Color Balance adjustment layer to an image, you can experiment with different colors repeatedly, because the change occurs only on the adjustment layer. If you decide to return to the original pixel values, you can hide or delete the adjustment layer.

You've used adjustment layers in other lessons. Here, you'll add a Hue/Saturation adjustment layer to change the color of the purple flower. An adjustment layer affects all layers below it in the image's stacking order unless a selection is active when you create it or you create a clipping mask.

1 Select the Flower2 layer in the Layers panel.

2 In the Adjustments panel, scroll to the Single Adjustments list and click Hue/Saturation, to add a Hue/Saturation adjustment layer.

3 In the Properties panel, apply the following settings:

- Hue: **43**
- Saturation: **19**
- Lightness: **0**

The changes affect the Flower2, Pineapple Copy, Pineapple, Clouds, and Background layers. The effect is interesting, but you want to change only the Flower2 layer.

4 In the Properties panel, click the Create Clipping Mask button (⤺□). It's the first button along the bottom of the panel, and you see it when the Properties panel displays options for a layer that can become a clipping mask, such as an adjustment layer.

▶ **Tip:** You can also find the Create Clipping Mask and Release Clipping Mask commands (and their keyboard shortcut) on the Layer menu, on the Layers panel menu, and by right-clicking the layer name. You can also create a clipping mask for a layer by Alt-clicking (Windows) or Option-clicking (macOS) the line under that layer in the Layers panel.

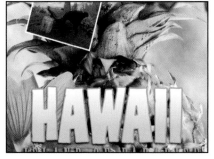

An arrow appears in the Layers panel, indicating that the adjustment layer applies only to the Flower2 layer. You'll learn more about clipping masks in Lesson 6, "Masks and Channels," and Lesson 7, "Typographic Design."

Updating layer effects

Layer effects are automatically updated when you make changes to a layer. You can edit the text and watch how the layer effect updates to match.

1 Select the Island Paradise layer in the Layers panel.

2 In the Tools panel, select the Horizontal Type tool (**T**).

3 In the options bar, change the Size by a few points, and press Enter or Return.

You changed the settings for the entire type layer, even though you didn't select the text by highlighting the characters (as you would have to do in a word processing program). This worked because in Photoshop, you can change settings for an entire type layer by selecting it in the Layers panel, as long as a type tool is selected.

If you add more text to a layer that has a layer effect applied to it, the new text takes on the same layer effect. Changing the type size may leave too little space above the Island Paradise and HAWAII type layers, so if you need to, you can adjust that.

4 Select the Move tool (✛), and drag the Island Paradise type layer as needed.

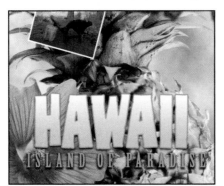

When you add text, layer effects are automatically applied to the new characters.

Reposition the text beneath the word "HAWAII."

5 Choose File > Save.

Creating a border from a selection

The Hawaii postcard is nearly done. The elements are almost all arranged correctly in the composition. You'll finish up by positioning the postmark and then adding a white postcard border.

1 Select the Move tool, and in the options bar, make sure Auto-Select is disabled.

2 Select the Postage layer, and then use the Move tool (✛) to drag it to the middle right of the image, as in the illustration.

Note: The Auto-Select option can save time by letting you select a layer by clicking it with the Move tool, instead of having to select it in the Layers panel. But in documents where many layers overlap, if clicking keeps selecting the wrong layer, try turning off Auto-Select.

3   Select the Island Paradise layer in the Layers panel, and then click the Create A New Layer button (⊞) at the bottom of the panel.

4   Choose Select > All.

5   Choose Select > Modify > Border. In the Border Selection dialog box, type **10** pixels for the Width, and click OK.

A 10-pixel border is selected around the entire image. Now, you'll fill it with white.

6   Select white for the Foreground Color, and then choose Edit > Fill.

7   In the Fill dialog box, choose Foreground Color from the Contents menu, and click OK.

8   Choose Select > Deselect.

9   Double-click the Layer 1 name in the Layers panel, and rename the layer **Border**.

Use layer comps to store and switch among design ideas

The Layer Comps panel (choose Window > Layer Comps) lets you store different views of a multilayered image file. A layer comp is simply a saved state of the settings in the Layers panel. Whenever you want to preserve a specific combination of layer properties, create a new layer comp. Then, by switching from one layer comp to another, you can quickly review the two designs. The beauty of layer comps becomes apparent when you want to demonstrate a number of possible design arrangements. When you've created a few layer comps, you can review the design variations without having to tediously select and deselect eye icons or change settings in the Layers panel.

For example, suppose you're designing a brochure, and you're producing a version in English as well as in French. You might have the French text on one layer and the English text on another in the same image file. To create two different layer comps, you would simply turn on visibility for the French layer and turn off visibility for the English layer and then click the Create New Layer Comp button in the Layer Comps panel. Then you'd do the inverse—turn on visibility for the English layer, turn off visibility for the French layer, and click the Create New Layer Comp button—to create an English layer comp. To view the different layer comps, click the Layer Comp box for each comp in the Layer Comps panel in turn.

Layer comps can be especially valuable when you want to save complex combinations of states of multiple layers. If some aspects need to stay consistent among layer comps, you can change the visibility, position, or appearance of one of its layers and then sync it to see that change reflected in all the other layer comps.

Flattening and saving files

When you finish editing all the layers in your image, you can merge or *flatten* layers to reduce the file size. Flattening combines all the layers into a single background layer. However, you cannot edit layers once you've flattened them, so you shouldn't flatten an image until you are certain that you're satisfied with all your design decisions. Rather than flattening your original PSD files, it's a good idea to save a copy of the file with its layers intact, in case you need to edit a layer later.

Note: If the sizes do not appear in the Status Bar, click the Status Bar pop-up menu arrow, and choose Document Sizes.

To appreciate what flattening does, notice the two numbers for the file size in the Status Bar at the bottom of the document window. The first number represents

what the file size would be if you flattened the image. The second number represents the file size without flattening. This lesson file, if flattened, would be 2–3MB, but the current file is much larger. So flattening is well worth it in this case.

1 Select any tool except the Type tool (**T**) to be sure that you're not in text-editing mode. Then choose File > Save (if it is available) to be sure that all your changes have been saved in the file.

2 Choose Image > Duplicate.

3 In the Duplicate Image dialog box, name the file **04Flat.psd**, and click OK.

4 Leave the 04Flat.psd file open, but close the 04Working.psd file.

5 Choose Layer > Flatten Image.

Only one layer, named Background, remains in the Layers panel.

▶ **Tip:** The Flatten Image command is also on the Layer menu and on the context menu when you right-click/Control-click a layer name.

6 Choose File > Save. Even though you chose Save rather than Save As, the Save As dialog box appears, because this document has not yet been saved to storage.

7 Make sure the location is on your computer in the Lessons/Lesson04 folder, and then click Save to accept the default settings and save the flattened file.

You have saved two versions of the file: a one-layer, flattened copy as well as the original file, in which all the layers remain intact.

You've created a colorful, attractive postcard. This lesson only begins to explore the vast possibilities and the flexibility you gain when you master the art of using Photoshop layers. You'll get more experience and try different techniques for layers in almost every lesson as you move forward in this book.

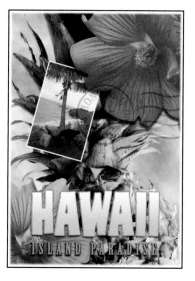

▶ **Tip:** Flattening always means merging all layers into one. If you want to merge only some of the layers in a file, click the eye icons to hide the layers you don't want to merge, and then choose Merge Visible from the Layers panel menu.

Extra credit

Exploring design options with Adobe Stock

Visualizing different ideas for a design project is easier when you can experiment with images. The Libraries panel in Photoshop gives you direct access to millions of Adobe Stock images. We'll add a stock image of a ukulele to this lesson's composition.

1 In the Lesson04 folder, open 04End.psd. Save it as **04End_Stock**.

2 In the Layers panel, select the Beach layer.

3 In the Libraries panel, open or create a library, type **ukulele** into the search field, set the search field menu (∨) to Adobe Stock, and locate any vertical image of a ukulele on a white background.

4 Drag the ukulele image into the document. Drag a corner handle to proportionally scale the image to about 25% of its original size. Apply the changes to finish importing the image.

Adobe Stock search results.

5 Choose Current Library from the search field menu (∨). The image was added to your library. Click the ✕ to clear the search.

6 Now remove the background. With the ukulele layer selected, choose the Object Selection tool ([]) in the Tools panel (it may be hidden in its tool group). Hover the pointer over the ukulele until a magenta highlight appears, and then click to select the outline of the ukulele. Click the Add Layer Mask button ([]) at the bottom of the Layers panel.

7 With the Move tool, drag the ukulele to the upper-left corner so that it partially overlaps the small photo of the beach view. You've just added an Adobe Stock photo to your postcard image!

Stock image in document.

Licensing an image

Until it's licensed, the ukulele image is a low-resolution version with an Adobe Stock watermark. You don't have to license the ukulele image for this lesson, but you must license images used in a real project. With the ukulele layer (not mask) selected in the Layers panel, click License Asset in the Properties panel and follow the prompts. After licensing, the image is automatically replaced with a high-resolution version without a watermark. If you plan to license many images, consider an Adobe Stock monthly plan or a pack of credits.

You've added a new element to your postcard using Adobe Stock!

Review questions

1 What is the advantage of using layers?

2 When you create a new layer, where does it appear in the Layers panel stack?

3 How can you make artwork on one layer appear in front of artwork on another layer?

4 How can you apply a layer style?

5 To edit a Gradient Fill layer by dragging on-canvas controls, what two things should you make sure to do?

6 Where can you see detailed options for editing a Gradient Fill layer?

Review answers

1 Layers let you move and edit different parts of an image as discrete objects. You can also hide individual layers as you work on other layers.

2 In the Layers panel, a new layer always appears immediately above the selected layer. If no layer is selected, a new layer appears at the top of the layer list.

3 You can make artwork on one layer appear in front of artwork on another layer by dragging layers up or down the stacking order in the Layers panel or by using the Layer > Arrange commands—Bring To Front, Bring Forward, Send Backward, and Send To Back. However, you can't change the layer position of a background layer unless you convert it to a regular layer (unlock it or double-click to rename it).

4 To apply a layer style, select the layer, and then click the Add A Layer Style button in the Layers panel, or choose Layer > Layer Style > [style].

5 Make sure the Gradient Fill layer is selected, and if you also make sure the Gradient tool is selected, the on-canvas gradient editor appears.

6 Detailed options for a Gradient Fill layer are displayed in the Gradient Controls section of the Properties panel, when a Gradient Fill layer is selected.

5 QUICK FIXES

Lesson overview

In this lesson, you'll learn how to do the following:

- Remove red eye.

- Brighten an image.

- Adjust the features of a face.

- Combine images to create a panorama.

- Crop and straighten an image and fill in any resulting empty areas.

- Blur the area around a subject.

- Merge images to extend depth of field (focus stack).

- Apply optical lens correction to a distorted image.

- Adjust the perspective of an image to match another image.

 This lesson will take about an hour to complete. To get the lesson files used in this chapter, download them from the web page for this book at peachpit.com/PhotoshopCIB2024. For more information, see "Accessing the lesson files and Web Edition" in the Getting Started section at the beginning of this book.

As you work on this lesson, you'll preserve the start files. If you need to restore the start files, download them from your Account page.

PROJECT: RED EYE REDUCTION

PROJECT: CORRECTING
IMAGE DISTORTION

PROJECT: PANORAMA FROM MULTIPLE IMAGES

Sometimes just one or two clicks in Photoshop can
turn an image from so-so (or worse) to awesome.
Quick fixes get you the results you want without a lot
of fuss.

Getting started

Not every image requires a complicated makeover using advanced features in Photoshop. In fact, once you're familiar with Photoshop, you can often improve an image quickly. The trick is to know what's possible and how to find what you need.

In this lesson, you'll make quick fixes to several images using a variety of tools and techniques. You can use these techniques individually or team them up when you're working with an image that needs just a little more help.

1 Start Photoshop, and then immediately hold down Ctrl+Alt+Shift (Windows) or Command+Option+Shift (macOS) to restore the default preferences. (See "Restoring default preferences" on page 5.)

2 When prompted, click Yes to delete the Adobe Photoshop Settings file.

Improving a snapshot

If you're sharing a snapshot with family and friends, you may not need it to look professional. But you probably don't want glowing eyes, and it would be good if the picture isn't too dark to show important detail. Photoshop gives you the tools to make quick changes to a snapshot.

Correcting red eye

Red eye occurs when the retina of a subject's eye is reflected by the camera flash. It commonly occurs in flash photographs taken in a dark room, because the subject's irises are wide open. Fortunately, red eye is easy to fix in Photoshop. In this exercise, you will remove the red eye from the woman's eyes in the portrait.

● **Note:** If you haven't installed Bridge, you'll be prompted to do so when you choose Browse In Bridge. For more information, see page 3.

You'll start by viewing the before and after images in Adobe Bridge.

1 Choose File > Browse In Bridge to open Adobe Bridge.

2 In the Favorites panel in Bridge, click the Lessons folder. Then, in the Content panel, double-click the Lesson05 folder to open it.

● **Note:** If Bridge asks you if you want to import preferences from a previous version of Bridge, click No.

3 Adjust the thumbnail slider, if necessary, so that you can see the thumbnail previews clearly. Then look at the RedEye_Start.jpg and RedEye_End.psd files.

RedEye_Start.jpg   *RedEye_End.psd*

Red eye is not the only problem with the image; it's also underexposed. Both are easy to correct in Photoshop.

4 Double-click the RedEye_Start.jpg file to open it in Photoshop. Close any messages that appear about new features.

5 Choose File > Save As, choose Photoshop for the Format, name the file **RedEye_Working.psd**, and click Save.

6 Select the Zoom tool (Q), and then drag to zoom in to see the woman's eyes. If Scrubby Zoom isn't selected, drag a marquee around the eyes to zoom in.

7 Select the Red Eye tool (⁺⊙), hidden under the Spot Healing Brush tool (🩹).

8 In the options bar, reduce the Pupil Size to **23%** and the Darken Amount to **62%**.

The Darken Amount specifies how dark the pupil should be.

9 Click the pupil in the woman's left eye. The red reflection disappears.

10 Click the pupil in the woman's right eye to remove the red reflection there, too.

If the red reflection is directly over the pupil, clicking the pupil usually removes it. If it doesn't, you can try clicking the highlight or try dragging the Red Eye tool around the entire pupil.

11 Choose View > Fit On Screen to see the entire image, and save your work.

Brightening an image

The woman's eyes no longer glow red, but the overall image is a bit dark. You can brighten an image in several different ways, as you've already seen. You can try adding adjustment layers for Brightness/Contrast, Levels, and Curves, depending on the degree of adjustment you want to make. For a quick fix or a good starting point, try the Auto button or the presets, which are available in both the Levels and Curves adjustments. Let's try a Curves adjustment layer for this image.

1 In the Adjustments panel, scroll to the Single Adjustments list and click Curves.

2 Click Auto. In this example, the automatic correction adds a midpoint on the curve and raises its value, lightening the image mostly around the midtones.

3 Choose Lighter (RGB) from the Preset menu. The curve changes slightly. The difference is that a preset applies the same curve to every image, while Auto analyzes the layer and creates a curve customized for it.

4 Click the Reset To Adjustment Defaults button (↺) at the bottom of the Properties panel to revert to the unadjusted image.

5 Select the on-image adjustment tool (☝) in the Curves panel, and then click the center of the forehead and drag up. Clicking with that tool adds a curve point that corresponds to the tonal level you clicked in the image. When you drag up, you raise that point and the curve, brightening the image from that tonal level.

> **Tip:** If you want to use the Auto button or the white point or black point samplers (eyedropper icons) in the Curves or Levels adjustments, use them before applying manual adjustments. Like presets, adjustments by those tools replace manual adjustments.

> **Tip:** To see how much you've brightened the image, hide the Curves layer, and then show it again.

You've just tried three different ways to adjust brightness using Curves.

6 Choose Layer > Flatten Image, and save the file.

Adjusting facial features with Liquify

The Liquify filter is useful when you want to distort only part of an image. It includes Face-Aware Liquify options that can automatically recognize faces in images and then lets you easily adjust facial features such as the size of or distance between the eyes. This can be useful for photos used in advertising and fashion, when portraying a certain look or expression may be more important than faithfully representing a specific person.

1 With RedEye_Working.psd still open, choose Filter > Liquify.

2 In the Properties panel, if the Face-Aware Liquify options are collapsed (hidden), click the right-facing triangle to expand them.

3 Make sure the Eyes section is expanded and that the link icon (𝟠) is selected for both Eye Size and Eye Height. Enter **32** for Eye Size and **10** for Eye Height.

▶ **Tip:** When the Face tool (𝕏) is selected in the Liquify toolbar, handles appear as you hover the pointer over different parts of the face. You can drag those handles to adjust different parts of the face directly, as an alternative to dragging the Face-Aware Liquify sliders.

When the link icon (⧉) is not selected for an Eyes option, you can set different values for the left and right eyes.

4 Make sure the Mouth section is expanded, and then enter **5** for Smile and **9** for Mouth Height.

5 Make sure the Face Shape section is expanded, and then enter **40** for Jawline and **50** for Face Width.

6 Deselect and reselect the Preview option to compare the image before and after your changes.

Before Face-Aware Liquify

After Face-Aware Liquify

▶ **Tip:** The Face-Aware Liquify options have a limited range because they're designed for subtle, believable distortions. If you want to exaggerate faces into caricatures or extreme expressions, you may want to use the more advanced manual tools along the left side of the Liquify dialog box. Or try the face-altering filters in Filter > Neural Filters, which you'll explore in Lesson 15, "Exploring Neural Filters."

Feel free to experiment with any of the Face-Aware Liquify options to get a better sense of the possibilities for quick, easy alterations.

7 Click OK to exit Liquify. Close the document, and save your changes.

The Face-Aware Liquify features are available only when Photoshop recognizes a face in an image. It may not recognize a face that is turned too far away from the camera or partially covered by hair, sunglasses, or a hat shadow.

When a workspace totally changes

Some Photoshop features, such as Liquify, open a dedicated workspace—a maximized dialog box covering most of the screen. If you're new to Photoshop, this can be confusing, because panels that were open may be temporarily inaccessible. For example, if panels such as Layers and Color were open before using Liquify, the dedicated Liquify workspace covers those panels as long as Liquify is open.

When a dedicated workspace is open, how do you restore the regular workspace? Look for OK and Cancel buttons. For example, when your Liquify edits are complete, click OK to apply your changes and return to the normal Photoshop workspace.

Blurring around a subject

The interactive blurs in the Blur Gallery let you customize a blur as you preview it on your image. You'll apply an elliptical blur effect to focus the viewer's attention on the unblurred center of the effect—in this case, the egret. You'll apply the blur as a Smart Filter so that you have the option of changing it later.

You'll start by looking at the start and end files in Bridge.

1 Choose File > Browse In Bridge to open Adobe Bridge.

2 In the Favorites panel in Bridge, click the Lessons folder. Then, in the Content panel, double-click the Lesson05 folder to open it.

3 Compare the Egret_Start.jpg and Egret_End.psd thumbnail previews.

Egret_Start.jpg.

Egret_End.psd.

▶ **Tip:** The Iris Blur option in this example is strictly elliptical in shape, and the other Blur Gallery options are similarly geometric. If you want background blur to recognize and avoid a subject's outline, try the Depth Blur Neural Filter with Focus Subject selected. You'll explore Neural Filters in Lesson 15.

In the final image, the egret stands out more, because its reflection and the grass around it have been blurred. Iris Blur, one of the interactive blurs in the Blur Gallery, makes the task easy.

4 Choose File > Return To Adobe Photoshop, and choose File > Open As Smart Object.

5 Select the Egret_Start.jpg file in the Lesson05 folder, and click OK or Open.

Photoshop opens the image. There is one layer in the Layers panel, and it's a Smart Object, as indicated by the badge on the layer thumbnail icon.

6 Choose File > Save As, choose Photoshop for the Format, name the file **Egret_Working.psd**, and click Save. Click OK in the Photoshop Format Options dialog box.

7 Choose Filter > Blur Gallery > Iris Blur. The Blur Gallery dialog box opens.

A blur ellipse is centered on your image. You can adjust the location and scope of the blur by moving the center pin, feather handles, and ellipse handles. At the top-right corner of the Blur Gallery task space, you also see the expandable Field Blur, Tilt-Shift Blur, Path Blur, and Spin Blur panels; those are additional types of blur you can apply.

8 Drag the center pin so that it's at the bottom of the bird's body.

9 Click the ellipse, and drag inward to tighten the focus around the bird.

▶ **Tip:** Background blur is most convincing when the amount of blur is higher for more distant objects, but the effects in Blur Gallery aren't tied to real depth. Some cameras can record actual depth info so that software can use it. For example, if you have a smartphone camera that can include an HEIF depth map with a photo, you can create a more realistic background blur effect by loading the depth map into the Lens Blur filter (choose Filter > Blur > Lens Blur).

A. *Center* **B.** *Ellipse* **C.** *Feather handle* **D.** *Blur*

10 Press Alt (Windows) or Option (macOS) as you click and drag the feather handles to match those in the first image after step 11. Pressing Alt or Option lets you drag each handle separately.

11 Click and drag on the Blur ring to reduce the amount of blur to **5** px, creating a gradual but noticeable blur. You can also change the same value by moving the Blur slider in the Iris Blur area of the Blur Tools panel.

12 Click OK in the options bar to apply the blur.

The blur may be a little too subtle. You'll edit the blur to increase it slightly.

13 Double-click Blur Gallery in the Egret layer in the Layers panel to open it again. Adjust the blur to **6** px, and click OK in the options bar to apply it.

The egret is accentuated by blurring the rest of the image. Because you applied the filter to a Smart Object, you can hide or edit the effect without altering the original image.

14 Save the file, and then close it.

Blur Gallery

The Blur Gallery includes five interactive blurs: Field Blur, Iris Blur, Tilt-Shift, Path Blur, and Spin Blur. Each gives you on-image selective motion blur tools, with an initial blur pin. You can create additional blur pins by clicking on the image. You can apply a single blur or a combination of blurs, and you can create a strobe effect for path and spin blurs.

Before   *After*

Before   *After*

Field Blur applies a gradient blur to areas of the image, defined by pins you create and settings you specify for each. When you first apply Field Blur, a pin is placed in the center of the image. You can adjust the blur relative to that point by dragging the blur handle or specifying a value in the Blur Tools panel; you can also drag the pin to a different location.

Iris Blur progressively blurs everything outside the focus ring. Adjust the ellipse handles, feather handles, and blur amount to customize the iris blur. It can be a quick way to approximate a shallow depth-of-field blur effect.

Before   *After*

Before   *After*

Tilt-Shift simulates an image taken with a tilt-shift lens, where the image has very shallow depth of field with the focus point in the distance. This blur defines a plane of sharpness and then fades outward to a blur. You can use this effect to simulate photos of miniature objects.

Spin Blur is a radial-style blur measured in degrees. You can change the size and shape of the ellipse, re-center the rotation point by pressing Alt or Option as you click and drag, and adjust the blur angle. You can also specify the blur angle in the Blur Tools panel. Multiple spin blurs can overlap. This blur can be useful for illustrating the rotation of propellers, wheels, or gears.

Before   *After*

Path Blur creates motion blurs along paths you draw. You control the shape and amount of the blur.

When you first apply a Path Blur, a default path appears. Drag the end point to reposition it. Click the center point and drag to change the curve. Click to add additional curve points. The arrow on the path indicates the blur's direction.

You can also create a multiple-point path or a shape. Blur shapes describe the local motion blurs, similar to camera shake. The Speed slider in the Blur Tools panel determines the speed for all the path blurs. The Centered Blur option ensures that the blur shape for any pixel is centered on that pixel, resulting in more stable-feeling motion blurs; to make the motion appear more fluid, deselect this option.

If you wanted to illustrate the blurs of individual animal legs moving in different directions, you could add a separate instance of Path Blur to each leg.

Some blur types provide additional options in the Effects tab, where you specify the bokeh parameters to control the appearance of blurred areas. Light Bokeh brightens the blurred areas; Bokeh Color adds more vivid colors to lightened areas that aren't blown out to white; Light Range determines the range of tones that the settings affect.

Before   *After*

You can add a **strobe effect** to spin and path blurs. Select the Motion Effects tab to bring its panel forward. The Strobe Strength slider determines how much blur shows between flash exposures (0% gives no strobe effect; 100% gives full strobe effect with little blur between exposures). Strobe Flashes determines the number of exposures.

Before   *After*

Applying a blur will smooth out visible digital image noise or film grain that's in the original image, and this mismatch between the original and blurred areas can make the blur appear artificial. You can use the Noise tab to restore noise or grain so that blurred areas match up with unblurred areas. Start with the Amount slider, and then use the other Noise options to match the character of the original grain. Increase the Color value if the original has visible color noise, and lower the Highlights value if you need to balance the noise level in the highlights compared to the shadows.

Creating a panorama

Sometimes a vista is too large for a single shot. Photoshop makes it easy to combine multiple images into a panorama so that your viewers can get the full effect.

Once again, you'll take a look at the end file first to see where you're going.

1   Choose File > Browse In Bridge.

Tip: In Bridge, you can preview a selected image in full-screen mode by pressing the spacebar. This is useful for previewing detailed or large images such as a panorama. Press the spacebar again to close the preview.

2   Navigate to the Lesson05 folder, if you're not there already. Then, look at the Skyline_End.psd thumbnail preview.

Skyline_End.psd.

You'll combine four shots of the Seattle skyline into a single wide panorama image so that viewers get a sense of the whole scene. Creating a panorama from multiple images requires only a few clicks. Photoshop does the rest.

Tip: You can also open selected images from Bridge directly into Photomerge by choosing Tools > Photoshop > Photomerge.

3   Return to Photoshop.

4   With no files open in Photoshop, choose File > Automate > Photomerge.

5   In the Source Files area, click Browse, and navigate to the Lesson05/Files For Panorama folder.

6   Shift-select all the images in the folder, and click OK or Open.

7   In the Layout area of the Photomerge dialog box, select Perspective.

The best option for merging photos isn't always Perspective; it depends on how the originals were photographed. If you're not completely happy with the result of a particular merge, you can always try again with a different Layout option. If you're not sure which one to use, you can simply click Auto.

8   At the bottom of the Photomerge dialog box, select Blend Images Together, Vignette Removal, Geometric Distortion Correction, and Content Aware Fill Transparent Areas. Then click OK.

Blend Images Together blends images based on the optimal borders between them, instead of creating a simple rectangular merge. Vignette Removal helps ensure consistent brightness when merging images that are darker around their edges. Geometric Distortion Correction compensates for barrel, pincushion, or fish-eye distortion. Content Aware Fill Transparent Areas automatically patches the empty areas between the merged image edges and the sides of the canvas.

Photoshop creates the panorama image. It's a complex process, so you may have to wait a few moments while Photoshop works. When it's finished, you'll see the full vista in the document window with five layers in the Layers panel. The bottom four layers are the original four images you selected. Photoshop identified the overlapping areas of the images and matched them, correcting any angular discrepancies. The top layer, containing "(merged)" in the layer name, is a single panorama image blended from all of the images you selected, combined with formerly empty areas filled in by Content Aware Fill. Those areas are indicated by the selection.

Note: Photomerge requires more time when you merge more images, or images with large pixel dimensions. Photomerge works faster on computers that are newer or that have more RAM.

▶ **Tip:** If you want to see how the panorama looks without the areas created by Content Aware Fill, hide the top layer.

Getting the best results with Photomerge

Tip: If you plan to create panoramas of interiors or with objects close to the camera, rotating a camera by hand or on a tripod may introduce parallax errors where items don't line up. You can avoid such errors by using a tripod attachment (sometimes called a *nodal slide*) that precisely rotates the camera around the entrance pupil of the specific lens you use.

If you know you're going to create a panorama when you take your shots, keep the following guidelines in mind to get the best result:

Overlap images by 15% to 40%. Sufficient overlap helps Photomerge blend edges seamlessly. Over 50% overlap won't help and makes you take too many images.

Use a consistent focal length. If you use a zoom lens, keep the focal length the same for all the pictures in the panorama.

Stay level. Keep the horizon at the same vertical position in each frame to avoid a tilted panorama. If your camera has a level indicator in the viewfinder, use it.

Use a tripod if possible. You'll get the best results if the camera is at the same height for each shot. A tripod with a rotating head makes that easier.

Take the photos from the same position. If you're not using a tripod with a rotating head, try to stay in the same position as you take the photos so that they are taken from the same viewpoint.

Avoid lenses that produce creative distortion. They can interfere with Photomerge. (The Auto option does adjust for images you take with fisheye lenses.)

Use the same exposure and aperture. Images blend more smoothly if the exposure is consistent across frames; auto-exposure may create unexpected exposure variations. Using the same aperture setting maintains consistent depth of field.

Try different layout options. If you don't like the results, try again using a different layout option. Often, Auto selects the appropriate option, but sometimes you'll get a better image with one of the other options.

9 Choose Select > Deselect.

10 Choose Layer > Flatten Image.

Tip: In the finished panorama files, the layers created from the original images have masks. Photoshop created the masks to blend the edges where adjacent images match. You can edit those masks, but if you won't need to, flattening the image results in a smaller file size.

11 Choose File > Save As. Choose Photoshop for the Format, and name the file **Skyline_Working.psd**. Save the file in the Lesson05 folder. Click Save.

The panorama looks great, but it's a little dark. You'll add a Levels adjustment layer to brighten it a little bit.

12 In the Adjustments panel, scroll down to the Single Adjustments list and click Levels to add a Levels adjustment layer.

13 Select the White Point eyedropper in the Properties panel, and then click a white area of the clouds.

The entire image brightens. The sky appears more blue, because the image was originally a little warm. The White Point eyedropper neutralized the warm cast.

14 Save your work. Click OK in the Photoshop Format Options dialog box.

It's that easy to create a panorama!

● **Note:** Step 13 works when you click an area that is close to, but not exactly, pure white. If an image doesn't change when you click it with the White Point eyedropper, you probably clicked an area that can't become any whiter and there is no color cast to correct. That happens when the pixel values where you clicked are already pure white in all color channels (such as RGB 255,255,255).

● **Note:** In step 14, the Photoshop Format Options alert may appear because a layer was added. The Photoshop Format Options dialog box usually won't appear for Photoshop documents containing only a Background layer.

Filling empty areas when cropping

The panorama image looks great except for two things: The horizon is slightly tilted, and the lower handrail is incomplete where the rocks on the right descend into the water. If you were to rotate the image, empty areas might appear at the corners, requiring a tighter crop and losing parts of the image. Fortunately, the same Content-Aware technology that filled in empty areas resulting from the panorama merge can also fill in empty areas that can result from straightening and cropping.

1 Make sure **Skyline_Working.psd** is open, and make sure the Background layer is selected in the Layers panel.

2 Choose Layer > Flatten Image.

3 In the Tools panel, select the Crop tool. The crop rectangle and its handles appear around the image.

▶ Tip: In step 4, you can also try the older Content-Aware option in the Fill menu in the options bar and compare its result to selecting Generative Fill.

4 In the options bar, select the Straighten icon (⬒), and in the Fill menu, make sure Generative Expand is selected.

Generative Expand will intelligently fill empty areas when you apply the crop.

5 Position the Straighten pointer on the horizon at the left edge of the image, and drag to the right to create a Straighten line that's aligned with the horizon; release the mouse button when you reach the end of the horizon at the right edge of the image.

Straightening the image rotated it, creating empty space at the top-left and bottom-right corners. Those will be filled by the Fill option you chose in step 4.

6   Click the Commit button in the options bar (✔) to apply the crop settings.

A progress bar appears as Generative Expand creates alternatives for filling in the empty corners. When it's finished, the Layers panel includes a new Generative Expand layer, and the Properties panel displays the three Variations created by Generative Expand. The selected Variation is the one currently applied to the Generative Expand layer.

▶ **Tip:** If you do a lot of cropping, you can simply press Enter or Return to apply the current crop settings, if you find that easier than moving the pointer up to the Commit button in the options bar.

7   In the Properties panel, click each of the three Variations while watching the top-left and bottom-right corners, and select the variation that you think is the best.

If you don't like any of them, click Generate to create three more variations, and select one of those.

That's how easy it is to fill in empty areas created by cropping!

8   Save your changes, and close the document.

Replacing a sky

When you find the right subject for a photo illustration or composite but it doesn't have quite the right sky to match the mood or time of day you want to convey, you can easily swap out the sky in Photoshop. Sky Replacement does many of the tough parts for you, such as creating a mask for the sky and making colors more consistent between the photo and the new sky.

1 In the Lesson05 folder, open the document Skyline_End.psd, and then choose Edit > Sky Replacement.

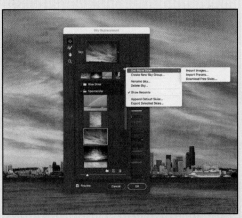

2 Select an image from the Sky list. The sky updates in the document; you can compare the original and new sky by clicking the Preview option. To use your own sky image, click the gear icon in the Sky list and choose Get More Skies > Import Images.

3 Check the quality of the automatically composited image. Are the colors of the two images consistent? Do you see any issues with the edge quality of the automatic sky mask? You can zoom in to check edges.

4 If you notice problems, use the Sky Replacement options. For example, you can reposition the sky image with the Sky Move tool, edit the mask edge with the Sky Brush tool, or change the Scale value in Sky Adjustments.

5 When you are satisfied with the Sky Replacement settings, make sure New Layers is selected in the Output To menu, and click OK.

If Output is set to New Layers, notice in the Layers panel that Sky Replacement automatically created layers to add the new sky and adjustments separately from the original layer. After you click OK in Sky Replacement, you can edit the layers and masks it created (you'll learn more about layer masks in Lesson 6, "Masks and Patterns"). Hiding the new layers reveals the original sky.

Correcting image distortion

The Lens Correction filter fixes common camera lens flaws, such as barrel and pincushion distortion, chromatic aberration, and vignetting. *Barrel distortion* is a lens defect that causes straight lines to bow out toward the edges of the image. *Pincushion distortion* is the opposite effect, causing straight lines to bend inward. *Chromatic aberration* appears as a color fringe along the edges of image objects. *Vignetting* occurs when the edges of an image, especially the corners, are darker than the center.

The Lens Correction filter contains an Auto Correction tab, which can automatically correct for some combinations of camera models and lenses. If your camera or lens isn't listed, or if you want more control, you can use the Custom tab, which contains options that can compensate for many types of lens distortions such as geometric distortion, chromatic aberration, and vignetting.

1 Choose File > Browse In Bridge.

2 Navigate to the Lesson05 folder if you're not already there, and then look at the Columns_Start.psd and Columns_End.psd thumbnail previews.

▶ **Tip:** If you capture photos with your camera set to save raw files, the Adobe Camera Raw plug-in module (for processing raw files in Photoshop and Bridge) has similar lens correction options in its Optics panel. Also, many more lens profiles are available for camera raw images than for Photoshop documents. You'll learn more about this in Lesson 12, "Working with Camera Raw."

Columns_Start.psd.

Columns_End.psd.

In this case, the original image of a Greek temple is distorted, with the columns appearing to be bowed. This photo was shot at a range that was too close with a wide-angle lens. You'll quickly correct the lens barrel distortion.

3 Double-click the Columns_Start.psd file to open it in Photoshop.

4 Choose File > Save As. In the Save As dialog box, name the file **Columns_Working.psd**, and save it in the Lesson05 folder. Click OK if the Photoshop Format Options dialog box appears.

5 Choose Filter > Lens Correction. The Lens Correction dialog box opens.

▶ **Tip:** If the crop rectangle from the previous exercise is still visible and distracting, switch to a tool such as the Hand tool.

6 At the bottom of the dialog box, make sure Show Grid and Preview are selected.

An alignment grid overlays the image. To the right are options for automatic corrections based on lens profiles. In the Custom tab are manual controls for correcting distortion, chromatic aberration, and perspective.

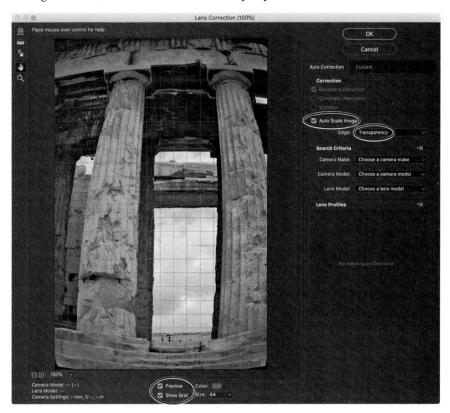

The Lens Correction dialog box includes auto-correction options. You'll adjust one setting in the Auto Correction tab and then customize the settings.

7 In the Correction area of the Auto Correction tab, make sure Auto Scale Image is selected and that Transparency is selected from the Edge menu.

8 Select the Custom tab.

▶ **Tip:** Watch the alignment grid as you make these changes so that you can see when the vertical columns are straightened in the image.

9 In the Custom tab, drag the Remove Distortion slider to about **+52.00** to remove the barrel distortion in the image. Alternatively, you could select the Remove Distortion tool (🔲) and drag in the image preview area until the columns are straight. The adjustment causes the image borders to bow inward. Because you selected Auto Scale Image, the Lens Correction filter automatically scales the image to adjust the borders.

10 The horizontal lines aren't parallel with the edges of the frame, so drag the Horizontal Perspective slider to about +14.

11 Deselect the Preview option to review how the image looked before these corrections, and then select the Preview option again to see how well the corrections improved the image.

Tip: A keyboard shortcut for toggling the Preview option is to press the P key.

The curving distortion caused by the wide-angle lens and low shooting angle is reduced.

12 Click OK to apply your changes and close the Lens Correction dialog box.

Tip: If the photo file contains lens information saved by a digital camera or if you know the exact lens that was used, options in the Auto Correction tab may provide a better starting point. When the correct Lens Model and Lens Profiles are selected, the profile may provide precise corrections for that lens, which you can refine in the Custom tab.

13 Choose File > Save to save your changes, click OK if the Photoshop Format Options dialog box appears, and then close the image.

 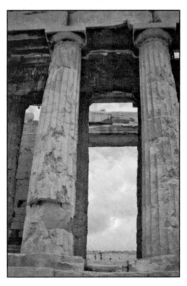

The temple looks much more stable now!

Extending depth of field

Sometimes you have to choose to focus on either the background or the foreground of a scene because the *depth of field*—the range of distances in focus—is narrow. If you want more depth of field but it isn't possible because of limitations of the equipment or the location, you can take a set of photos focused along the range of distances you want to appear sharp. You can merge the photos in Photoshop using a process sometimes called *focus stacking*. This produces a single image with the combined depth of field of the image set.

▶ **Tip:** See if your camera has a feature with a name such as "focus bracketing" that, with a single press of the shutter button, takes multiple shots focused at a series of distances. This feature makes it easier to photograph a consistent image set for focus stacking.

Because you'll need to align the images exactly, it's helpful to use a tripod to keep the camera steady. You might still be able to get good results with a handheld camera if you compose the images consistently. In this exercise, you'll add depth of field to an image of a wine glass in front of a beach.

1 Choose File > Browse In Bridge.

2 Navigate to the Lesson05 folder, if you're not there already, and then look at the Glass_Start.psd and Glass_End.psd thumbnail previews.

Glass_Start.psd.

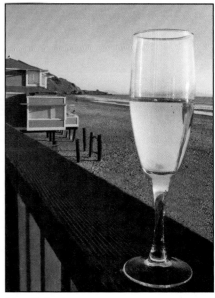

Glass_End.psd.

The first image has two layers. Depending on which layer is visible, either the glass in the foreground or the beach in the background is in focus. You'll extend the depth of field to make both clear.

3 Double-click the Glass_Start.psd file to open it.

4 Choose File > Save As. Name the file **Glass_Working.psd**, and save it in the Lesson05 folder. Click OK if the Photoshop Format Options dialog box appears.

5 In the Layers panel, hide the Beach layer so that only the Glass layer is visible. The glass is in focus, but the background is blurred. Then, show the Beach layer again. Now the beach is in focus, but the glass is blurred.

You'll merge the layers, using the part of each layer that is in focus. First, you need to align the layers.

6 In the Layers panel, Shift-click to select both of the layers.

7 Choose Edit > Auto-Align Layers.

Because these images were shot from the same angle, Auto will work just fine.

Tip: When aligning layers that are not involved in a panorama, Reposition is often the best alignment option to use. In this exercise, Reposition is the projection that the Auto option chose.

8 Select Auto, if it isn't already selected. Make sure neither Vignette Removal nor Geometric Distortion is selected. Then click OK to align the layers.

Now that the layers are perfectly aligned, you're ready to blend them.

9 Make sure both layers are still selected in the Layers panel. Then choose Edit > Auto-Blend Layers.

Tip: The technique in this exercise, called *focus stacking*, is useful for macro photography, where depth of field is typically very shallow. Multiple images with shallow depth of field are shot at different focus distances and then merged.

10 Select Stack Images and Seamless Tones And Colors, if they aren't already selected. Make sure Content Aware Fill Transparent Areas is not selected, and then click OK.

Both the wine glass and the beach behind it are in focus, because Auto-Blend Layers combined the sharpest parts of each image. In the Layers panel, notice that both original layers are preserved, and the blending is achieved by masks that hide the out-of-focus areas of each image so that only the sharp areas of each are visible.

11 Save your work, and close the file.

Adjusting perspective in an image

The Perspective Warp feature lets you adjust the way objects in your image relate to the scene. You can correct distortions, change the angle from which an object appears to be viewed, or shift the perspective of an object so that it merges smoothly with a new background.

Using the Perspective Warp feature is a two-step process: defining the planes and adjusting them. You start in Layout mode, drawing *quads* to define two or more planes; it's a good idea to align the edges of the quads so that they are parallel with the lines of the original object. Then you switch to Warp mode and manipulate the planes you defined.

You'll use Perspective Warp to merge images with different perspectives.

1 Choose File > Browse In Bridge.

2 Navigate to the Lesson05 folder, if you're not there already, and then look at the Bridge_Start.psd and Bridge_End.psd thumbnail previews.

Bridge_Start.psd.

Bridge_End.psd.

In the Bridge_Start.psd file, the image of the train has been combined with the image of a trestle bridge, but their perspectives don't match. If you're illustrating a story about a flying train that is making a landing on a trestle bridge, this might be perfect. But if you want a more realistic image, you'll need to adjust the perspective of the train to put it firmly on the tracks. You'll use Perspective Warp to do just that.

3 Double-click the Bridge_Start.psd file to open it in Photoshop.

4 Choose File > Save As, and rename the file **Bridge_Working.psd**. Click OK in the Photoshop Format Options dialog box.

5 Select the Train layer.

The tracks are on the Background layer. The train is on the Train layer. Because the Train layer is a Smart Object, you can apply Perspective Warp and then modify the results if you're not satisfied.

Note: Perspective Warp can work faster on a computer that qualifies for graphics acceleration. To see if your computer qualifies, see the "Getting Started" section for a link to the Photoshop system requirements.

6 Choose Edit > Perspective Warp.

A small animated tutorial appears, showing you how to draw a quad, which defines a plane.

7 Watch the animation, and then close it.

Now you'll create quads to define the planes of the train image.

8 Draw the quad for the side of the train: Click above the top of the smokestack, drag down to the railroad tie below the front wheel, and then drag across to the end of the caboose.

9 Drag a second quad for the front of the train, dragging across the cowcatcher at the bottom and into the trees at the top. Drag it to the right until it attaches to the left edge of the first quad.

Tip: Not sure if you've properly drawn the perspective of quads around a subject? They should look like a shipping container fitted to the subject.

10 Drag the corners of the planes to match the angles of the train. The bottom line of the side plane should run along the bottom of the train wheels; the top edge should border the top of the caboose. The front plane should mirror the lines of the cowcatcher and the top of the light.

Now that the quads are drawn, you're ready for the second step: warping.

11 Click Warp in the options bar. Close the tutorial window that appears.

12 Click the Automatically Straighten Near Vertical Lines button, next to Warp in the options bar.

Lines close to vertical are made vertical, making it easier to adjust its perspective.

13 Drag the handles to manipulate the planes, moving the back end of the train down and into perspective with the tracks. Exaggerate the perspective toward the caboose for a more dramatic result.

14 Warp other parts of the train as needed. You may need to adjust the front of the train. Pay attention to the wheels; make sure you don't distort them as you warp the perspective.

While there are precise ways to adjust perspective, in many cases you may need to trust your eyes to tell you when it looks right. Remember that you can return to tweak it again later, because you're applying Perspective Warp as a Smart Filter.

15 When you're satisfied with the perspective, click the Commit Perspective Warp button (✔) in the options bar.

16 To compare the changed image with the original, hide the Perspective Warp filter in the Layers panel. Then show the filter again.

If you want to make further adjustments, double-click the Perspective Warp filter in the Layers panel. You can continue to adjust the existing planes or click Layout in the options bar to reshape them. Remember to click the Commit Perspective Warp button to apply your changes.

17 Save your work, and close the file.

Changing the perspective
of a building

In the exercise, you applied Perspective Warp to one layer to change its relationship with another. But you can also use Perspective Warp to change the perspective of an object in relationship to others in the same layer. For example, you can shift the angle from which you view a building.

In this case, you apply Perspective Warp the same way: In Layout mode, draw the planes of the object you want to affect. In Warp mode, manipulate those planes. Of course, because you're shifting angles within a layer, other objects on the layer will change too, so you need to watch for any irregularities.

In this image, as the perspective of the building shifts, so does the perspective of the trees surrounding it.

Extra credit

Transformations with the Content-Aware Move tool

With the Content-Aware Move tool, you need only a few quick steps to duplicate a thistle so that it combines seamlessly with the background and is also different enough that it doesn't look like an exact copy of the original.

1 Open Thistle.psd in your Lesson05/Extra Credit folder, and save it as **Thistle_Working.psd**.

2 Select the Content-Aware Move tool (✂) (grouped with the healing brush and Red Eye tools).

3 In the options bar, choose Extend from the Mode menu. Choosing Extend duplicates the thistle; if you just want to reposition the single thistle, you would choose Move.

4 With the Content-Aware Move tool, draw a selection around the thistle, with a margin large enough to include a little of the grass around it.

5 Drag the selection to the left, and drop it in the empty area of grass.

6 Right-click (Windows) or Control-click (macOS) the dragged thistle, and choose Flip Horizontal.

7 Drag the top-left transformation handle to make the thistle smaller. If you think the copy of the thistle should be farther from the original, position the pointer inside the transformation rectangle and drag the thistle copy slightly to the left.

8 Press Enter or Return to apply the transformations. Leave the content selected so you can adjust the Structure and Color options in the Options bar to improve how the duplicated thistle blends with the background.

9 Choose Select > Deselect, save your changes, and close the document.

Tips for using the Content-Aware Move tool

The Content-Aware Move tool defaults to the Move mode, which helps blend moved selections into their new background (see "Extra credit" on page 151).

When set to Extend mode, the Content-Aware Move tool can expand areas of regular or randomized visual repetition such as meadows, solid-colored walls, sky, wood grains, or water. The Extend mode can also be useful with architectural subjects, especially when they're shot on a plane parallel to the camera; it's less effective for subjects shot at an angle.

If you're working with an image that has multiple layers, select Sample All Layers in the options bar to include them all in the selection.

The Structure and Color options define how closely the results reflect the existing image patterns. In the Structure settings, 1 is the loosest and 7 the strictest. The Color settings range from 0 (no color adaptation) to 10 (matching the color as closely as possible). Experiment with the options while the object is still selected to see which give you the best results in a particular image. You may want to hide the selection edges (choose View > Show > Selection Edges or View > Extras) to see how the object integrates into its new position.

Review questions

1 What is red eye, and how do you correct it in Photoshop?

2 Why might some parts of the Photoshop workspace become inaccessible or hidden, such as the Color and Layers panels? And how do you return to the normal workspace?

3 How can you create a panorama from multiple images?

4 Which common camera lens flaws can the Lens Correction filter fix?

Review answers

1 Red eye occurs when a camera flash is reflected in the retinas of a subject's eyes. To correct red eye in Photoshop, zoom in to the subject's eyes, select the Red Eye tool, and then click or drag around each eye.

2 If standard panels can't be opened, you are probably working in a dedicated workspace that provides options only for a specific task, such as applying Liquify or Blur Gallery effects. Many menu commands and panels aren't available in a dedicated workspace. To exit a dedicated workspace and keep the edits you made in it, look for an OK button and click it. (When not in a dedicated workspace, panels can be opened and hidden using the Window menu or by a preset on the Window > Workspace menu.)

3 To blend multiple images into a panorama, choose File > Automate > Photomerge, select the files you want to combine, and click OK.

4 The Lens Correction filter can fix common camera lens flaws such as barrel and pincushion distortion, in which straight lines bow out toward the edges of the image (barrel) or bend inward (pincushion); chromatic aberration, where a color fringe appears along the edges of image objects; and vignetting at the edges of an image, especially corners, that are darker than the center.

6 MASKS AND PATTERNS

Lesson overview

In this lesson, you'll learn how to do the following:

- Select a subject in one click.
- Use Select and Mask to remove the background around a subject.
- Refine a mask to include complex edges.
- Manipulate an image using Puppet Warp.
- Create a star by customizing a vector shape layer.
- Create an adjustable pattern from a vector shape layer.

 This lesson will take about an hour to complete. To get the lesson files used in this chapter, download them from the web page for this book at peachpit.com/PhotoshopCIB2024. For more information, see "Accessing the lesson files and Web Edition" in the Getting Started section at the beginning of this book.

As you work on this lesson, you'll preserve the start files. If you need to restore the start files, download them from your Account page.

PROJECT: PODCAST EPISODE GRAPHICS

Masks are essential for building a composite image. Create masks to hide unwanted areas of each layer, such as backgrounds, so that what's visible on the layers are only the subjects you want to composite.

Why masks are useful

Out of the camera, a digital image is an opaque rectangle. To composite that image with others, you need to hide unwanted areas. Or you might want an adjustment layer or filter to be visible only on some areas of a layer. The recommended way to do both is by using a *mask*, a way to mark areas of a layer as transparent.

Using a mask is more useful than deleting or erasing unwanted areas of a layer, because a mask is reversible. For example, if you accidentally trimmed off part of the subject with a mask, editing the mask lets you restore the trimmed area.

A mask is similar to a selection, but there are important differences. A selection is temporary, affects only the selected layer, and is lost when you close a document. In contrast, one layer (pixel) mask and one vector mask can be saved with each layer. You can easily convert a selection to a mask, and vice versa.

Getting started

First, you'll view the image that you'll create using masks.

1 Start Photoshop, and then simultaneously hold down Ctrl+Alt+Shift (Windows) or Command+Option+Shift (macOS) to restore the default preferences. (See "Restoring default preferences" on page 5.)

2 When prompted, click Yes to delete the Adobe Photoshop Settings file.

3 Choose File > Browse In Bridge to open Adobe Bridge.

4 Click the Favorites tab on the left side of the Bridge window. Select the Lessons folder, and then double-click the Lesson06 folder in the Content panel.

5 Study the 06End.psd file. To enlarge the thumbnail so that you can see it more clearly, move the thumbnail slider at the bottom of the Bridge window to the right.

In this lesson, you'll create a graphic for a podcast. The model was photographed in front of a different background. You'll use Select And Mask to quickly isolate the model over the final background. You'll also tilt the model's head up a little more and create a pattern for the background.

6 Double-click the 06Start.psd thumbnail to open it in Photoshop. Click OK if you see an Embedded Profile Mismatch dialog box, and close any messages that appear about new features.

7 Choose File > Save As, rename the file to **06Working.psd**, and click Save. Click OK if the Photoshop Format Options dialog box appears.

Saving a working copy of the file lets you preserve the original, if you need it later.

About masks and channels

Alpha channels, quick masks, clipping masks, layer masks, vector masks—what's the difference? They're all variations of the same idea: an image overlay that uses white, black, and gray areas to control which areas of a layer are visible or transparent. Choose the right one by understanding the following important differences:

- A **color channel** stores one of the visible components of a color image. For example, an RGB image has three color channels: red, green, and blue.

- An **alpha channel** stores a selection as a grayscale image. You can convert alpha channels to and from selections, masks, and vector paths. In some file formats such as PNG, an alpha channel marks transparent areas of an image in a way that other applications recognize.

- A **layer mask** is an alpha channel attached to a specific layer in Photoshop, controlling which parts of the layer are revealed or hidden. It appears as a white thumbnail next to the layer thumbnail in the Layers panel until you paint black in it; an outline around the layer mask thumbnail indicates that it's selected.

- A **vector mask** is a layer mask made of resolution-independent vector objects, not pixels, useful when a geometrically perfect mask edge is more important than editing a mask with a brush. You create vector masks using the commands on the Layer > Vector Mask submenu and using the Pen tool or shape tools.

- A **clipping mask** uses one layer's content to mask another layer. For example, if you want to fill type characters with an image, setting up the type characters as a clipping mask shows the image only inside the characters.

- A **channel mask** is a mask manually built using tones from one or more color channels, such as the green channel in an RGB image. Channel masks are useful in advanced techniques for masking, color correction, and sharpening. For example, the edge between trees and sky may be clearest in the blue channel.

- A **quick mask** is a temporary mask you create to restrict painting or other edits to a specific area of a layer. It's a selection in pixel form; instead of editing the selection marquee, you edit a quick mask using painting tools.

▶ **Tip:** Because masks mark which areas of a layer are visible, they also control where your edits are visible. For example, if you paint a masked layer with the Brush tool, the brush strokes are visible only on the unmasked (white) areas of a layer.

Using Select And Mask and Select Subject

Photoshop provides a set of tools focused on creating and refining masks, collected in a task space called Select And Mask. Inside Select And Mask, you'll use the Select Subject tool to get a fast head start on the mask that will separate the model from the background. Then you'll refine the mask using other Select And Mask tools, such as the Quick Selection tool.

1 In the Layers panel, make sure both layers are visible and the Model layer is selected.

2 Choose Select > Select And Mask.

▶ **Tip:** When any selection tool is active, the Select And Mask button is available in the options bar. You can choose Select > Select and Mask when the Select and Mask button is not shown.

Tip: The first time you use Select And Mask, a tutorial tip may pop up. You may view it before you continue with the lesson, or you can click Later or Close.

Select And Mask opens with the image (notice how the panels changed). A semi-transparent "onion skin" overlay indicates masked areas, currently covering the entire image because nothing is revealed by the mask yet.

Tip: When a selection tool is active, you can also open Select And Mask by clicking the Select And Mask button in the options bar, instead of having to find the command in the menus.

3 Click the View menu in the View Mode section of the Properties panel, and choose Overlay. The masked area is now shown as a semitransparent red color instead of the onion skin. It's solid because nothing is masked yet.

Tip: Quickly cycle through the View Modes by pressing the F key. Viewing different modes helps you spot selection mistakes that might not be obvious in other modes. Also, the View Mode menu lists a single-key shortcut for each mode.

The different View Modes are provided so that you can see the mask more easily over various backgrounds. In this case, the red overlay will make it easier to see missed areas and edges later, where edges and loose hair aren't properly masked.

4 In the options bar, click the Select Subject button.

Using advanced machine learning technology, the Select Subject feature is trained to identify typical subjects of a photo, including people, animals, and objects, and then create a selection. The selection may not be perfect, but it's often close enough for you to refine easily and rapidly with other selection tools.

5 Click the View menu in the View Mode section of the Properties panel, and choose Black & White. This View Mode helps make the mask edge easier to see.

6 Click the View menu in the View Mode section of the Properties panel, and choose Overlay to better compare the edge to the actual image.

Notice that there are a few areas over the chest that were missed by Select Subject. You can easily add them to the selection using the Quick Selection tool.

7 Make sure the Quick Selection tool (✒) is selected. In the options bar, set up a brush with a size of **15** px.

8 Drag the Quick Selection tool over the missed areas (without extending into the background) to add the missed areas to the selection. Notice that the Quick Selection tool fills in the selection as it detects content edges, so you don't have to be exact. It's okay if you release the mouse button and drag more than once.

Note: You can choose how to process Select Subject in the Select Subject button drop-down list. Cloud processing may produce better results, using a larger machine learning model on a powerful remote computer. Processing on your device is usually faster but less precise. Changing this setting affects the next time you click Select Subject; you can set this permanently in the Image Processing panel of the Preferences dialog box.

Tip: You don't have to be in the Select And Mask dialog box to use the Select > Subject command. Also, it's OK to use Select Subject first and then enter Select And Mask to refine the selection. Or, if Select Subject doesn't work, try the Object Selection tool.

Tip: If you don't like the initial selection, in addition to trying cloud processing (see first tip above), you can also try a different Refine Mode in the Properties panel. Compare Color Aware and Object Aware and see which works better.

▶ **Tip:** When editing a selection, increase the magnification if it helps you see missed areas.

Where you drag teaches the Quick Selection tool which areas should be revealed and are not part of the mask. Do not drag the Quick Selection tool over or past the model's edge to the background, because this teaches the Quick Selection tool to include part of the background in the mask. If you accidentally add unwanted areas to the mask, either choose Edit > Undo or reverse the edit by painting over it with the Quick Selection tool in Subtract mode. To enable Subtract mode for the Quick Selection tool, click the Subtract From Selection icon (⊖) in the options bar.

▶ **Tip:** You can adjust the opacity of the onion skin by dragging the Transparency slider under the View Mode options.

As you drag the Quick Selection tool over the model, the overlay disappears from the areas that you are marking to be revealed. Don't worry about perfection yet.

9   Click the View menu in the View Mode section again, and choose On Layers. This shows you how the current Select And Mask settings look over any layers that are behind this layer. In this case, you're previewing how the current settings will mask the Model layer over the Episode Background layer.

Inspect the edges around the model at a high magnification, such as 400%. Some of the original light background may still show between the model's edge and the podcast background, but overall the Select Subject and Quick Selection tools should have created clean edges for the shirt and face. Don't be concerned about edge gaps or imperfect hair edges, because you'll take care of those next.

Getting better and faster results with Select And Mask

When using Select And Mask, it's important to use different tools for image areas that should be fully revealed, for areas that should be fully masked, and for partially masked edges (such as fuzzy dog hair). Try these recommendations:

- The Select Subject button can be a fast way to create an initial selection.

- The Quick Selection tool is useful for rapidly touching up a selection produced by Select Subject or for creating an initial selection. As you drag the tool, it uses edge detection technology to find mask edges automatically. Don't drag it on or over a mask edge; keep it fully inside (in Add mode) or outside (in Subtract mode) the areas that should be revealed.

- To paint solid mask edges manually (without using automatic edge detection), use the Brush, Lasso, or Polygonal Lasso tool. These have an Add mode for marking revealed areas and a Subtract mode for marking masked areas.

- Instead of having to switch between Add and Subtract modes with the options bar, you can leave a tool in Add mode, and when you want to temporarily use the tool in Subtract mode, hold down the Alt (Windows) or Option (macOS) key.

- To improve the mask along edges containing complex transitions such as hair, drag the Refine Edge Brush along those edges. Do not drag the Refine Edge brush over areas that should be fully revealed or fully masked.

- You don't have to do all of your selecting inside Select And Mask. For example, if you've already created a selection with another tool such as Color Range, leave that selection active, and then if you want to clean up the selection, click Select > Select And Mask in the options bar.

▶ **Tip:** In Select And Mask, the Polygonal Lasso tool is grouped with the Lasso tool.

Refining a mask

The mask is pretty good so far. The Select Subject mask even correctly masked the hole within the loop of hair over the back of the shirt. But just above that loop is another gap within hair, and that gap should also be part of the mask so that the blue background shows through. In Select And Mask, the Refine Edge Brush tool can help mask areas and edges that are fuzzy.

1 At a magnification of 300% or higher, inspect the empty areas within the hair, comparing the large hole inside the lower hair loop with the smaller gap in the hair above it.

The blue background should also be showing through the upper gap, but the gap is currently not masked out. This gap would not be easy to mask with a normal (solid color) brush tool because of the fine hairs along its edges, but the Refine Edge Brush tool is designed to recognize and mask these types of subtle edges.

Julieanne Kost is an official Adobe Photoshop evangelist.

Tool tips from the Photoshop evangelist

Zoom tool shortcuts

Often when editing an image, you'll need to zoom in to work on a detail and then zoom out again to see the changes in context. Here are several keyboard shortcuts that make zooming faster and easier:

- With any tool selected, press Ctrl (Windows) or Command (macOS) with the plus sign (+) to zoom in, or with the minus sign (–) to zoom out.
- Double-click the Zoom tool in the Tools panel to return the image to 100% view.
- When Scrubby Zoom is selected in the options bar, just drag the Zoom tool to the left to zoom out or to the right to zoom in.
- Press Alt (Windows) or Option (macOS) to change the Zoom In tool to the Zoom Out tool, and click the image. Each Alt/Option-click reduces the image by the next preset increment, centering the image where you clicked.

2   Select the Refine Edge Brush tool (). In the options bar, set up a brush with a size of **20** px and Hardness of **100**%.

▶ **Tip:** Depending on the image, clicking the Refine Hair button can reduce the amount of manual brushing you need to do with the Refine Edge Brush tool.

3   Drag the Refine Edge Brush tool over the enclosed area that should be transparent. Gaps in the hair should become masked as transparent, and fine hairs are added to the visible edge.

4 Click the View option, and choose Black & White to more clearly evaluate the current mask edge. Inspect the mask at different magnifications. When you're done, choose View > Fit On Screen. Black areas indicate transparency.

▶ Tip: Gray pixels should appear only along transitional (semitransparent) mask edges. All areas fully outside the subject should be solid black, and all areas fully inside should be solid white.

▶ Tip: A quick way to remember which foreground color to paint in a mask is the mnemonic phrase "black conceals, white reveals."

If you see hairs or other details that should be more visible, drag the Refine Edge brush over them. The finer the details you want to mask, the smaller you should set the Refine Edge brush size. It's okay if the brush size is slightly larger than the details you want to mask, and you don't have to drag the Refine Edge Brush tool precisely.

If you see Refine Edge Brush tool mistakes that need to be erased, such as inner areas incorrectly added to the mask, drag the Refine Edge Brush tool over the mistakes while holding down the Alt (Windows) or Option (macOS) key.

If you see individual spots or discrete areas that need to be fully visible or fully transparent, you can paint them out using the Brush tool, the third one down in the toolbox. To make areas visible, paint them with white; to make areas hidden, paint them with black. You can also drag the Lasso tool to enclose any areas you want to add, subtract, or intersect with the mask, depending on its mode in the options bar.

Adjusting Global Refinements

At this point the mask is good but needs to be tightened up a little. You can tune the overall appearance of the mask edge by adjusting the Global Refinements settings.

1 Click the View menu in the View Mode section of the Properties panel, and choose On Layers. This lets you preview adjustments over the Episode Background layer, which is behind the Model layer.

2 In the Global Refinements section, move the sliders to create a smooth, unfeathered edge along the face. The optimal settings depend on the selection you created, but they'll probably be similar to ours. We moved the Smooth slider to 1 to reduce the roughness of the outline, Contrast to 20% to sharpen the transitions along the selection border, and Shift Edge to –15% to move the selection border inward and help remove unwanted background colors from selection edges. (Adjusting Shift Edge to a positive number would move the border outward.)

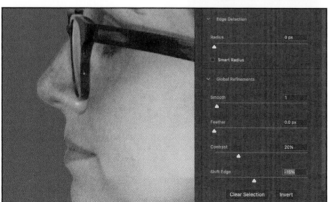

3 Take one more look at this preview of the current mask over the background layer, and make any remaining corrections as needed.

Note: Pay attention to details while using Global Refinements. For example, if you adjust Smooth and the mask edge starts to round corners or grind down important details, that means Smooth is set too high. Similarly, setting Feather too high can create unsightly halos along the edge.

Completing the mask

▶ **Tip:** If you mask many images that need similar Properties panel settings, click the Preset menu and choose Save Preset to create a named preset that you can apply at any time.

When you're satisfied with the mask, you can apply it to the document as a selection, a layer with transparency, a layer mask, or a new document. For this project, we want to use this as a layer mask on the Model layer, which was selected when you entered Select And Mask.

1 If the Output Settings are hidden, click the disclosure icon (⟩) to reveal them.

2 Zoom in to 200% or more so that you can more easily see the light fringing around the face edge that's due to the Model layer's original background color seeping in behind the mask.

3 Select Decontaminate Colors to suppress those color fringes. If Decontaminate Colors creates unwanted artifacts, reduce the Amount until the effect looks the way you want. We set Amount to 25%.

4 Choose New Layer With Layer Mask from the Output To menu. Then click OK.

5 In the Layers panel, the Model Copy layer now has a layer mask (pixel mask) that was generated by Select And Mask.

The layer was copied because using the Decontaminate Colors option requires generating new pixels. The original Model layer is preserved and automatically hidden. If you wanted to start over, you could delete the Model Copy layer, make the original Model layer visible again and selected, and open Select And Mask again.

If the mask isn't perfect, you can continue to edit it at any time. When a layer mask thumbnail is selected in the Layers panel, you can click the Select And Mask button in the Properties panel, click it in the options bar (if a selection tool is active), or choose Select > Select And Mask.

6 Save your work.

● **Note:** If you had not selected Decontaminate Colors, it would have been possible to choose a Layer Mask output option that would have added a layer mask to the Model layer without copying it.

Manipulating an image with Puppet Warp

The Puppet Warp feature gives you flexibility in manipulating an image. You can reposition areas, such as hair or an arm, just as you might pull the strings on a puppet. Place pins wherever you want to control movement. You'll use Puppet Warp to tilt the model's head back so she appears to be looking up.

Note: Photoshop provides several different ways to warp a layer. You'll use Puppet Warp because it's the easiest way to pivot part of an image, such as tilting the head back in this example.

1 Zoom out so you can see the entire model.

2 With the Model Copy layer selected in the Layers panel, choose Edit > Puppet Warp.

A mesh appears over the visible areas in the layer—in this case, the model. On the mesh, you'll place pins where you want to control movement (or to ensure there is no movement).

Note: Your mesh may be slightly different. It's OK if your pin positions are slightly different than what is shown here.

3 Click to add pins around the body and along the base of the head, as shown below. Each time you click, Puppet Warp adds a pin. About 10 to 12 pins should work.

The pins you've added around the shirt will keep it in place as you tilt the head.

Tip: The ability of Puppet Warp to pivot part of a layer makes it different than the other Photoshop distortion tools, such as Filter > Liquify and the Edit > Transform submenu commands.

4 Click the pin at the nape of the neck to select it. A blue dot appears in the center of the pin to indicate that it's selected.

5   Press Alt (Windows) or Option (macOS). A larger circle appears around the pin, and a curved double arrow appears next to it. Continue pressing Alt or Option as you drag the pointer to rotate the head backwards. You can see the angle of rotation in the options bar; you can enter **170** there to rotate the head back.

6   When you're satisfied with the rotation, click the Commit Puppet Warp button (✓) in the options bar, or press Enter or Return.

Note: Be careful not to Alt-click or Option-click the dot itself, or you'll delete the pin.

▶ **Tip:** On your own, you can compare the difference between dragging the pin itself, and Alt/Option-dragging to pivot the layer around the pin.

7   Delete the Model layer (the one without the mask). It's no longer needed.

8   Choose File > Save to save your work so far.

Creating a pattern for the background

The design for the episode graphic incorporates a pattern into the background. You'll quickly create the pattern by customizing a vector graphic shape.

Customizing a polygon shape

The background is based on star shapes. There is no star tool in Photoshop, but you can easily create a star by customizing a shape drawn with the Polygon tool.

1 In the Lesson06 folder, open the document 06Pattern.psd. It opens in a separate document tab.

2 Select the Polygon tool (⬠), which is grouped with the Rectangle tool. In the options bar, make sure the tool is set to **Shape**.

3 Hold down Shift and draw a polygon shape about 340 pixels wide. If it isn't centered on the canvas, after drawing you can reposition it with the Move tool.

4 With the shape layer still selected, in the Appearance section of the Properties panel set the Fill to No Color, set the Stroke to **20px**, and apply a blue Stroke color slightly darker than the background; we used R=23, G=49, B=153.

● **Note:** If you can't see the polygon options, they may be out of view. Try scrolling down the Properties panel or making the panel taller.

5 Set the polygon Number Of Sides to **8**, and set the Star Ratio to **70%**. When the Star Ratio is less than 100%, the number of sides becomes the number of points.

A. *Rotate angle*
B. *Number of sides*
C. *Star ratio*

6 In the Layers panel, duplicate the star shape layer by dragging and dropping it on the Create A New Layer button.

7 In the Transform section of the Properties panel, change the Rotate angle to **24**.

8 Choose Edit > Free Transform Path, and hold down the Alt (Windows) or Option (macOS) key as you drag a corner handle to shrink the duplicate star layer to fit inside the larger star. Press Enter or Return to apply the transformation.

▶ **Tip:** The Edit > Free Transform Path command may appear as Free Transform if you switched to the Move tool in step 3. The command is Free Transform Path when the current tool can edit paths or shapes.

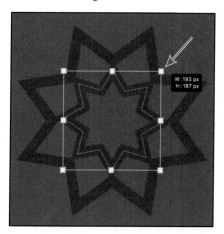

9 Choose View > Pattern Preview to see how the design looks as a pattern. If a message appears, click OK. Only the original shape on the canvas is editable, but Pattern Preview updates to account for any changes you make.

10 Select the Move tool, select Polygon 1 (the large star) in the Layers panel, and look for a small circular handle inside the top-right star point. If you don't see the handle, make sure Show Transform Controls is selected in the options bar, and increase the view magnification.

11 Drag the handle to change the sharp star points to rounded points. We used a radius of 20 pixels. The pattern preview updates.

12 In the Layers panel, select Polygon 1 copy (the small star). In the Properties panel, set the Number Of Points to **15** and reduce the Stroke Width to **15 px**.

13 Click the eye icon for the Background layer to hide it so that the pattern will have a transparent background.

▶ **Tip:** If you wanted this pattern to always have its own blue background, blocking layers behind it, you'd leave the Background layer visible when defining the pattern.

14 Choose Edit > Define Pattern, name it **Podcast Pattern**, and click OK. This creates a pattern preset that you can use in any Photoshop document.

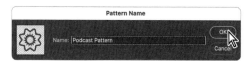

15 Choose File > Save As, rename the file to 06Pattern_Working.psd, and click Save. Click OK if the Photoshop Format Options dialog box appears.

16 Switch to 06Working.psd, and select the Episode Background layer.

17 In the Layers panel, click the Create New Fill Or Adjustment Layer button, and choose Pattern.

▶ **Tip:** If you want to create a pattern from just an area of a document, use the Rectangular Marquee tool to draw a selection before choosing Edit > Define Pattern.

18 In the Pattern Fill dialog box, click the pattern picker, and at the bottom of the list, select the blue pattern you created. Set Angle to **45** degrees, set Scale to **35%**, and click OK.

▶**Tip:** If you want a pattern to cover a partial area of the document, apply a mask to the pattern fill layer. Or, select an area of a layer, choose Edit > Fill, and choose Pattern from the Contents pop-up menu.

19 Save your work. Your podcast background is ready for the next step!

▶**Tip:** This example creates a pattern using vector shape layers, but you can also create a pattern that includes other kinds of layers, such as photos, type, and paintings.

Review questions

1 How is a mask similar to and different than a selection?

2 What's a quick way to precisely select the most prominent item in an image?

3 Why is Select and Mask useful?

4 How do you use a layer mask to make parts of a layer transparent?

5 After you define a pattern, how do you apply it to the image as an adjustable pattern?

Review answers

1 A mask and a selection both let you mark areas of a layer to restrict visibility or edits. A mask belongs to a specific layer and is saved with the document; a selection is temporary and is lost when a document is closed.

2 Select Subject identifies an image's main subject and creates a precise selection around the subject in one click.

3 Select and Mask offers specialized tools to improve the edge of a selection or mask.

4 You make parts of a layer transparent (hidden) by painting black in a layer mask. White areas mark layer areas that are to be opaque (visible), and gray shades indicate semi-transparent areas.

5 Apply a pattern to the image by creating a pattern fill layer.

7 TYPOGRAPHIC DESIGN

Lesson overview

In this lesson, you'll learn how to do the following:

- Use guides to position text in a composition.

- Make a clipping mask from type.

- Merge type with other layers.

- Preview fonts.

- Format text.

- Flow text along a path.

- Control type and positioning using advanced features.

 This lesson will take less than an hour to complete. To get the lesson files used in this chapter, download them from the web page for this book at peachpit.com/PhotoshopCIB2024. For more information, see "Accessing the lesson files and Web Edition" in the Getting Started section at the beginning of this book.

As you work on this lesson, you'll preserve the start files. If you need to restore the start files, download them from your Account page.

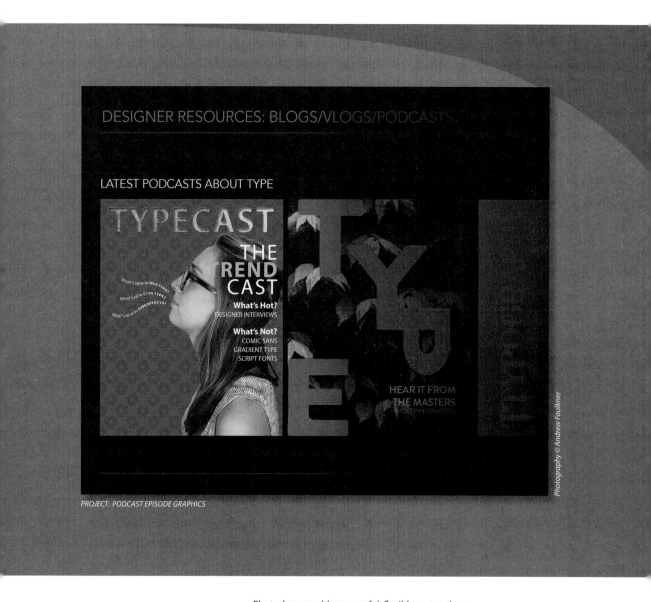

DESIGNER RESOURCES: BLOGS/VLOGS/PODCASTS

LATEST PODCASTS ABOUT TYPE

TYPECAST

THE
TREND
CAST

What's Hot?
DESIGNER INTERVIEWS

What's Not?
COMIC SANS
GRADIENT TYPE
SCRIPT FONTS

WHAT'S NEW IN WEB TYPE?
WHAT'S NEW IN 3D TYPE?
WHAT'S NEW IN TYPE EFFECTS?

TYPE

HEAR IT FROM
THE MASTERS
AVOID TYPE DISASTERS

PROJECT: PODCAST EPISODE GRAPHICS

Photoshop provides powerful, flexible text tools so
you can add type to your images with great control
and creativity.

About type

Note: If some fonts installed on your computer aren't available in Photoshop, check to see if they are PostScript Type 1 fonts, which are an old font format that is no longer supported. Consider licensing OpenType versions of those fonts, which may be available as Adobe Fonts.

A Photoshop type layer consists of vector-based shapes that describe the letters, numbers, and symbols of a typeface. Many typefaces are available in more than one format. The TrueType format is widely used, and the OpenType format is preferred by professionals (see "OpenType in Photoshop" on page 195, later in this lesson).

Photoshop preserves the vector-based character outlines, so type renders at the full resolution of the Photoshop document as you edit, scale, or resize type layers. However, the pixel dimensions of the document limit how sharp type can be. As you magnify a document, jagged type edges appear sooner in a document with smaller pixel dimensions, such as in low-resolution graphics designed for websites.

Getting started

Note: Though this lesson starts where Lesson 6 left off, use the 07Start.psd file. We've included a path and a sticky note In the start file that won't be in the 06Working.psd file you saved.

In this lesson, you'll work on a design that represents an episode of a podcast series about typography. You'll start with the artwork you created in Lesson 6: The episode artwork has a model, her shadow, and the blue background. You'll add and stylize type for the episode artwork, including warping the text.

You'll start the lesson by viewing an image of the final composition.

Note: If Bridge is not installed, you'll be prompted to download and install it. See page 3 for more information.

1   Start Photoshop, and then simultaneously hold down Ctrl+Alt+Shift (Windows) or Command+Option+Shift (macOS) to restore the default preferences. (See "Restoring default preferences" on page 5.)

2   When prompted, click Yes to delete the Adobe Photoshop Settings file.

3   Choose File > Browse In Bridge to open Adobe Bridge.

4   In the Favorites panel on the left side of Bridge, click the Lessons folder, and then double-click the Lesson07 folder in the Content panel.

5   Select the 07End.psd file. Increase the thumbnail size to see the image clearly by dragging the thumbnail slider to the right.

You'll apply the type treatment in Photoshop to finish the episode artwork. All of the type controls you need are available in Photoshop, so you don't have to switch to another application to complete the project.

Note: If Photoshop displays a dialog box telling you about the difference between saving to Cloud Documents and On Your Computer, click Save On Your Computer. You can also select Don't Show Again, but that setting will deselect after you reset Photoshop preferences.

6   Double-click the 07Start.psd file to open it in Photoshop. Click OK if you see an Embedded Profile Mismatch dialog box, and close any messages that appear about new features.

7   Choose File > Save As, rename the file **07Working.psd**, and click Save.

8   Click OK in the Photoshop Format Options dialog box.

9 Choose Graphic and Web from the Workspace Switcher in the options bar.

The Graphic and Web workspace displays the Character and Paragraph panels that you'll use in this lesson, along with the Glyphs and Layers panels. The Tools panel may look different than it has in other lessons, because the Graphic and Web workspace includes a customized Tools panel.

> **Tip:** You can easily customize the Tools panel for your needs. Choose Edit > Toolbar and then hide, show, or arrange the tools the way you want.

Creating a clipping mask from type

A *clipping mask* is an object or a group of objects whose shape masks other artwork so that only areas within the clipping mask are visible. In effect, you are clipping the artwork to the visible pixels of the layer. In Photoshop, you can create a clipping mask from shapes or letters. In this exercise, you'll use letters as a clipping mask to allow an image in another layer to show through.

Adding guides to position type

You'll be adding multiple type layers that need to line up on the canvas. To simplify alignment, you'll start by adding nonprinting guides to help position the type.

Tip: The View >
Actual Size command
makes the Photoshop
ruler match a real-world
ruler. Actual Size works
best with print docu-
ments, not documents
measured in pixels.

1 Choose View > Fit On
Screen to see the whole
canvas clearly.

2 Choose View > Rulers to
display rulers along the
left and top borders of
the document window.

3 If the rulers aren't
displaying in inches,
right-click (Windows)
or Control-click (macOS) the rulers, and choose Inches.

Tip: If you find it
difficult to position
the vertical ruler guide
exactly at 4.25", holding
down Shift will snap the
guide to the 4.25" ruler
tick mark.

4 Drag a vertical guide from the left ruler to the center of the document (4.25").

Adding point type

Now you're ready to add type to the composition. You can enter *point type* (short
text anchored to a point) or *paragraph type* (multiple lines that can recompose as
you resize their text container). First, you'll create point type.

1 In the Layers panel, select the Pattern Fill layer.

2 Select the Horizontal Type tool (**T**), and, in the options bar, do the following:

- Choose a serif typeface, such as Minion Pro Regular, from the Font Family
  pop-up menu.

- Type **115 pt** for the Size, and press Enter or Return.

- Click the Center Text button.

3 In the Character panel, change the Tracking value to **50**.

Tracking specifies the space between selected letters, which affects type density.

4   Position the pointer over the center guide you added to set an insertion point, roughly where the guide crosses the edge of the model's shadow, click, and then type **TYPECAST** in all capital letters. Then click the Commit Any Current Edits button (✔) in the options bar.

Note: After you type, you must commit your editing in the layer by clicking the Commit Any Current Edits button, switching to another tool or layer, or clicking away from the text layer. You cannot commit to current edits by pressing Enter or Return; doing so would create a new line of type.

The word "TYPECAST" is added, and it appears in the Layers panel as a new type layer named TYPECAST. You can edit and manage the type layer as you would any other layer. You can add or change the text, change the orientation of the type, apply anti-aliasing, apply layer styles and transformations, and create masks. You can move, restack, and copy a type layer, or edit its layer options, just as you would for any other layer.

The text is big enough, but not modern enough, for this design. Try a different font:

5   Double-click the "TYPECAST" text to edit it.

6   In the options bar or Contextual Task Bar, open the Font Family pop-up menu by clicking the arrow to the right of the font name. Hover the pointer over items in the font list.

When the pointer is over a font name, Photoshop temporarily applies that font to the selected text so you can preview the font in context.

Tip: When a type layer is selected in the Layers panel, the Properties panel displays type settings—another place you can change type options such as the font.

7 Select Myriad Pro Semibold or a similar font, and then click the Commit Any Current Edits button (✔) in the options bar.

That's much more appropriate.

8 If needed, use the Move tool to drag the "TYPECAST" text to adjust its position close to the top of the design.

9 Choose File > Save to save your work so far.

Making a clipping mask and applying a shadow

You added the letters in black, the default text color. However, you want the letters to appear to be filled with a texture from an image, so you'll use the letters to make a clipping mask that will allow another image layer to show through.

1 In the Layers panel, make sure the TYPECAST layer is selected.

2 Choose File > Place Embedded, navigate to the Lesson07 folder, and double-click the Metal.tif file. It appears with a bounding box so that you can scale it or move it into place.

3 With the bounding box still active, drag the Metal layer up until it's aligned with the top of the canvas. Then press Enter or Return to finish placing the file.

4 With the Metal layer selected, choose Create Clipping Mask from the Layers panel menu (☰).

▶ **Tip:** You can also create a clipping mask by holding down the Alt (Windows) or Option (macOS) key and clicking between the Metal and TYPECAST type layers. Or, choose Layer > Create Clipping Mask when the Metal layer is selected.

Creating a clipping mask restricts the Metal layer to the non-transparent areas of the next layer down (the TYPECAST layer). In the Layers panel, a small arrow and an underlined layer name indicate the two layers used in the clipping mask.

Next, you'll add an inner shadow to give the letters depth.

5 Select the TYPECAST layer. Then, click the Add A Layer Style button (*fx*) at the bottom of the Layers panel, and choose Inner Shadow from the pop-up menu.

6 In the Layer Style dialog box, set the Blend Mode to Multiply, and set Opacity to **48**%, Angle to **120**°, Distance to **18**, Choke to **0**, and Size to **16**. Then click OK.

The Inner Shadow option adds a sense of dimension to the title text.

7 Choose File > Save to save your work so far.

Julieanne Kost is an official Adobe Photoshop evangelist.

Tool tips from the Photoshop evangelist

Type tool tricks

- If clicking a type tool isn't creating a new type layer because it's activating an existing type layer nearby, Shift-click the tool to create the new type layer.

- To select all of the characters on a type layer, in the Layers panel double-click the layer's thumbnail icon.

- To check spelling across all type layers, choose Edit > Check Spelling. You can also choose Check Spelling from the context menu that appears when you right-click (Windows) or Control-click (macOS) a type tool on the canvas.

Paragraph and character styles

If you need to consistently format a large amount of type in a Photoshop document, you can use paragraph and character styles to consistently format more text in less time. Use a paragraph style to apply a named preset of type options to one or more paragraphs with a single click. Use a character style to apply a preset of type options to one or more selected characters. You can use these styles by opening their panels: Choose Window > Paragraph Styles and Window > Character Styles.

Type styles in Photoshop are similar to type styles in page layout applications such as Adobe InDesign and word-processing applications such as Microsoft Word, but there are a few differences in Photoshop. For the best results working with type styles in Photoshop, keep the following in mind:

- By default, all text you create in Photoshop has the Basic Paragraph style applied. The Basic Paragraph style is defined by your text defaults, but you can change the style definition by double-clicking the style name.

- Deselect all layers before you create a new style.

- If the selected text was changed from the current paragraph style (usually the Basic Paragraph style), those changes (considered overrides) persist even when you apply a new style. To ensure that all the attributes of a paragraph style are applied to text, apply the style, and then click the Clear Override button (↻) in the Paragraph Styles panel.

- Want to use the styles from another Photoshop document? Open the Paragraph Styles or Character Styles panel menu, choose Load Styles, and select the document containing the styles you want. To save the current styles as defaults for all new documents, choose Type > Save Default Type Styles. To use your default styles in an existing document, choose Type > Load Default Type Styles.

Creating type on a path

In Photoshop, you can create type that follows along a path that you draw with a pen or shape tool. The direction the type flows depends on the order in which anchor points were added to the path. When you use the Horizontal Type tool to add text to a path, the letters are perpendicular to the baseline of the path. If you change the location or shape of the path, the type moves with it.

You'll create type on a path to make it look as if questions are coming from the model's mouth. We've already created the path for you; we stored it in the Paths panel.

1 In the Layers panel, select the Model layer.

2 Choose Window > Paths to show the Paths panel.

▶ **Tip:** To learn about drawing paths with the Pen tool, see Lesson 8, "Vector Drawing Techniques."

3 In the Paths panel, select Speech Path to make it active and visible.

The path appears to be coming out of the model's mouth.

4 Select the Horizontal Type tool.

5 In the options bar, click the Right Align Text button.

6 In the Character panel, select the following settings:

- Font Family: Myriad Pro
- Font Style: Regular
- Font Size (T): **14** pt
- Tracking (): **–10**
- Color: White
- All Caps (**TT**)

● **Note:** The path won't print or export because it isn't a shape layer—it exists only in the Paths panel. But the text on the path is a type layer, so the type will print and export.

7 Move the Horizontal Type tool over the path. When a small curved line appears across the I-bar, click near the end of the path closest to the model's mouth, and type **What's new in 3D type?**.

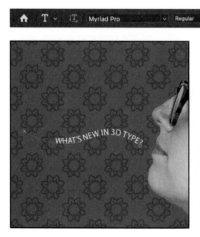

As you type on the path, the text is added from the right because Right Align Text was selected in step 5.

8   With the Horizontal Type too, select "3D TYPE?" and change its font style to Bold. Click the Commit Any Current Edits button (✔) in the options bar.

9   In the Layers panel, select the What's new in 3D type? layer, choose Duplicate Layer from the Layers panel menu, and click OK.

You can't see the duplicate text layer yet, because it's exactly on top of the original text layer. But the Layers panel shows that the duplicate layer has the word "copy" at the end of the layer name. You'll move the copy away from the original.

10 Choose Edit > Free Transform Path. Rotate the path approximately 15 degrees, and then shift the path up above the first path and a little to the right, as in the following figure. Click the Commit Transform button in the options bar.

11 With the Type tool, select "3D" in the upper copy of the text layer, and replace it with **web**. Click the Commit Any Current Edits button in the options bar.

When you edit the characters on a text layer, the layer name automatically updates to match. (The layer name will not update if you edited the layer name to differ from the actual text on the layer.)

● **Note:** If you can't remember how to rotate using a transform bounding box, position the pointer near the outside of the transform bounding box until the pointer changes to a rotate icon (an arc with two arrows), and drag.

12 Repeat steps 9–11, replacing the words "3D type" with **type effects**. Rotate the left side of the path about –15 degrees, and move it below the original path.

13 Choose File > Save to save your work so far.

Warping point type

The text on a curvy path is more interesting than straight lines would be, but you'll warp the text to make it more playful. *Warping* lets you distort type into a variety of shapes, such as an arc or a wave. The warp style you select is an attribute of the type layer—you can change a layer's warp style at any time to change the overall shape of the warp. Warping options give you precise control over the orientation and perspective of the warp effect.

1 If necessary, zoom or scroll to move the visible area of the document window so that the sentences to the left of the model are in the center of the screen.

2 Select the What's new in 3D type? layer.

Note: You can also choose Warp Text from the context menu that appears when you right-click/Control-click a type layer (not the layer thumbnail) in the Layers panel.

3 Choose Type > Warp Text.

4 In the Warp Text dialog box, choose Wave from the Style menu, and select the Horizontal option. Specify the following values: Bend, +**33**%; Horizontal Distortion, –**23**%; and Vertical Distortion, +**5**%. Then click OK.

The Bend slider specifies how much warp is applied. Horizontal Distortion and Vertical Distortion determine the perspective of the warp.

▶ **Tip:** Do you want to simulate type wrapping around a beverage can? With a type layer selected, choose Edit > Transform > Warp, and then choose Cylinder from the Warp pop-up menu in the options bar.

The words "What's new in 3D type?" appear to float like a wave on the design.

5 Repeat steps 3 and 4 to warp the other two text layers you typed on a path. Feel free to try different settings.

6 Save your work.

Designing paragraphs of type

All of the text you've added so far has been point type because it's a single line. However, many designs call for full paragraphs of text. You can add paragraph type and apply paragraph styles. You don't have to switch to a dedicated page layout program for sophisticated paragraph type controls.

Using guides for positioning

You will add paragraphs to the design. First, you'll add some guides to the work area to help you position the paragraphs.

1   If necessary, zoom or scroll so that you can see the entire top half of the document.

2   Drag a guide from the left vertical ruler, placing it approximately ¼" from the right edge of the canvas.

3   Drag a guide down from the top horizontal ruler, placing it approximately 2" from the top of the canvas.

Adding paragraph type from a sticky note

You're ready to add the text. In a real-world design environment, text might be provided to you in a comment (in an online Photoshop review using File > Share for Review) or in an email message. It's also possible for someone to open the document and enter text into a sticky note, as we've done for you here.

1 Position the Move tool near the edge of the yellow sticky note in the lower-right corner of the image window, and when it appears as a black pointer only (▶), double-click to open the Notes panel.

 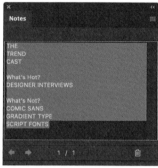

2 All nine lines of the text should be selected; if they aren't, click in the note text and choose Select > All. Choose Edit > Copy, and close the Notes panel.

3 Select the Model layer. Then, select the Horizontal Type tool (**T**).

4 Position the pointer where the guides intersect at about ¼" from the right edge and 2" from the top of the canvas. Hold down the Shift key as you start to drag a text box down and to the left. Then release the Shift key, and continue dragging until the box is about 4 inches wide by 6 inches high. The new text layer is created in front of the Model layer that was selected (above the Model layer in the Layers panel).

5 Choose Edit > Paste to add the text from the note.

6 Select the first three lines ("The Trend Cast"), and then apply the following settings in the Character panel:

- Font Family: Myriad Pro (or another sans serif font)
- Font Style: Regular
- Font Size (⇥T): **70** pt
- Leading (⇴A): **55** pt
- Tracking (🅑): **50**
- Color: White

▶ **Tip:** You create notes using the Note tool, which is hidden when the Graphics and Web workspace is active. You can find the Note tool quickly by choosing Edit > Search. However, if you want to collect comments from multiple people, it may be easier to use the cloud-based Share for Review online comment feature (choose File > Share for Review).

▶ **Tip:** In step 4, the reason you press Shift is to make sure you create a new type layer. If you don't press Shift, the Horizontal Type tool might instead select text in the nearby text layer containing the "TYPECAST" headline.

⬤ **Note:** If the text isn't visible, make sure the new type layer is above the Model layer in the Layers panel.

▶ **Tip:** If you paste text and it includes unwanted formatting, you can instead choose the Edit > Paste Without Formatting command in Photoshop to remove all formatting from the pasted text.

7 With the text still selected, click the Right Align Text button in the options bar or Paragraph panel.

8 Select just the word "Trend," and change the Font Style to Bold.

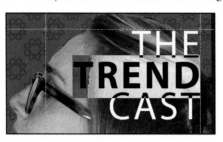

You've formatted the title. Now you'll format the rest of the text.

9 Select the rest of the text you pasted. In the Character panel, select the following:

- Font Family: Myriad Pro
- Font Style: Regular
- Font Size: **22** pt

● **Note:** *Leading* (pronounced "ledding") determines the vertical space between lines.

- Leading: **28** pt
- Tracking: **0**
- Deselect All Caps (**TT**)

The text looks good, but it's all the same. You'll make the headlines stand out more.

10 Select the "What's Hot?" text, change the following in the Character panel, and then press Enter or Return:

- Font Style: Bold
- Font Size: **28** pt

▶ **Tip:** To quickly select an entire paragraph, triple-click it when a type tool is selected.

11 Repeat step 10 for the "What's Not!" subhead.

12 Select the word "TREND." Then, in the Character panel, change the text color to blue. We used R=0, G=174, B=239 (or #00aeef in hexadecimal RGB).

13 Click the Commit Any Current Edits button in the options bar.

14 Save your changes.

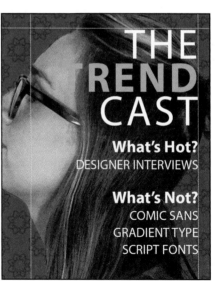

Saving as Photoshop PDF

The type you've added consists of vector-based outlines, which remain crisp and clear as you zoom in or resize them. However, if you save the file as a JPEG or TIFF image, Photoshop rasterizes the type, so you lose that flexibility. When you save a Photoshop PDF file, vector type is preserved. However, type resolution is always limited to the document resolution. For example, in a 300 × 200 px document even a vector type layer is likely to look jaggy because a document of those pixel dimensions simply doesn't have many pixels for resolving curves and details.

You can preserve other Photoshop editing capabilities in a Photoshop PDF file too. For example, you can retain layers, color information, and even notes.

To ensure you can edit the document later, select Preserve Photoshop Editing Capabilities in the Save Adobe PDF dialog box. This will result in a larger PDF file.

To preserve any notes in the file and convert them to Acrobat comments when you save to PDF, select Notes in the Save area of the Save As dialog box.

You can open a Photoshop PDF file in Acrobat or Photoshop, place it in another application, print it, or upload it to a website. For more information, see "Saving the Image as Photoshop PDF" in Lesson 14, "Producing and Printing Consistent Color."

Finishing up

Now, you'll clean up a bit before saving the finished project.

1   With the Move tool, right-click (Windows) or Control-click (macOS) near the top-left corner of the yellow note icon, and choose Delete Note from the context menu; click Yes to confirm that you want to delete the note.

2   Hide the guides: Choose View > Show > Guides to deselect the command. Then choose View > Fit on Screen to get a nice look at your work.

3   Choose File > Save.

Congratulations! You've added and stylized all of the type. Now that the design is ready to go, you'll export a copy to upload to the podcast service.

> **Tip:** Want a design to have a familiar look but not with the exact font that look is known for? Try Font Similarity. Choose a font in the Font Family menu in either the Type tool options bar or the Character panel. You'll see options at the top of the font list; click the Show Similar Fonts button.

The font list will now show the 20 most similar fonts available either on your system or from Adobe Fonts.

> **Tip:** The keyboard shortcut for hiding and showing guides (View > Show > Guides) is Ctrl+; (Windows) or Command+; (macOS).

The Glyphs panel

The Glyphs panel (Window > Glyphs) lists all characters available for a font, including specialized characters and alternate versions such as swashes. At the top is a row of recently used glyphs (empty if you haven't used any glyphs yet). Use the menu below the font name to specify a writing system such as Arabic, or a category such as punctuation. To use a glyph, position a flashing text cursor in a text layer and then double-click a glyph. A black dot in the bottom-right corner of a glyph's box indicates that alternates are available; click and hold the mouse on that box to view or select alternate glyphs.

4 Choose File > Export > Export As, choose JPG from the Format menu, leave the rest of the settings as they are, and click Export. Change the filename to **07Upload.jpg**, go to the Lesson07 folder, and click Save.

5 Close the document window and save any changes.

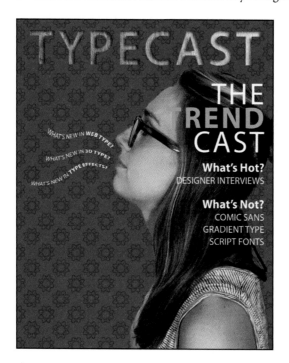

OpenType in Photoshop

OpenType is a cross-platform font file format developed jointly by Adobe and Microsoft. The format uses a single font file for both Mac and Windows, so you can move files from one platform to another without font substitution or reflowed text. OpenType offers expanded character sets and layout features, such as swashes and discretionary ligatures, that aren't available in traditional PostScript and TrueType fonts. This, in turn, provides richer linguistic support and advanced typography control. You can identify OpenType fonts in the Photoshop font menu because they appear with an OpenType icon (*O*). Here are some highlights of OpenType:

The OpenType menu. The Character panel menu includes an OpenType submenu that displays all available features for a selected OpenType font, including ligatures, alternates, and fractions. Dimmed features are unavailable for that typeface; check marks appear next to features that have been applied.

Discretionary ligatures. To add a discretionary ligature to two OpenType letters, such as to "th" in the Bickham Script Standard typeface, select them in the file, and choose OpenType > Discretionary Ligatures from the Character panel menu.

Swashes. Adding swashes or alternate characters works the same way as discretionary ligatures: Select the letter, such as a capital "T" in Bickham Script, and choose OpenType > Swash to change the ordinary capital into an ornate (swash) "T."

True fractions. To create true fractions, type the fraction's characters—for example, 1/2. Then, select the characters, and from the Character panel menu, choose OpenType > Fractions. Photoshop applies the true fraction (½).

Color fonts. While you can apply a color to a font in Photoshop, a format called OpenType-SVG allows multiple colors and gradients to be part of the font design itself. For example, a color font may provide the letter "A" in solid blue as well as solid red and in a blue-to-green gradient.

Emoji fonts. Another example of OpenType-SVG fonts are emoji fonts, made possible because OpenType-SVG allows vector graphics to be used as font characters. The Photoshop font family menu indicates color and emoji fonts with an OpenType SVG icon (⬛SVG).

Variable fonts. When you want a certain font weight but Regular is too thin and Bold is too thick, you can use a variable font that lets you customize attributes such as weight, width, and slant in the Properties panel. The Photoshop font family menu indicates variable fonts with an OpenType VAR icon (⬛VAR).

Note that some OpenType fonts have more options than others.

▶ **Tip:** Want to know if a character has OpenType alternates? Just select it. If a thick bar appears under a selected character, right-click (Windows) or Control-click (macOS) the bar and select Show Alternatives for Selection to reveal the alternate glyphs available for that character in the font applied to it. You can select from those glyphs just as you can in the Glyphs panel, or you can click a triangle to open the Glyphs panel.

Extra credit

Using Match Fonts to keep your projects consistent

We want to identify a font that was used in another design and apply it to text that says "Premiere Episode" (see the file MatchFont.jpg in the Lesson07 folder). We'd like to use that font for another episode. But the only available file is flattened, so the original type layer is lost. Because no type layer is available, it's impossible to select the text to find out which font was used. Fortunately, you don't have to guess which font is in the image because, in Photoshop, you can let the Match Font feature figure it out for you. Thanks to the magic of intelligent imaging analysis, using just a picture of a Latin font, Photoshop can use machine learning to detect which font it is. Match Font then shows you a list of similar fonts. Match Font is also useful for identifying fonts in photos, such as in the text on a sign in a street scene.

1 Open MatchFont.jpg in the Lesson07 folder.

2 Use the Rectangular Marquee tool to tightly select the area containing the mystery font.

3 Choose Type > Match Font. Photoshop displays a list of fonts similar to the font in the image, including active fonts on your system and Adobe Fonts.

4 To list only the fonts on your computer, deselect Show Fonts Available To Activate From Adobe Fonts.

5 Select a script font that most closely resembles the font in the image from the list of fonts that Match Font determined to be similar. Your Match Font results may look different than ours.

6 Click OK. Photoshop selects the font you clicked, so you can now create new text with it.

Review questions

1 How is a Photoshop text layer different than a pixel (image) layer?

2 What are the two kinds of text layers in Photoshop? How are they different?

3 What is a clipping mask, and how do you make one from type?

Review answers

1 Text in Photoshop consists of vector-based shapes that describe the letters, numbers, and symbols of a typeface. When you add type to an image in Photoshop, the characters appear on a text layer at the same resolution as the document. As long as it's a type layer, Photoshop preserves the type outlines so that the text remains sharp when you scale or resize type, save a Photoshop PDF file, or print the image at high resolution.

2 You can create point type or paragraph type. Point type is anchored to a point created where you click a type tool. Paragraph type can contain multiple lines that can recompose as you resize their text container; you create it by dragging a type tool.

3 A clipping mask is an object or group that uses the visible pixels of one layer to mask another—you see only the areas of the layer that overlap the visible pixels of the clipping mask. To use a text layer as a clipping mask, make sure the layer you want to reveal is directly above the text layer, select the layer you want to show through the letters, and apply the Create Clipping Mask command (found on the Layer menu, the Layers panel menu, or the layer's context menu).

8 VECTOR DRAWING TECHNIQUES

Lesson overview

In this lesson, you'll learn how to do the following:

- Understand the difference between bitmap and vector graphics.

- Draw straight and curved paths using the Pen tool.

- Save paths.

- Draw and edit shape layers.

- Draw custom shapes.

- Use Smart Guides.

 This lesson will take about 90 minutes to complete. To get the lesson files used in this chapter, download them from the web page for this book at peachpit.com/PhotoshopCIB2024. For more information, see "Accessing the lesson files and Web Edition" in the Getting Started section at the beginning of this book.

As you work on this lesson, you'll preserve the start files. If you need to restore the start files, download them from your Account page.

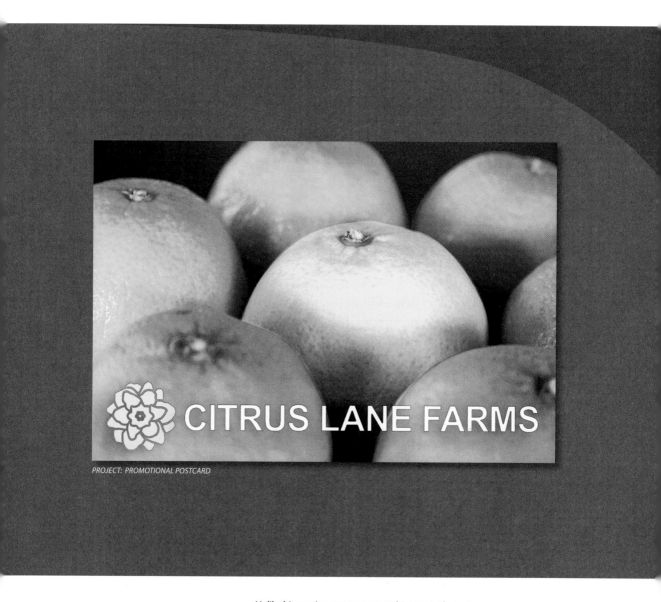

PROJECT: PROMOTIONAL POSTCARD

Unlike bitmap images, vector graphics retain their crisp edges when you enlarge them to any size. You can draw vector shapes and paths in your Photoshop images and add vector masks to control what is shown in an image.

About bitmap images and vector graphics

Before working with vector shapes and vector paths, it's important to understand the basic differences between the two main categories of computer graphics: *bitmap images* and *vector graphics*. You can use Photoshop to work with either kind of graphic; in fact, you can combine both bitmap and vector data in an individual Photoshop image file.

Bitmap images, technically called *raster images*, are based on a grid of dots known as *pixels*. Each pixel is assigned a specific location and color value. In working with bitmap images, you edit groups of pixels rather than objects or shapes. Because bitmap graphics can represent subtle gradations of shade and color, they are appropriate for continuous-tone images such as photographs or artwork created in painting programs. A disadvantage of bitmap graphics is that they contain a fixed number of pixels. As a result, they can lose detail and appear jagged when scaled up onscreen or printed at a lower resolution than they were created for.

Vector graphics are made up of lines and curves defined by mathematical objects called *vectors*. These graphics retain their crispness whether they are moved, resized, or have their color changed. Vector graphics are appropriate for illustrations, type, and graphics such as logos that may be scaled to different sizes.

In the lessons so far, you've worked with bitmap images on Photoshop layers. A different type of layer—a shape layer—contains vector graphics in Photoshop.

Logo drawn as vector art.

Logo rasterized as bitmap art.

About paths and the Pen tool

In Photoshop, the outline of a vector shape is called a *path*. A path is a curved or straight line segment you draw using the Pen tool, the Freeform Pen tool, the Curvature Pen tool, or a shape tool. The Pen and Curvature Pen tools draw paths with great precision; shape tools create rectangles, ellipses, and other shape paths; and the Freeform Pen tool draws paths as if you were drawing with a pen on paper.

Paths can be open or closed. An open path (such as a wavy line) has two distinct endpoints. A closed path (such as a circle) is continuous. The type of path you draw affects how it can be selected and adjusted.

Unlike the pixels created by the painting tools, a path doesn't make a printable mark on its own. A path is more like a selection marquee in vector form, so you can use a path to mark an area of a layer with pixels using a *fill* (color, pattern, or other content) or a *stroke* (outline). To use a path as a vector object that you can fill, stroke, print, export, and continue to edit as a vector object, create it as a *shape* layer.

Julieanne Kost is an official Adobe Photoshop evangelist.

Tool tips from the Photoshop evangelist

Accessing tools quickly

Each tool in the Tools panel has a single-letter keyboard shortcut. Type the letter, get the tool. Press Shift with the shortcut key to cycle through any nested tools in a group. For example, press P to select the Pen tool, and press Shift+P to toggle between the Pen, Freeform Pen, and Curvature Pen tools.

Getting started with vector drawing

In this lesson, you'll create a postcard that will help promote a citrus fruit farm. You've been given an image of oranges, but because the farm wants to convey the idea that they grow more than just oranges, it's been decided that one of the oranges will be recolored to look like a lemon. Recoloring one item requires isolating it by creating a mask of its outline, and one quick and precise way to create a clean outline of that item is using the Pen tool to draw a vector path.

Before you begin, view the image you'll be creating.

1 Start Photoshop, and then simultaneously hold down Ctrl+Alt+Shift (Windows) or Command+Option+Shift (macOS) to restore the default preferences. (See "Restoring default preferences" on page 5.)

2 When prompted, click Yes to delete the Adobe Photoshop Settings file.

3 Choose File > Browse In Bridge.

4 In the Favorites panel, click the Lessons folder, and then double-click the Lesson08 folder in the Content panel.

5 Select the 08End.psd file, and press the spacebar to see it in full-screen view.

To create this postcard, you'll trace an image and use that tracing to make a vector mask that lets you change the color of one of the oranges. First, you'll practice making paths and selections using the Pen tool.

6 When you've finished looking at the 08End.psd file, press the spacebar again. Then double-click the 08Practice_Start.psd file to open it in Photoshop, and close any messages that appear about new features.

7 Choose File > Save As, rename the file **08Practice_Working.psd**, and click Save. If the Photoshop Format Options dialog box appears, click OK.

Note: If Bridge isn't installed, the File > Browse In Bridge command in Photoshop will start the Creative Cloud desktop app, which will download and install Bridge. After installation completes, you can start Bridge. For more information, see page 3.

Note: If Photoshop displays a dialog box telling you about the difference between saving to Cloud Documents and On Your Computer, click Save On Your Computer. You can also select Don't Show Again, but that setting will deselect after you reset Photoshop preferences.

Drawing a shape with the Pen tool

The Pen tool is commonly used for creating vector graphics on a computer. You'll find the Pen tool in many applications, including Adobe Illustrator (which first featured the Pen tool in 1987), Adobe Photoshop, and Adobe InDesign. Even video applications such as Adobe Premiere Pro and Adobe After Effects include the Pen tool, because you can use it to draw precise shapes, masks, and paths for motion graphics and visual effects. The Pen tool may not be easy to learn, but trust us: Knowing how to use the Pen tool is worth the effort and investment to learn, because it's a marketable skill across many creative digital disciplines.

Tip: The Curvature Pen tool offers a potentially simpler way to draw precise vector paths; consider learning it if you find the Pen tool to be challenging to use. The Pen tool is taught in this lesson because it's a traditional and industry-standard tool for precisely drawing vector graphics.

The Pen tool works a little differently than a brush or pencil tool. We've created a practice file that you'll use to learn how to draw a straight path, a simple curve, and an S-curve with the Pen tool.

Creating paths with the Pen tool

You can use the Pen tool to create paths that are straight or curved, open or closed. If you're unfamiliar with the Pen tool, it can be confusing to use at first. Understanding the elements of a path and how to create those elements with the Pen tool makes paths much easier to draw.

To create a straight path, click the mouse button. The first time you click, you set the first *anchor point*. Each time that you click thereafter, a straight line is drawn between the previous anchor point and the current one. To draw complex straight-segment paths with the Pen tool, click each time you want to add a new segment.

Creating a straight line.

To create a curved path, drag to both place an anchor point and extend a direction line for that point, and then click or drag to place the next anchor point. Each direction line ends in two direction points; the positions of direction lines and points determine the size and shape of the curved segment. Moving the direction lines and points reshapes the curves in a path.

Smooth curves are connected by anchor points called *smooth points*. Sharply curved paths are connected by *corner points*. When you move a direction line on a smooth point, the curved segments on both sides of the point adjust simultaneously, but when you move a direction line on a corner point, only the curve on the same side of the point as the direction line is adjusted.

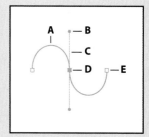

A. *Curved line segment*
B. *Direction point*
C. *Direction line*
D. *Selected anchor point*
E. *Unselected anchor point*

You can move path segments and anchor points, either individually or as a group. When a path contains multiple segments, you can drag individual anchor points to adjust individual segments of the path, or select all anchor points in a path to edit the entire path. Use the Direct Selection tool (▷) to select and adjust an anchor point, a path segment, or an entire path.

Creating a closed path differs from creating an open path, in the way that you end it. To end an open path, press Enter or Return. To create a closed path, position the Pen tool pointer over the starting point, and click. Closing a path automatically ends the path. After the path closes, the Pen tool pointer appears with a small *, indicating that your next click will start a new path.

Creating a closed path.

When you first draw a path, it appears in the Paths panel as a Work Path, which is only temporary. Save any work path you want to use again in the future, especially if you want to use multiple paths in the same document. To save a work path, double-click it in the Paths panel, type a name in the Save Path dialog box, and click OK. It's added as a new named path in the Paths panel and remains selected. If you don't save a work path, it's lost as soon as you deselect it and then start drawing again. (Saving the path isn't necessary when you draw a path as a shape, because a shape is created as a named layer.)

First, you'll configure the Pen tool options and the work area.

1 In the Tools panel, select the Pen tool (⌀).

2 In the options bar, select or verify the following settings:

- Choose Shape from the Tool Mode pop-up menu.

- In the Path Options menu, make sure that Rubber Band is not selected.

- Make sure that Auto Add/Delete is selected.

- Choose No Color from the Fill pop-up menu.

- Choose a green color from the Stroke pop-up menu. We used the green swatch in the CMYK presets group.

▶ **Tip:** The Align stroke option controls whether the stroke width sits entirely to one side of a path or the other or is centered over the path.

- Enter **4 pt** for the stroke width.

- In the Stroke Options window, choose Center (the second option) from the Align menu.

A. *Tool Mode menu*
B. *Stroke Width menu*
C. *Stroke Options menu*
D. *Path Options menu*
E. *Auto Add/Delete*

Drawing a straight line

You'll start by drawing a straight line. Anchor points mark the ends of path segments; the straight line you'll draw is a single path segment with two anchor points.

1 Drag the Paths panel tab out of the Layers panel group so that you can see both it and the Layers panel at the same time. You can dock the Paths panel with another panel group.

The Paths panel displays thumbnail previews of the paths you draw. Currently, the panel is empty, because you haven't started drawing.

2 If necessary, zoom in so that you can easily see the lettered points and red circles on the shape template. Make sure you can see the whole template in the document window, and after you zoom, make sure the Pen tool is selected.

3 On the first shape, click point A, and release the mouse button. You've created an anchor point.

4 Click point B. You've created a straight line with two anchor points.

5 Press Enter or Return to stop drawing.

Note: If a tutorial pops up for the Curvature Pen tool, you don't need to read it at this time. It will probably close on its own, or you can close it.

Create an anchor point.

Click to create a straight line.

Complete the path.

The path you drew appears in the Paths panel and as a new layer in the Layers panel.

Note: The new path appears in both the Paths and Layers panels because the Tool Mode menu in the options bar is set to Shape, so drawing a new path also creates a new shape layer. If the Tool Mode menu was set to Path, the new path would be added to the Paths panel only.

Drawing curves

On curved segments, selecting an anchor point displays one or two direction lines, depending on the shapes of adjacent segments. You adjust the shape of a curved segment by dragging the direction point at the end of a direction line, and the direction line shapes the curve. You'll create curved lines, using smooth points.

1 Click A on the semicircle, and release the mouse to create the first anchor point.

2 Click point B, but don't release the mouse button. Instead, drag to the open red circle to the right of point B to create a curved path segment and a smooth anchor point. Then release the mouse button.

Tip: The red circles indicate where you should stop dragging an anchor point's direction point to form the desired shape of the curve. If you drag the direction point to a different location, the curve will have a different shape.

Create an anchor point.

Click and hold.

Drag to curve the path segment.

Smooth anchor points have two linked direction lines. When you move one, the curved segments on both sides of the path adjust simultaneously.

3 Position the pointer over point C, click and drag down to the open red circle below, and then release the mouse button. You've created a second curved path segment and another smooth point.

4 Click point D, and release the mouse to create the final anchor point. Press Enter or Return to complete the path.

  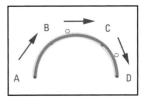

Click C to create a point.   *Drag to curve the segment.*   *Click D to finish the semicircle.*

▶ **Tip:** What's the advantage of drawing paths using points and handles, instead of drawing directly as with a real pen or pencil? For most people, it's difficult to draw curves and straight lines without bumps or other errors. Points and handles let you draw perfect curves and straight lines. If you prefer to draw normally, you can use the Freeform Pen tool.

When you draw your own paths using the Pen tool, use as few points as possible to create the shape you want. The fewer points you use, the smoother the curves are, and the easier it is to edit the shape later.

Using the same techniques, you'll draw an S-shaped curve.

5 Click point A, and then click and drag from point B to its open red circle.

6 Continue with points C, D, E, and F, in each case clicking the point and then dragging to the corresponding open red circle.

7 Click point G to create the final anchor point, and then press Enter or Return to complete the path.

Each of the three shapes is on its own layer in the Layers panel. Only one path is in the Paths panel, because the Paths panel shows only the Shape Path for the layer that's currently selected in the Layers panel.

Notice that the curves you drew with the Pen tool are much smoother and easier to precisely control than if you had drawn them freehand.

Drawing a more complex shape

Now that you've got the idea, you'll draw a more complex object.

1 Click point A on the shape on the right side to set the first anchor point.

2 Press the Shift key as you click point B. Pressing the Shift key constrains the line to 45-degree angles, which in this case ensures you'll get a horizontal line.

3 Press the Shift key as you click points C, D, and E to create straight path segments.

4 Click point F, and drag to the open red circle to create a curve. Then release the mouse button.

5 Click point G, and drag to the open red circle to create another curve. Then release the mouse button.

6 Click point H to create a corner point.

When you move a direction line on a corner point, only the curve on the same side of the point as the direction line is adjusted, so you can create a sharp transition between two segments.

7 Click point A to draw the final path segment and close the path. Closing a path automatically ends the drawing; if you click or drag the Pen tool, it will create a new path. After you close a path, you don't need to press Enter or Return unless you also want to deselect the path.

▶ **Tip:** If you notice that you slightly missed the red dot on the template while dragging a curve point, you can reposition the point without starting over. Keeping the mouse button down, hold down the spacebar and drag until the point is in the right place. Then release the spacebar to continue dragging the direction lines of that anchor point.

Start with straight segments.

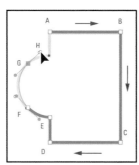
Drag to create a curve.

Close the path.

8 Close the file (you don't have to save changes for this exercise). You have successfully used the Pen tool to draw both curves and straight lines.

Drawing a path traced from a photo

Now you're ready to draw a path around a real object. You'll use the techniques you've practiced to draw a path around the edge of one orange out of several. The path you draw will later be converted into a layer mask so that you can change the color of that orange. The orange is partially covered by surrounding oranges, so the path you draw will be a combination of curved and straight segments, like the shapes you've practiced on. Later, you'll combine the altered image with text and a shape layer to create a promotional postcard for a citrus farm.

1   From Photoshop or Bridge, open the 08Start.psd file.

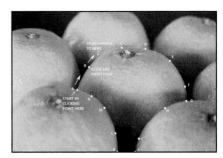

The image includes two layers: the background layer and a template layer named Path Guide that you will trace to draw the path.

2   Choose File > Save As, rename the file **08Working.psd**, and click Save. If the Photoshop Format Options dialog box appears, click OK.

3   Select the Pen tool, and then, in the options bar, choose Path from the Tool Mode pop-up menu.

Because Path is now selected in the options bar instead of Shape, what you see when you draw will be different than in the practice exercise. You'll be drawing a path, not a shape. The path you draw will appear as a temporary work path in the Paths panel, and a shape layer won't be created.

The reason you're switching to a path is because you won't need to print or export the path you're about to draw. You'll use the path as a starting point for creating a mask, so the path itself doesn't need to be a visible part of the final document. For more information about shapes and paths, see the sidebar "Comparing shapes, paths, and pixels."

Comparing shapes, paths, and pixels

When you use the Pen tool or the tools grouped with it, or the Rectangle tool or any of the tools grouped with it, a menu in the options bar lets you choose whether you want the tool to draw a shape, a path, or, in some cases, pixels.

This is an important decision, because each option has different advantages:

Shape. A shape is a vector object created on its own layer in the Layers panel. You can apply the same layer effects, masks, and other properties that you would to a pixel layer. The difference is that you can continue to edit the shape as a vector path, using path editing tools such as the Pen tool and the Direct Selection tool. You can't edit a shape layer using pixel-based tools such as brushes. You can change a shape layer's fill and stroke. Because a shape is a layer, when its layer visibility is enabled, it's visible and will print and export.

A selected shape layer also displays its path in the Paths panel.

Path. A path is a vector object that doesn't display, print, or export, so it doesn't appear in the Layers panel; you'll find it in the Paths panel. A path is useful for creating type along a path, clipping paths, and in other "backstage" roles where editing a vector path saves time. For example, sometimes it's faster to create a selection by first drawing and editing a path and then converting that to a selection.

Because a path is not a layer, it's visible in the document window only when it's selected in the Paths panel, and it can't have a stroke and fill. If it's hard to see, you can improve its visibility by clicking the Path Options menu (the gear) in the options bar and adjusting the path's Thickness and Color. Because a path isn't visible in a printed or exported image, those options affect only the visibility of the path while drawing in Photoshop.

Pixels. Some tools, such as the Rectangle tool and the tools grouped with it, also offer a Pixels option. Drawing with the Pixels option creates pixels on the currently selected layer, without creating a vector path or shape layer.

The Pixels option creates a pixel layer, so you won't be able to edit the resulting layer using path editing tools. Instead, edit it with pixel-based tools such as the brushes, eraser, and selection tools.

4 With the Pen tool selected, click point A. A new temporary Work Path appears in the Paths panel.

5 Click point B, and drag to the open circle on the right to create the initial curve.

6 Click point C, and drag to the open circle to its right.

7 Continue tracing the orange, clicking and dragging curve segments for points D through F.

8 Click point G (do not drag). This creates the corner at point G.

9 At points H and I, click and drag to their corresponding open circles to create their curved segments.

▶ **Tip:** When tracing along a well-defined edge, the Pen tool is not the only useful tool. For some shapes and edges, you might find it easier to use the Magic Lasso tool, the Object Selection tool, or the Quick Selection tool.

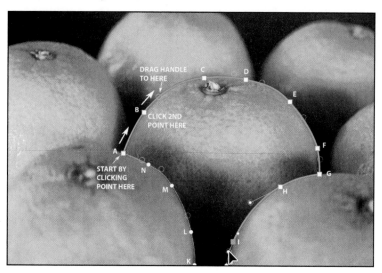

10 Click point J to create a corner.

11 Hold down Shift to create a perfectly level segment as you click point K.

12 At points L, M, and N, click and drag to their corresponding open circles to create their curved segments.

13 Position the pointer over point A, and when you see a small circle by the Pen tool pointer, click to close the path. The circle indicates that the pointer is close enough to close the path.

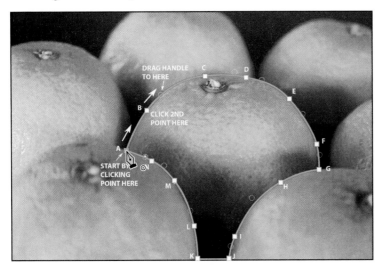

14 Evaluate your path. If you want to adjust any segments, do step 15; otherwise skip to step 16.

15 Select the Direct Selection tool (⟩) (grouped with the Path Selection tool (⟩)), and then press the Esc key (or click in the document window away from the path) so that no points are selected but you can still see the path. Then do any of the following with the Direct Selection tool as needed:

- To reposition a point or a straight segment, drag it.

- To change the shape of a curved segment between two points, drag the segment (not points).

- To change the shape of a curved segment extending from a point, drag its direction point to adjust the angle of that direction line.

16 When you're done, leave the path selected, and save your work so far.

▶ **Tip:** To move the entire path, drag it with the Path Selection tool, grouped with the Direct Selection tool.

Converting a path to a selection and a layer mask

▶ **Tip:** If you'd prefer to create a mask that you can always edit as a path, create a vector mask for the layer instead. Skip step 2, and then, in step 4, make sure the Lemon path is selected in the Paths panel when you add the new Hue/Saturation adjustment layer.

Using the Pen tool made it easy to create a precise outline of the orange in the center of the image. But the goal is to change the color of that orange without changing the others, through a layer mask. Creating the layer mask requires making a selection. Fortunately, it's easy to convert a path to a selection.

The path is a work path, which is temporary; it will be replaced if you draw another path. You can still create a selection from a work path, but first, it's a good practice to save any path you might want to use again in the future.

1 In the Paths panel, double-click Work Path. In the Save Path dialog box, type **Lemon** for the name, and click OK.

2 Make sure the Lemon path is selected in the Paths panel, and then click the Load Path as a Selection button (⬡) at the bottom of the Paths panel.

Photoshop creates a selection from the path. You'll change the color of the selected orange to lemon yellow, using a Hue/Saturation adjustment layer through a layer mask of the orange. The selection you just created will make it quick and easy to create the layer mask, because an active selection is automatically converted to a layer mask when you add an adjustment layer.

▶ **Tip:** It's just as easy to convert a selection into a path. When a selection is active, click the Make Work Path from Selection button in the Paths panel; it's the button to the right of the one you clicked in step 2.

3 In the Layers panel, hide the Path Guide layer, because you no longer need it, and select the Background layer.

4 In the Adjustments panel, scroll down to the Single Adjustments list, and click Hue/Saturation (⬛). A new Hue/Saturation adjustment layer appears in the Layers panel, and the selection becomes a mask for that new adjustment layer.

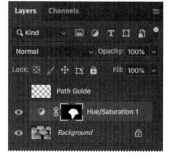

5   In the Properties panel, change the Hue setting so that the orange in the center changes to a lemon yellow color. We entered a Hue value of **+17**.

6   Save the document.

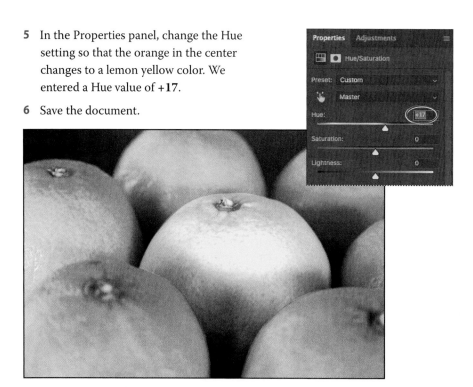

▶ **Tip:** After you change the color of the center orange, you may notice minor errors along the edges of the layer mask. Remember that you can edit a layer mask: Click the layer mask thumbnail in the Layers panel to select it, and then use the Brush tool to paint white where you want the color applied by the adjustment layer to be visible, or paint black where you want the color of the Background layer to be visible. (If it was still a vector mask, you would edit it using the Direct Selection tool and Pen tool.)

You used the Pen tool to quickly and precisely draw a path that traced the outline of an object in an image. You converted the path into a selection so that when you added a new adjustment layer, the selection became a layer mask that isolated the object for the adjustment layer. Well done!

Creating a logo with text and a custom shape

Now you'll create a logo that will overlay the image, using text and a shape layer.

1   If the rulers aren't visible, choose View > Rulers to display them.

2   Right-click (Windows) or Control-click (macOS) the rulers, and if they are currently displaying in pixels, choose Inches. This document will become a printed postcard, and Inches is an appropriate unit of measure for print.

3   In the Layers panel, make sure the Hue/Saturation adjustment layer is selected so that the layer you're about to create will be added above it.

Tip: For step 4, a quick way to find a font is to type **bold** or **heavy** into the font menu. The list will display only font names containing the word you entered, so all you have to do is pick one.

4 Select the Horizontal Type tool (**T**), and, in the options bar, do the following:

- Choose a bold or heavy typeface from the Font Family pop-up menu. We used Arial Bold; you can choose another font that looks good as a logo.

- Type **55 pt** for the Size, and press Enter or Return.

- Click the Right Align Text button, because you'll soon add a graphic element to the left of the text.

- Click the color swatch and set the text color to white.

5 Drag the Horizontal Type tool to create a text layer across the bottom of the canvas, inset about half an inch away from the sides and bottom. Ours is about 9 inches wide by 1 inch tall.

6 Type **Citrus Lane Farms** to replace the placeholder text, click the Commit button (✓) in the options bar, and leave the text layer selected in the Layers panel.

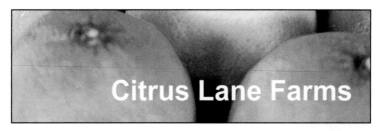

7 This font looks better with tighter letter spacing. With the text selected, in the Character or Properties panel, apply a negative Tracking value; for our font we used **–25**.

8 In the Properties panel, select the All Caps button (**TT**) in the Type Options group. If you don't see this option, scroll down in the Properties panel.

9 If needed, use the Move tool to reposition the text layer so that it looks better relative to the bottom and right sides. Leave space to the left of the text for a graphic you're about to add.

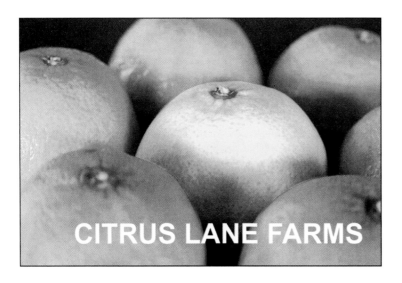

CITRUS LANE FARMS

Adding a preset shape

When you need a shape such as a symbol or object, one place you can turn to is the Shapes panel, which contains a wide selection of premade graphics. When you add a shape to a document, it becomes a shape layer.

A shape is a vector object drawn using paths, which has two advantages. You can edit it using the same techniques you used to edit the paths you drew earlier in this lesson. Also, like a text layer, a path is resolution-independent, so it will always be as smooth and detailed as the document resolution allows.

You find shapes in the Shapes panel. It's easy to use, because it works like the other Photoshop panels that contain preset effects, such as the Swatches, Gradients, and Brushes panels: You see small visual previews of each preset, you can organize them in groups (folders), and you can create your own.

1 Choose Window > Shapes to open the Shapes panel. The Shapes panel includes groups of shape presets.

2 Expand the Flowers presets group.

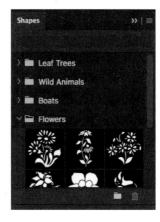

▶ **Tip:** Photoshop includes more preset groups than you see by default in a presets panel list. In the panel menu, choose Legacy Shapes and More to load additional preset groups, including presets that were available in previous versions of Photoshop.

Extra credit

Using Creative Cloud Libraries with linked Smart Objects

When you organize and share your design assets using Creative Cloud Libraries, you and your team can use those library items in many Creative Cloud desktop and mobile apps. Let's take a look:

1 Open 08End.psd. If the Libraries panel isn't open, choose Window > Libraries.

2 In the Libraries panel menu, click Create New Library, name it **Citrus Lane Farms**, and click Create.

3 In the Layers panel, select the Flower layer, and then hold down Shift as you click the Citrus Lane Farms text layer so that the two layers are selected.

4 Click the Add Elements button (+), and choose Graphic to add both layers as a single library item.

After the Libraries panel syncs the logo to Creative Cloud, it will be available in Creative Cloud desktop and mobile apps that use Creative Cloud Libraries.

The appearance of the Citrus Lane Farms text layer was adjusted to look good over the image of the oranges; it should be tested over a wide range of backgrounds and edited as needed for readability. A library item is a Smart Object linked to Creative Cloud, so you can edit it in Photoshop by double-clicking it in the Libraries panel. When you save changes, it updates in all documents that use it.

Adding a color

A library can store colors for use across Adobe applications.

1 With the Eyedropper tool, click the flower in the document window so that its color becomes the foreground swatch in the Tools panel.

2 At the bottom of the Libraries panel, click the Add Elements button (+), and click the Foreground Color swatch, adding it to the current library.

Collaborating

When you share a Creative Cloud Library, your team always has the current version of those assets. In the Libraries panel menu, choose Invite People. The Creative Cloud desktop app opens; fill in the Invite screen that appears. When the people you invited are signed into their Creative Cloud accounts, they will see your shared library in their Creative Cloud applications.

Adding assets to libraries using Adobe mobile apps

Use Adobe mobile apps—such as Adobe Capture—to use your phone or tablet camera to record color themes, shapes, and brushes from real life and add them to your Creative Cloud libraries. Library assets you add with mobile apps automatically sync to your Creative Cloud account, so you'll see the new assets in your Libraries panel when you return to your computer.

3 Drag the last shape preset, and drop it to the left of the Citrus Lane Farms logo.

The flower shape now appears in the Layers panel. The shape currently has a transform bounding box around it so that you can make adjustments before committing it to the document. And yes, there are some adjustments to be made.

▶ **Tip:** Want to save your own shape preset? Draw a path or shape, select it with the Path Selection tool, choose Edit > Define Custom Shape, name it, and click OK. It's added to the Shapes panel; if a shape group is active, it's added to that group.

4 Drag any handle on the shape to resize it to be about 1.5 inches tall.

5 Drag the flower to position it between the left edge of the document and the Citrus Lane Farms text.

6 Click the Commit Transform button (✔) in the options bar, or press Enter or Return. The transformation bounding box disappears.

A shape is added using the current fill and stroke settings for shapes, which were the ones set for the practice shape earlier. The flower shape is intended to have a solid yellow fill. That change could not be done while the bounding box was active, but now that it's been committed to the document, the colors can be changed.

7 Make sure the flower shape is still selected in the Layers panel.

8 In the Layers panel, double-click the name of the shape layer, type **Flower**, and press Return or Enter to rename the layer.

9 Select any shape tool, such as the Rectangle tool or any tool grouped with it. The options bar now displays settings for shapes.

▶ **Tip:** If the magenta Smart Guides prevent you from making precise adjustments, hold down the Control key as you drag.

▶ **Tip:** Do you wish one of the preset shapes was slightly different? All shapes are paths, so after you add a shape to the document, you can edit it by using the Pen tool or any of the tools grouped with it, or the Direct Selection tool.

10 In the options bar, click the Fill swatch, expand the RGB swatch presets group that appears in the drop-down menu, and click the yellow swatch.

11 In the options bar, click the Stroke swatch, and set it to No Color. Close the pop-up menu by pressing Enter or Return.

12 Choose Select > Deselect Layers. Now you can see the flower shape without its path being highlighted.

13 If needed, use the Move tool to reposition the flower and text, composing them relative to each other as a logo and relative to the edges of the document.

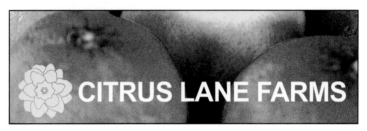

14 Save your work.

You've combined an image, a color adjustment layer masked with the help of a path you drew by hand, a pre-made shape, and a text layer. The postcard is ready to go!

Extra credit

Quickly adding color and effects using presets

You can use presets to quickly enhance the look of both the text and the flower in the logo. The way that you do this is similar to how you added the flower shape with the Shapes panel and changed its color using the Swatches panel.

1 Open 08Working.psd (if it isn't already open), and save it as **08StylePresets.psd**.

2 Start by applying a preset to the flower. In the Styles panel (Window > Styles), expand the Basics preset group.

3 Drag the second preset from the Basics group, and drop it on the flower in the document window. The style is applied to the flower shape layer. Then drag the same style and drop it on the text.

You can apply a preset by dragging and dropping it on a layer or by clicking a preset when the layer is selected. Either way is fine.

In this example, the Basic style applies a simple stroke and drop shadow. But the possibilities are much wider. Explore your design options by freely editing the presets in the Styles, Gradients, Patterns, and Swatches panels and applying them to layers until you get the look you want. And you can add your own presets to those panels.

You can see that the effects have been applied in the Layers panel, and you can fine-tune those effects in different ways:

- Click the eye icon for different layer effects to disable or enable them.

- Double-click an effect name to open the Layer Style dialog box, where you can edit effects.

- If you try to apply a style and it doesn't seem to change the layer, you may first need to delete effects already applied to the layer: In the Layers panel, drag that layer's Effects heading to the Delete (trash can) icon at the bottom of the Layers panel. Note that a preset may also alter a layer's Opacity and Fill Opacity, so you may have to set those back to the default of 100%.

- If you don't see any effects listed after a layer after applying a style, the preset may have been applied as a fill or stroke instead of a layer style. To edit it, double-click the shape layer thumbnail (not the name).

- If you applied a preset to a shape, select any shape tool, such as the Rectangle tool, to display shape options in the options bar. Click the Fill or Stroke swatch to edit the preset.

Extra credit

Using Smart Guides to maintain alignment and equal spacing

Let's take this design to the next level. You can use the Citrus Lane Farms logo to make a repeated motif for packaging or other signage. Smart Guides can help you position the images evenly.

1 Open 08End.psd, and save it as **08SmartGuides.psd**. Choose View > Show, and make sure there is a check mark next to the Smart Guides command, indicating that it's enabled. If not, select the Smart Guides command to enable it.

2 Select the Flower layer. Then select the Move tool, hold down the Alt (Windows) or Option (macOS) key as you drag a copy of the Flower layer up until the value in the magenta box indicates that it's about 3 inches away from the original, and then release the mouse button. Notice that the magenta Smart Guides help keep the Flower copy perfectly aligned with the original. Without Smart Guides, you'd have to also press Shift to keep the copy aligned. The Alt or Option key copies the selected layer.

3 In the Layers panel, change the Opacity of the Flower copy layer to 50%.

4 Make sure the Move tool and Flower copy layer are still selected. Hold down the Alt (Windows) or Option (macOS) key as you use the Move tool to drag a copy of the Flower copy layer to the right, until the magenta values indicate that the layer and its copy are about 1 inch apart and still aligned. Then release the mouse button.

5 This time, with the Flower copy 2 layer still selected, hold down Alt or Option as you drag the Flower copy 2 layer to the right; release the mouse when two transformation values boxes appear between the three flower layers across the top. The boxes let you know that the distance between the three flower layers is now equal. Using Smart Guides is a fast and easy way to make sure layers you drag are evenly spaced, without having to do math or use a distribution command.

6 Repeat step 4 so that you have four equally spaced flowers.

Review questions

1 What is the difference between a bitmap image and a vector graphic?

2 After using the Pen tool to add an anchor point to a path, how do you make sure the next path segment is a curve?

3 How can you add a preset shape to the document?

4 For paths and shapes, why would you use the Direct Selection tool instead of the Selection tool?

5 What are some ways to change the shape of a curved path segment?

Review answers

1 Bitmap, or raster, images are based on a grid of pixels and are appropriate for continuous-tone images such as photographs or artwork created in painting programs. Vector graphics are made up of shapes based on mathematical expressions and are appropriate for illustrations, type, and drawings that require clear, smooth lines.

2 Drag (instead of clicking) to create the next point with the Pen tool.

3 To add a preset shape, open the Shapes panel, find the shape, and drag it into the document window.

4 The Direct Selection tool lets you edit the points, segments, and direction lines of a path or shape. The Selection tool lets you move and resize an entire path or shape.

5 You can change the shape of a curved path segment by using the Direct Selection tool to drag either of a curved segment's two anchor points, the direction points for either anchor point, or the curved segment itself.

9 ADVANCED COMPOSITING

Lesson overview

In this lesson, you'll learn how to do the following:

- Apply and edit Smart Filters.

- Use the Liquify filter to creatively distort an image.

- Apply color effects to selected areas of an image.

- Apply filters to create various effects.

- Use the History panel to return to a previous state.

- Upscale a low-resolution image while maintaining quality.

 This lesson will take about an hour to complete. To get the lesson files used in this chapter, download them from the web page for this book at peachpit.com/PhotoshopCIB2024. For more information, see "Accessing the lesson files and Web Edition" in the Getting Started section at the beginning of this book.

As you work on this lesson, you'll preserve the start files. If you need to restore the start files, download them from your Account page.

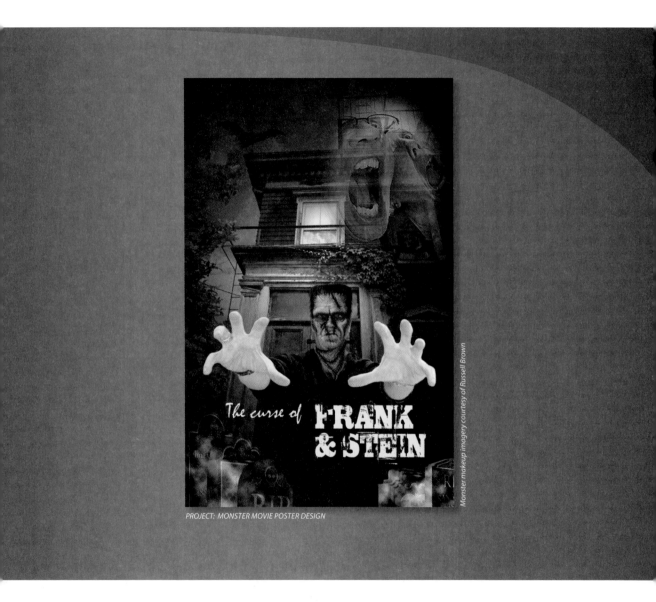

The curse of FRANK & STEIN

PROJECT: MONSTER MOVIE POSTER DESIGN

Monster makeup imagery courtesy of Russell Brown

Filters can transform ordinary images into extraordinary digital artwork. Smart Filters let you edit those transformations at any time. The wide variety of features in Photoshop lets you be as creative as you want to be.

Getting started

In this lesson, you'll assemble a montage of images for a movie poster as you explore filters in Photoshop. First, look at the final project to see what you'll be creating.

1. Start Photoshop, and then simultaneously hold down Ctrl+Alt+Shift (Windows) or Command+Option+Shift (macOS) to restore the default preferences. (See "Restoring default preferences" on page 5.)

2. When prompted, click Yes to delete the Adobe Photoshop Settings file.

3. Choose File > Browse In Bridge.

4. In Bridge, choose Favorites from the menu on the left, and then click the Lessons folder. Double-click the Lesson09 folder.

5. View the 09_End.psd thumbnail. Move the slider at the bottom of the Bridge window if you need to zoom in to see the thumbnail more clearly.

● **Note:** If Bridge isn't installed, the File > Browse In Bridge command in Photoshop will start the Creative Cloud desktop app, which will download and install Bridge. After installation completes, you can start Bridge.

This file is a movie poster that comprises a background, a monster image, and several smaller images. Each image has had one or more filters or effects applied to it.

The monster is composed of an image of a perfectly normal (though slightly threatening) guy with several ghoulish images applied. These monstrous additions are courtesy of Russell Brown, with illustration by John Connell.

6. In Bridge, navigate to the Lesson09/Monster_Makeup folder, and open it.

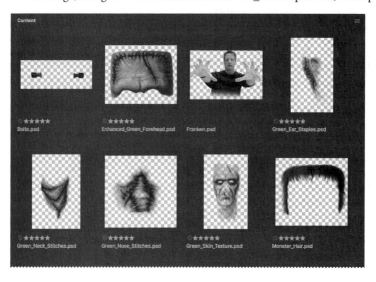

7   Shift-click the first and last items to select all the files in the Monster_Makeup folder, then choose Tools > Photoshop > Load Files Into Photoshop Layers, and finally close any messages that appear about new features.

Photoshop imports all the selected files as individual layers in a new Photoshop file. The designer used a red layer color to indicate components of the monster's look.

8   In Photoshop, choose File > Save As. Choose Photoshop for the Format, and name the new file **09Working.psd**. Save it in the Lesson09 folder. Click OK in the Photoshop Format Options dialog box.

Note: If Photoshop displays a dialog box telling you about the difference between saving to Cloud Documents and On Your Computer, click Save On Your Computer. You can also select Don't Show Again, but that setting will deselect after you reset Photoshop preferences.

Arranging layers

Your image file contains eight layers, imported in alphabetical order. In their current positions, they don't make a very convincing monster. You'll rearrange the layer order and resize their contents as you start to build your monster.

1   Zoom out or scroll so that you can see the entire document canvas. Also, if you can't see all of the layers in the Layers panel at once, drag the top edge of the Layers panel to make it taller.

2   In the Layers panel, drag the Monster_Hair layer to the top of the layer stack, if it isn't already on top.

3 Drag the Franken layer to the bottom of the layer stack.

● **Note:** If the wrong layer becomes selected when you try to drag the Franken layer to the bottom of the image, deselect Auto-Select in the options bar.

4 Select the Move tool (✛), and then in the document window, drag the Franken layer (the image of the person) to the bottom of the canvas.

▶ **Tip:** The keyboard shortcut for Free Transform is Ctrl+T (Windows) or Command+T (macOS). This is a good all-in-one shortcut to learn because you can use it to move, scale, or rotate selected layers.

5 In the Layers panel, Shift-select every layer except the Franken layer, and choose Edit > Free Transform.

6   Drag down from a corner of the selection to resize all the selected layers to about 50% of their original size. (Watch the width and height percentages in the options bar.)

7   With the Free Transform bounding box still active, position the layers over the head of the Franken layer. Then press Enter or Return to commit the transformation.

8   Zoom in to see the head area clearly.

9   Hide all layers except the Green_Skin_Texture and Franken layers.

10 Select only the Green_Skin_Texture layer, and use the Move tool to center it over the face.

▶ **Tip:** If magenta Smart Guides appear as you drag, making it difficult to position the Green_Skin_Texture layer, hold down the Control key to temporarily suppress snapping to Smart Guides as you drag. Or permanently disable them by deselecting the View > Show > Smart Guides command.

11 Choose Edit > Free Transform again to adjust the fit of the texture to the face. Using the eyes and mouth as a guide, press arrow keys to nudge the entire layer into position. Drag handles on the bounding box to adjust the width and height. (To adjust without preserving proportions, Shift-drag a handle.) When you've positioned the skin texture, press Enter or Return to commit the transformation.

12 Save your file.

Using Smart Filters

When you apply a filter (any command on the Filter menu), it permanently changes layer pixels. To be able to edit, hide, or remove filter settings at any time after applying the filter, you can apply a filter to a Smart Object layer, making it a nondestructive Smart Filter.

Applying the Liquify filter

You'll use the Liquify filter to tighten the eye openings and change the shape of the monster's face. To be able to adjust the filter settings later, you'll apply the Liquify filter as a Smart Filter. To make that possible, you'll first convert the Green_Skin_Texture layer to a Smart Object.

1 Make sure the Green_Skin_Texture layer is selected in the Layers panel, and then choose Filter > Convert For Smart Filters. This creates a Smart Object. Click OK if you're asked to confirm the conversion to a Smart Object.

2 Choose Filter > Liquify.

Photoshop displays the layer in the Liquify dialog box.

3 In the Liquify dialog box, if the Face-Aware Liquify group of options is expanded, click the disclosure triangle next to it to collapse the group.

You already explored Face-Aware Liquify in Lesson 5. While Face-Aware Liquify is a quick and powerful way to modify facial features, the amount of face editing you can do with those options is limited. In this lesson, you'll try some manual Liquify techniques, which you may prefer when you want to create a more expressive face. Hiding the Face-Aware Liquify options makes it easier to concentrate on the other options in the Liquify dialog box.

Note: Step 4 doesn't change the document; it just changes how much you see of other layers while you work on the layer that was selected when you entered the Liquify dialog box.

4   Select Show Backdrop, and then choose Behind from the Mode menu.
    Set the Opacity to **75**.

5   Select the Zoom tool (🔍) from the Tools panel on the left side of the dialog box, and zoom in to the eye area.

6   Select the Forward Warp tool (🖌) (the first tool).

The Forward Warp tool pushes pixels forward as you drag.

7   In the Brush Tool Options area, set Size to **150** and Pressure to **75**.

8 With the Forward Warp tool, pull the monster makeup's right eyebrow down to close the eye opening. Then pull up from under the eye.

9 Repeat step 8 on the left eyebrow and under-eye area. You might prefer to use the Forward Warp tool differently for each eye, to create an even scarier face.

10 When you've closed the gap around the eyes, click OK.

Because you've applied the Liquify filter as a Smart Filter, you can freely remove or change your Liquify edits later without losing image quality, by double-clicking the Smart Object in the Layers panel.

Positioning other layers

Now that you've got the skin texture in place, you'll move the other layers into position, working up from the lowest layers in the Layers panel.

1 Make the Green_Nose_Stitches layer visible, and select it in the Layers panel.

2 Choose Edit > Free Transform, and then position the layer over the nose, resizing it as necessary. Press Enter or Return to commit the transformation.

▶ **Tip:** To resize from the center of a selection, hold down Alt (Windows) or Option (macOS) as you drag a bounding box handle.

You'll repeat the process to position the rest of the layers.

3 Make the Green_Neck_Stitches layer visible, and select it. Then move it over the neck. If you need to adjust it, choose Edit > Free Transform, resize it, and press Enter or Return.

▶ **Tip:** If you only need to move a layer, you can simply drag it with the Move tool. In these steps, choosing Edit > Free Transform lets you both move and resize a layer.

4 Make the Green_Ear_Staples layer visible, and select it. Move the staples over his right ear. Choose Edit > Free Transform, resize and reposition the staples, and then press Enter or Return.

▶ **Tip:** Remember that you can position and size a selected layer using any combination of the Move tool, the Edit > Free Transform command, and the arrow keys. Use whatever tools get the job done!

5   Make the Enhanced_Green_Forehead layer visible, and select it. Move it over the forehead; it's probably a bit large. Choose Edit > Free Transform, resize the forehead to fit his head, and press Enter or Return.

6   Make the Bolts layer visible, and select it. Drag the bolts so they're positioned on both sides of the neck. Choose Edit > Free Transform, and resize them so that they fit snugly against the neck. When you have them in position, press Enter or Return to commit the transformation.

7   Finally, make the Monster_Hair layer visible, and select it. Move it over the forehead. Choose Edit > Free Transform, and then resize the hair so it fits properly against the forehead. Press Enter or Return to commit the change.

8   Save your work so far.

Editing a Smart Filter

With all the layers in position, you can further refine the eye openings and experiment with the bulges in the eyebrows. You'll return to the Liquify filter to make those adjustments.

1 In the Layers panel, double-click Liquify, listed under Smart Filters in the Green_Skin_Texture layer.

Photoshop opens the Liquify dialog box again. This time, all the layers are visible in Photoshop, so when Show Backdrop is selected, you see them all. Sometimes it's easier to make changes without a backdrop to distract you. Other times, it's useful to see your edits in context.

2 Zoom in to see the eyes more closely.

3 Select the Pucker tool (🖑) in the Tools panel, and click on the outer corner of each eye.

The Pucker tool moves pixels toward the center of the brush as you click or hold the mouse button, or drag.

4 Select the Bloat tool (🖑), and click the outer edge of an eyebrow to expand it; do the same for the other eyebrow.

The Bloat tool moves pixels away from the center of the brush as you click or drag.

5 Experiment with the Pucker, Bloat, and other tools in the Liquify filter to customize the monster's face.

Remember that you can change the brush size and other settings. You can undo individual steps using the Undo keyboard shortcut (Ctrl+Z on Windows and Command+Z on Mac) if the Edit menu isn't available. If you want to discard all current changes and start over, hold down the Alt (Windows) or Option (macOS) key to change the Cancel button into a Reset button, and click Reset.

▶ **Tip:** The Pucker, Bloat, and other tools on the left side of the Liquify panel provide more control over Liquify distortions than the Face-Aware Liquify options, and they work on any part of an image. But Face-Aware Liquify is easier for quick and subtle adjustments to facial features.

6 When you're happy with the monster's face, click OK, and save your work.

Painting a layer

There are many ways to paint objects and layers in Photoshop. One of the simplest is to paint with the Brush tool on a layer set to the Color blending mode. You'll use this method to paint the exposed skin green on your monster.

1 Select the Franken layer in the Layers panel.

2 Click the Create A New Layer button (⊞) at the bottom of the Layers panel.

Photoshop creates a new layer, named Layer 1.

▶ Tip: Be sure to distinguish the blending mode of a layer (shown in the Layers panel) from the blending mode of a tool (shown in the options bar). To learn more about blending modes, including a description of each one, see "Blending modes" in Photoshop Help.

3 With Layer 1 selected, choose Color from the Blending Mode menu at the top of the Layers panel.

The Color blending mode combines the luminance of the base color (the color already on the layer) with the hue and saturation of the color you're applying. It's a good blending mode to use when you're coloring monochrome images or tinting color images.

4 In the Tools panel, select the Brush tool (✏). In the options bar, select a **60**-pixel brush with a Hardness of **0**.

5 Hold down Alt or Option (to temporarily switch to the Eyedropper tool) as you click the forehead to sample a green color there. Then release the Alt or Option key to return to the Brush tool.

The sampled color becomes the new Foreground color, loaded into the Brush tool.

6 Ctrl-click (Windows) or Command-click (macOS) the thumbnail in the Franken layer to select its contents. Notice that a selection marquee appears on the layer.

▶ **Tip:** Step 6 selects nontransparent areas of a layer. The goal here to is to recolor the skin, so another approach is to choose Select > Color Range and choose Skin Tones from the Select menu. That would specifically select the skin and not the shirt.

Clicking a layer in the Layers panel selects Layer 1 for painting, but the goal here is to paint only over the exposed skin on the Franken layer. Ctrl-clicking (Windows) or Command-clicking (macOS) the Franken layer thumbnail is a quick way to create a selection based on the Franken layer's non-transparent pixels.

7 Make sure Layer 1 is still selected in the Layers panel, and then use the Brush tool to paint over the hands and arms. You can paint quickly where the hands are against transparent areas, because the selection restricts the paintable area. However, remember that the shirt is part of the selection, so as you paint the skin close to the shirt color, take care to paint only the skin and not the shirt.

▶ **Tip:** To change the brush size as you paint, press the bracket keys on your keyboard. The Left Bracket key ([) decreases the brush size; the Right Bracket (]) increases it.

8 Paint any areas of the face or neck where the original flesh color shows through the Green_Skin_Texture layer.

9 When you're happy with the green skin, choose Select > Deselect. Save your work.

Adding a background

You've got a good-looking monster. Now it's time to put him in his spooky environment. To easily move the monster onto a background, you'll first merge the layers.

▶ **Tip:** Merging or flattening layers permanently combines them into a single layer. That also reduces the file size of the Photoshop document. If you want to preserve the ability to edit selected layers separately, select layers and choose New Group from Layers instead of Merge Visible in step 1. Then, in step 6, drag that layer group from the Layers panel to the other document.

1 Make sure all the layers are visible. Then choose Layer > Merge Visible.

Photoshop merges all the visible layers into one. It's named Layer 1 because that was the selected layer at the time of the merge.

2 Rename Layer 1 **Monster**.

3 Choose File > Open. Navigate to and open the Backdrop.psd file in the Lesson09 folder.

4 Choose Window > Arrange > 2-Up Vertical to display both the monster and backdrop files.

5 Click the 09Working.psd file to make it active.

6 Select the Move tool (✛), drag the Monster layer, and then drop it onto the Backdrop.psd file. Position the monster so his hands are just above the movie title.

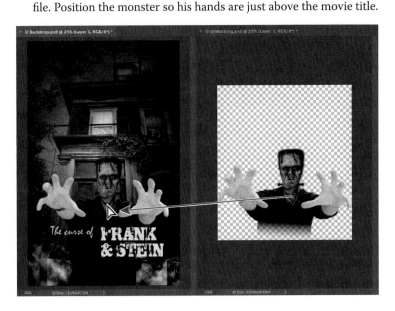

7 Close the 09Working.psd file, saving changes when prompted.

From now on, you'll work on the movie poster file itself.

8 Choose File > Save As, and save the file with the name **Movie-Poster.psd**. Click Save, and then click OK in the Photoshop Format Options dialog box.

Using the History panel to undo edits

You've used the Edit > Undo command to back out of the last change you applied. You can also choose Edit > Redo to reapply a change you just undid. Repeatedly choosing either command steps you back or forward through multiple edits.

For a before/after comparison of just your last edit, choose Edit > Toggle Last State, or press its keyboard shortcut: Ctrl+Alt+Z (Windows) or Command+Option+Z (macOS). This is a quick way to undo/redo with one command instead of two.

A more visual way to step backward and forward through your changes is to use the History panel; choose Window > History to see it. The History panel shows you a list of your changes. To go back to a certain edit (for example, four steps ago), just select it in the History panel, and continue working from that point.

Applying filters and effects

You'll add a tombstone to the poster, and you'll experiment with filters and effects to see what works, using the History panel to back up to an earlier edit state.

1   In Photoshop, choose File > Open.

2   Navigate to the Lesson09 folder, and double-click the T1.psd file to open it. If an Embedded Profile Mismatch message appears, click OK.

The tombstone image is plain, but you'll add some visual interest to it. You'll start by adding a little atmospheric texture to the tombstone.

3   Press the D key to restore the default foreground and background colors.

4   Choose Filter > Render > Difference Clouds.

The original is dull.   Clouds add drama.

You'll leave the top of the tombstone in focus but blur the rest using an iris blur.

▶ **Tip:** The D key is a shortcut for clicking the Default Foreground and Background Colors icon (⬛) in the Tools panel. The foreground and background colors are set because in step 4, Difference Clouds will use those colors.

⬤ **Note:** The Difference Clouds result you get may not match the figure shown; Difference Clouds renders uniquely each time you run it.

5 Choose Filter > Blur Gallery > Iris Blur. Photoshop enters the Blur Gallery task space that displays just the tools for certain blur effects.

6 In the document window, drag the Iris Blur ellipse up so that the top of the tombstone is sharp and the rest is not. Then click OK.

▶ **Tip:** If you want to change the shape and area of the blur effect, drag the handles. Dragging the circle near the center is an alternate way to control the Blur Amount option that you see in the Iris Blur options, on the right side of the Blur Gallery task space.

By default, the ellipse is centered. Shift the focus higher.

You'll use adjustment layers to make the image lighter and change its color.

7 In the Adjustments panel, scroll down to the Single Adjustments list and click Brightness/Contrast (☀). Then, in the Properties panel, move the Brightness slider to **70**.

8 In the Adjustments panel, click Channel Mixer (◐) in the Single Adjustments list.

9 In the Properties panel, choose Green from the Output Channel menu, and then change the Green value to **+37** and the Blue value to **+108**.

The tombstone takes on a green cast.

Note: The green channel is set as the Output Channel, so the adjustments changed the green channel to 37% of its original amount while adding 108% of the blue channel to the green channel.

The Channel Mixer is a useful option for correcting color balance, usually by applying much smaller values than you used here. The Channel Mixer is also an alternative to the Black & White adjustment for controlling how colors are converted to grayscale and for tinting effects. In this case, you used the Channel Mixer to make a purely creative color adjustment to an image.

10 In the Adjustments panel, scroll down to the Single Adjustments list and click Exposure (⚡). In the Properties panel, move the Exposure slider to **+.90** to brighten the lighter areas of the image.

Tip: The Exposure adjustment is primarily intended for correcting HDR images, but in this lesson it's used as a creative effect.

Undoing multiple steps

The tombstone certainly looks different than it did when you started, but it doesn't quite match the tombstones that are already in the poster. You'll use the History panel to revisit the steps you've taken.

1 If the History panel isn't already open, choose Window > History. Drag the bottom of the panel down so that you can see the entire list.

● **Note:** The History panel lists the steps you have done in the current session only. The list is reset when you close a document, so when you open a document, the History panel is empty.

The History panel records the recent steps you've performed on the image. The current state is selected.

2 Click the Blur Gallery state in the History panel.

The History states below the selected state are dimmed, and the image has changed. At the selected History state, the Difference Clouds filter was run, and the iris blur was applied. But the Layers panel doesn't show adjustment layers because the current History state is before the brightness and color changes were applied.

3 Click the Modify Channel Mixer Layer state in the History panel.

Many of the states are restored. The color has returned, along with the brightness and contrast settings. There are two adjustment layers in the Layers panel. However, the states below the one you selected remain dimmed, and the Exposure adjustment layer is not listed in the Layers panel.

You'll return almost to the beginning to apply different effects to the tombstone.

4 Click Difference Clouds in the History panel.

Everything following that state is dimmed.

5 Choose Filter > Noise > Add Noise.

Adding noise will give the tombstone a more stone-like texture.

6 In the Add Noise dialog box, set the Amount to **3**%, select Gaussian, and select Monochromatic. Then click OK.

> **Tip:** If the Noise adjustments are hard to see, click the magnifying glass icon in the Add Noise dialog box.

The states that were dimmed after the state you selected (Difference Clouds) are no longer in the History panel. They were replaced by the task you just performed (Add Noise). You can click any state to return to that point in the process, but as soon as you perform a new task, Photoshop replaces all dimmed states.

The tombstone is ready to join the others in your movie poster.

Note: A Paste Profile Mismatch dialog box may appear when you drag a layer between documents with different document color profiles. For this lesson, clicking OK is fine because it will convert the layer colors to match the destination document.

7 Choose Window > Arrange > Tile All Vertically.

8 With the Move tool, drag the tombstone you just created to the Movie-Poster.psd file. Click OK if you see a color management warning.

9 Drag the tombstone to the bottom-left corner, with the top third of it showing.

10 Choose File > Save to save the Movie-Poster.psd file. Then close the T1.psd file without saving it.

You've had a chance to try some new filters and effects and to use the History panel to backtrack. By default, the History panel retains only the last 50 states. You can change the number of levels in the History panel by choosing Edit > Preferences > Performance (Windows) or Photoshop > Settings > Performance (macOS) and entering a different value for History States.

Note: Setting the number of History states involves a trade-off. Maintaining more History states may cause Photoshop to use more memory or create a larger temporary scratch file.

Note: If you're using macOS 12 or earlier, the Settings command is named Preferences.

Improving a low-resolution image

You'll add another image to the movie poster. However, the only version available has small pixel dimensions, which may work for web pages and social media but will appear too coarse for high-quality printing. To address this, Photoshop can *resample* the image—change its pixel dimensions by creating or deleting new pixels based on existing ones. Increasing pixel dimensions is called *upsampling*, and decreasing them is called *downsampling*. Resizing an image by resampling is different than maintaining pixel dimensions and scaling by percentage or inches/centimeters.

The Super Zoom Neural Filter can upsample a low-resolution image using machine learning that can be more effective than older Photoshop resampling options. You'll use Super Zoom to improve a low-resolution image for the movie poster.

1 Choose File > Open, navigate to the Lesson09 folder, and open the Faces.jpg file.

2 Zoom in to 300% or more. At this magnification, pixels should be visible. If the Status Bar at the bottom of the document window is set to Document Dimensions, it will show that the pixel dimensions are 216 × 288 px—a very low number of pixels. (You can also verify this by choosing Image > Image Size.)

3 Choose Filter > Neural Filters. If a Welcome to Neural Filters message appears, click Skip Tour.

4 In the All Filters list, click Super Zoom to select it. If the filter is not loaded in the panel on the right, click Download.

5 At the bottom of the Neural Filters workspace, make sure the Output menu is set to New Document.

6 Under the Super Zoom preview on the right, click the Zoom In icon (⊕) until the label next to it says Zoom image (3x). Notice that the resolution on the large preview on the left improves as you increase the scaling factor.

7 Make sure Enhance Image Details, Remove JPEG Artifacts, and Enhance Face Details are selected, and set Noise Reduction to **3**.

Note: For typical resampling tasks, you can use one of the options in the Resample menu in the Image > Image Size dialog box. But the traditional Resample options are less effective at enhancing this very low resolution example, so the Super Zoom Neural Filter is used instead.

▶ **Tip:** You'll learn more about Neural Filters in Lesson 15, "Exploring Neural Filters."

Note: When Output is set to New Layer, the Zoom Image option maintains the current pixel dimensions and enlarges an enhanced portion of it. Here, you want to create a more detailed version of the image at larger pixel dimensions, and that requires choosing New Document in the Output menu.

8 Click the Show Original button to view the image as it is before opening Neural Filters, and then click it again to toggle back to previewing the image with the current options for all enabled Neural Filters.

Original image.   *Preview of Super Zoom settings.*

9 Click OK. Super Zoom creates a new, untitled document tab with the results. Its pixel dimensions are now 648 × 864 px, or 3x the original width and height.

10 Choose Select > All, and then choose Edit > Copy.

11 Select the Movie-Poster.psd tab to bring it to the front, and then select the Elliptical Marquee tool (○), hidden under the Rectangular Marquee tool (▭).

12 In the options bar, enter **50 px** for Feather to soften the edge of the pasted image.

13 Draw an oval in the upper-right corner of the poster, above the monster's head. The oval should overlap the window and fire escape.

14 Make sure Layer 1 is selected, and then choose Edit > Paste Special > Paste Into. If the Paste Profile Mismatch dialog box appears, click OK.

15 Select the Move tool (⊕), and center the pasted image in the feathered area.

16 In the Layers panel, choose Luminosity from the Blending Mode menu, and move the Opacity slider to **50**%.

▶ **Tip:** You can drag to recompose the pasted image behind its layer mask because the layer and its mask are unlinked. When you want to transform the layer and its mask together, in the Layers panel click the space between the layer and mask icons to enable the link icon, which is visible when enabled.

In the Layers panel, you'll see that Layer 2 is the image you just pasted, and that layer has a layer mask with a feathered elliptical mask shape. When you used the Edit > Paste Into command, Photoshop created the layer mask from the feathered elliptical selection you drew.

17 You've finished the poster! Close the Movie-Poster.psd document, saving changes. Then close the Faces.jpg file and its untitled copy without saving them.

Review questions

1 What are the differences between using a Smart Filter and a regular filter to apply effects to an image?

2 What do the Bloat and Pucker tools in the Liquify filter do?

3 What does the History panel do?

4 What is the relationship of the Undo and Redo commands to the History panel?

Review answers

1 Smart Filters are nondestructive: They can be adjusted, enabled and disabled, and deleted at any time without altering original layer pixels. In contrast, regular filters permanently change a layer; once applied, the original state of that layer can't be restored (except by using Edit > Undo command). A Smart Filter is a filter applied to a Smart Object layer.

2 The Bloat tool moves pixels away from the center of the brush; the Pucker tool moves pixels toward the center of the brush.

3 The History panel records recent steps you've performed in Photoshop during the current session. You can return to an earlier step by selecting it in the History panel.

4 The Undo and Redo commands move back or forward, respectively, through the steps in the History panel.

10 PAINTING WITH THE MIXER BRUSH

Lesson overview

In this lesson, you'll learn how to do the following:

- Customize brush settings.

- Clean the brush.

- Mix colors.

- Create a custom brush preset.

- Use wet and dry brushes to blend color.

 This lesson will take about an hour to complete. To get the lesson files used in this chapter, download them from the web page for this book at peachpit.com/PhotoshopCIB2024. For more information, see "Accessing the lesson files and Web Edition" in the Getting Started section at the beginning of this book.

As you work on this lesson, you'll preserve the start files. If you need to restore the start files, download them from your Account page.

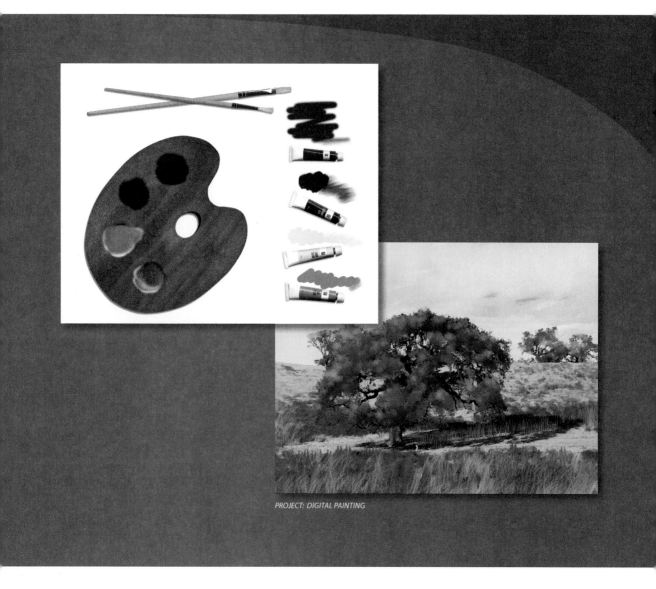

PROJECT: DIGITAL PAINTING

The Mixer Brush tool gives you flexibility, color-mixing
abilities, and brush strokes as if you were painting on
a physical canvas.

About the Mixer Brush

In previous lessons, you've used brushes in Photoshop to perform various tasks. The Mixer Brush is unlike other brushes in that it lets you mix colors with each other. You can change the wetness of the brush and how it mixes the brush color with the color already on the canvas.

Some Photoshop brush types can have realistic bristles, so you can add textures that resemble those in paintings you might create in the physical world. While this is a great feature in general, it's particularly useful when you're using the Mixer Brush. Combining different bristle settings and brush tips with different wetness, paint-load, and paint-mixing settings gives you opportunities to create exactly the look you want.

Getting started

In this lesson, you'll get acquainted with the Mixer Brush as well as the brush tip and bristle options available in Photoshop. Start by taking a look at the final projects you'll create.

1 Start Photoshop, and then simultaneously hold down Ctrl+Alt+Shift (Windows) or Command+Option+Shift (macOS) to restore the default preferences. (See "Restoring default preferences" on page 5.)

2 When prompted, click Yes to delete the Adobe Photoshop Settings file.

3 Choose File > Browse In Bridge to open Adobe Bridge.

4 In Bridge, click Lessons in the Favorites panel. Double-click the Lesson10 folder in the Content panel.

5 Preview the Lesson10 end files.

You'll use the palette image to explore brush options and learn to mix colors. You'll then apply what you've learned to transform the landscape image into a painting.

6 Double-click 10Palette_Start.psd to open the file in Photoshop.

7 Choose File > Save As, and name the file **10Palette_Working.psd**. Click OK if the Photoshop Format Options dialog box appears.

Note: If Bridge isn't installed, the File > Browse In Bridge command in Photoshop will start the Creative Cloud desktop app, which will download and install Bridge. After installation completes, you can start Bridge.

Note: If Photoshop displays a dialog box telling you about the difference between saving to Cloud Documents and On Your Computer, click Save On Your Computer. You can also select Don't Show Again, but that setting will deselect after you reset Photoshop preferences.

8   Click the Choose a Workspace icon at the top-right corner of the application frame, and choose the Painting workspace.

● **Note:** You can paint more naturally and expressively by using a stylus and a graphics tablet. If the stylus can sense attributes such as pressure and angle, you can use Photoshop brush settings to apply them to your brush strokes.

Selecting brush settings

The practice image includes a palette and four tubes of color, which you'll use to sample the colors you're working with. You'll change settings as you paint different colors, exploring brush tip settings and wetness options.

1   Select the Zoom tool (⌕), and zoom in on the four tubes of paint, leaving some empty space above the red tube.

2   Select the Eyedropper tool (𝄕), and click the red tube to sample its color.

The foreground color changes to red.

3   Select the Mixer Brush tool (⌗) in the Tools panel. (When another workspace is selected, you may find the Mixer Brush hidden under the Brush tool [✏].)

● **Note:** When you hold down the Eyedropper tool on the image, Photoshop displays a sampling ring that previews the color you're selecting. The sampling ring is available if Photoshop can use the graphics processor on your computer (see the Performance panel in Photoshop preferences).

4   Choose Window > Brush Settings to open the Brush Settings panel. Select the first brush.

The Brush Settings panel contains brush presets and several options for customizing brushes.

▶ **Tip:** Looking for a specific brush name in the Brush Settings panel? Hover the pointer over a brush thumbnail, and its name will pop up in a tool tip.

Experimenting with wetness options and brushes

The effect of the brush is determined by the Wet, Load, and Mix fields in the options bar. *Wet* controls how much paint the brush picks up from the canvas. *Load* controls how much paint the brush holds when you begin painting (as with a physical brush, it runs out of paint as you paint with it). *Mix* controls the ratio of paint from the canvas and paint from the brush.

You can change these settings separately. However, it's faster to select a standard combination from the pop-up menu.

1   In the options bar, choose Dry from the pop-up menu of blending brush combinations.

When you select Dry, Wet is set to 0%, Load to 50%, and Mix is not applicable. With the Dry preset, you paint opaque color; you can't mix colors on a dry canvas.

2   Paint one continuous zigzag stroke in the area above the red tube. As you continue painting without releasing the mouse, the red paint eventually fades and runs out.

Note: You can also sample paint by Alt-clicking or Option-clicking the Mixer Brush tool. This samples the area within the brush size as an image, unless you selected Load Solid Colors Only in the Current Brush Load menu in the options bar.

3   With the Eyedropper tool, sample the blue color from the blue tube of paint.

4   Select the Mixer Brush. For the blue paint, in the Brush Settings panel we chose the Round Sketch Ballpoint Pen brush (the first brush in the second row). Choose Wet from the pop-up menu in the options bar.

If the brush you select doesn't match the one shown here, resize the Brush Settings panel so that the brush thumbnails display six columns across.

5 Paint above the blue tube. The paint mixes with the white background.

● **Note:** If you aren't getting the same results from the brushes, make sure the Background layer is selected in the Layers panel.

6 Choose Dry from the menu in the options bar, and then paint again above the blue tube. A much darker, more opaque blue appears and doesn't mix with the white background.

7 Sample the yellow color from the yellow paint tube, and then select the Mixer Brush. For the yellow paint, in the Brush Settings panel we chose the Pencil KTW 1 brush (the fourth brush in the second row). Choose Dry from the menu in the options bar, and then paint in the area over the yellow paint tube.

● **Note:** If the brushes in your Brush Settings panel don't match the ones shown in this lesson, open the Brushes panel, Shift-select all brushes and brush folders in the list, click the Delete Brush button (🗑), click OK to confirm, and then choose Restore Default Brushes from the Brushes panel menu.

8 Choose Very Wet from the menu in the options bar, and then paint some more. Now the yellow mixes with the white background.

9 Sample the green color from the green paint tube, and then select the Mixer Brush. For the green paint, in the Brush Settings panel we chose the Hard Round 30 brush (the sixth brush in the fifth row). Choose Dry from the menu in the options bar.

10 Paint a brush stroke above the green paint tube. Experiment on your own, painting over the green stroke with a different color, using different Mixer Brush settings, particularly the Wet amount.

Mixing colors

Note: Depending on the complexity of your project and the performance of your computer, you may need to be patient. Mixing colors can be an intensive process.

You've used wet and dry brushes, changed brush settings, and mixed the paint with the background color. Now, you'll focus more on mixing colors with each other as you add paint to the painter's palette.

1 Zoom out just enough to see the full palette and the paint tubes.

2 Select the Paint mix layer in the Layers panel so the color you paint won't blend with the brown palette on the Background layer.

The Mixer Brush tool mixes colors only on the active layer unless you select Sample All Layers in the options bar.

3 Use the Eyedropper tool to sample the red color from the red paint tube, and then select the Mixer Brush. In the Brush Settings panel, select the Soft Round 30 brush (the first brush in the first row). Then choose Wet from the pop-up menu in the options bar, and paint in the top circle on the palette.

4 Click the Clean The Brush After Each Stroke icon (✖) in the options bar to deselect it.

Tip: If the paint tubes are covered by the Brush Settings panel, feel free to rearrange your workspace to make room. For example, collapse or close panels you aren't using. But make sure you can still see the Layers panel.

Tip: You can use the Eyedropper tool to sample a color even if the layer that contains the color isn't selected.

5 Use the Eyedropper tool to sample the blue color from the blue paint tube, and then use the Mixer Brush tool to paint in the same circle, mixing the red with the blue until the color becomes purple.

6 Use the Eyedropper tool to sample the purple color from the circle you just painted, and then paint in the next circle.

7 In the options bar, choose Clean Brush from the Current Brush Load pop-up menu. The preview changes to indicate transparency, meaning the brush has no paint loaded.

▶ **Tip:** Use the Eyedropper tool to sample the color, since it's on a different layer.

To remove the paint load from a brush, you can choose Clean Brush in the options bar. To replace the paint load in a brush, sample a different color.

If you want Photoshop to clean the brush after each stroke, select the Clean The Brush After Each Stroke icon (✘) in the options bar. To load the brush with the foreground color after each stroke, select the Load The Brush After Each Stroke icon (✒) in the options bar. By default, both of these options are selected.

8 Use the Eyedropper tool to sample the blue color from the blue paint tube, and then use the Mixer Brush to paint blue in half of the next circle.

9 Sample the yellow color from the yellow paint tube, and slowly paint over the blue with a wet brush to mix the two colors.

▶ **Tip:** When switching tools often as in these steps, it's useful to watch the pointer icon to make sure the active tool is the one you currently want.

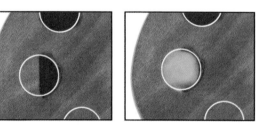

10 Fill the last circle with yellow and red paint, mixing the two with a wet brush to create an orange color.

11 Hide the Circles layer in the Layers panel to remove the outlines on the palette. You've mixed paint colors on a digital palette!

12 Choose File > Save, and close the document.

Julieanne Kost is an official Adobe Photoshop evangelist.

Tool tips from the Photoshop evangelist

Mixer Brush shortcuts

There are no default keyboard shortcuts for the Mixer Brush tool, but you can create your own.

To create custom keyboard shortcuts:

1 Choose Edit > Keyboard Shortcuts.

2 Choose Tools from the Shortcuts For menu.

3 Scroll down to the bottom of the list.

4 Select a command, and then enter a custom shortcut. You can create shortcuts for the following commands:

- Load Mixer Brush
- Clean Mixer Brush
- Toggle Mixer Brush Auto-Load
- Toggle Mixer Brush Auto-Clean
- Toggle Mixer Brush Sample All Layers
- Sharpen Erodible Tips

Mixing colors with a photograph

When you come up with a great brush, you probably want to save all of its settings so that you can use that brush again in a later project. While Photoshop already has a tool preset feature that lets you save tool settings, brushes have more options than most tools. For this reason, Photoshop has convenient brush presets that can remember everything about a brush.

Earlier, you mixed colors with a white background and with each other. Now, you'll use a photograph as your canvas. You'll add colors and mix them with each other and with the background colors to transform a photograph of a landscape into a painting.

1 Choose File > Open. Double-click the 10Landscape_Start.jpg file in the Lesson10 folder to open it.

2 Choose File > Save As. Rename the file **10Landscape_Working.jpg**, and click Save. Click OK in the JPEG Options dialog box.

Photoshop includes numerous brush presets, which are very handy. But if you need a different brush for your project, you might find it easier to create your own brush preset or download brush presets that another artist has created and shared online. In the following exercises, you'll load, edit, and save custom brush presets.

Loading custom brush presets

The Brushes panel displays visual samples of the strokes created by different brushes. If you already know the name of the brush you want to use, it can be easier to display the brushes by name. You'll list them by name now, so you can find your preset for the next exercise.

1 In the Brushes panel (choose Window > Brushes if it's not open), expand one of the brush preset groups to see how the brushes are organized.

Now you'll load brush presets that you'll use for this exercise. Loading brush presets is how you use brush presets that you've downloaded or purchased.

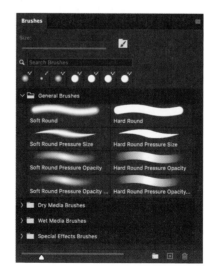

▶ **Tip:** If you have enough space on your screen, you can see more brushes at once by making the Brushes panel wider or taller.

2 Click the Brushes panel menu, and choose Import Brushes.

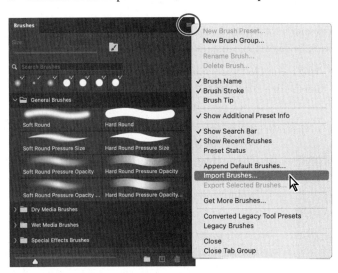

► Tip: If you want to share your custom brushes with others or back them up, select the brushes or brush groups, and choose Export Selected Brushes from the Brushes panel menu.

3 Navigate to the Lesson10 folder, select CIB Landscape Brushes.abr, and click Open or Load. The CIB Landscape Brushes group appears at the end of the Brushes panel list.

4 Click to expand the CIB Landscape Brushes group, revealing the brushes it contains.

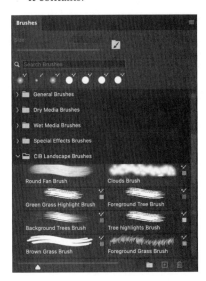

Some of the presets contain not only a stroke preview and a name, but also a color swatch. That's because a color can be part of a brush preset.

Creating a custom brush preset

For the next exercise, you'll create and save a variation on a brush preset that exists in the CIB Landscape Brushes you just imported.

1 Select the Mixer Brush, and then, in the CIB Landscape Brushes group in the Brushes panel, select the Round Fan Brush. You'll use this brush preset as the starting point for the brush preset you'll create.

2 Change the following settings in the Brush Settings panel:

- Size: **36** px

- Shape: Round Fan

- Bristles: **35%**

- Length: **32%**

- Thickness: **2%**

- Stiffness: **75%**

- Angle: **0°**

- Spacing: **2%**

▶ **Tip:** In the Brush Settings panel, the Brush Tip Shape options include the Angle setting, which simulates the rotation angle at which you hold the brush handle. Some graphics tablets can use a stylus that lets you rotate the brush tip as you paint, by rotating the stylus. If you don't have such a stylus, you can rotate the brush tip angle by one degree as you paint, by pressing the Left Arrow or Right Arrow keys. Add the Shift key to rotate in 15-degree increments. The current brush angle is displayed at the end of the options bar.

3 Click the Foreground color swatch in the Tools panel. Select a medium-light blue color (we chose R=86, G=201, B=252).

4 Choose Dry from the pop-up menu in the options bar.

Now it's time to save the settings as a brush preset.

5 Choose New Brush Preset from the Brush Settings panel menu.

► Tip: The options in the New Brush dialog box make it possible to save the brush size, the tool settings, and the brush color in the preset.

6   Name the brush **Sky Brush**, select all of the options in the New Brush dialog box, and then click OK.

Your new brush is saved in the CIB Landscape Brushes group because it was based on a brush preset from that group. Feel free to reorganize your brush presets any way you like by dragging and dropping presets into brush preset groups within the Brushes panel. You can create a brush preset group by clicking the Create A New Group button (▢) at the bottom of the Brushes panel. You can change the order of the Brushes panel list and organize brush preset groups into subgroups.

Using brush presets to paint and mix colors

Now you'll use brush presets to interpret an existing image using your own painting style. You'll paint the sky first, using the brush preset you just created.

1   Select the Sky Brush from the Brushes panel.

Presets are saved on your system, so once added, they are always available.

2   Paint over the sky, moving in close to the trees. Because you're using a dry brush, the blue paint isn't mixing with the colors beneath it.

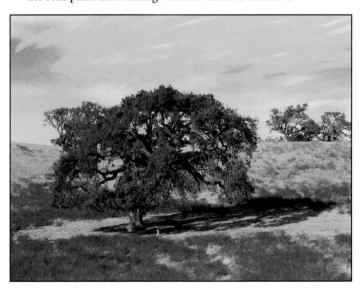

3 Select the Clouds Brush.

4 Use this brush to scrub diagonally in the upper-right corner of the sky, blending the color in the wet brush preset with the existing color on the layer.

▶ **Tip:** When using different brush presets, observe how brush behavior is affected by the settings in both the options bar and the Brush Settings panel. It's a good way to learn how to create your own brush presets.

When you're satisfied with the sky, move on to the grass and trees.

5 Select the Green Grass Highlight Brush. Then paint short vertical strokes over the darker green grass areas to add some bright green grass.

▶ **Tip:** Notice how Mixer Brush strokes look different depending on the colors under the brush when you start dragging. Experiment with painting blades of grass starting from the bottom compared to starting at the top.

▶ **Tip:** If you're using a stylus that senses angle, notice how the angle of some brush tips changes depending on how you hold the stylus. With those brush types, how your brush strokes look depends on the direction you drag relative to the brush tip angle.

Tip: You can paint brush strokes that are shorter and lighter for a more representational and textured image, or you can paint longer, more intensive strokes to create a bolder, more expressive image.

6 Select the Tree Brush, and then paint the darker areas of the tree. Then select the Background Trees Brush, and paint the two smaller trees on the right side of the painting. Select the Tree Highlights Brush, and paint the lighter areas of the trees. These are Wet brushes so that you can blend colors.

So far, so good. Now you can add some detail to the grasses.

Tip: Experiment by changing the brush size or options in the Brush Settings panel. If you're using a stylus that senses pressure or angle, experiment by varying them as you paint. Use the full range of Mixer Brush settings and techniques to create your personal painting style!

7 Select the Brown Grass Brush. Paint along the brown grass with up-and-down strokes for the look of a field. Use the same brush to paint the trunk of the tree.

8 Select the Foreground Grass Brush. Then paint using diagonal strokes to blend the colors in the grass.

9 Choose File > Save, and close the document.

Voilà! You've created a masterpiece with your paints and brushes, and there's no mess to clean up.

Brushes from Kyle T. Webster

In 2017, award-winning digital brush designer Kyle T. Webster joined Adobe. At the same time, Adobe acquired the popular brush collections at KyleBrush.com. Kyle has drawn for *The New Yorker*, *TIME*, *The New York Times*, *The Wall Street Journal*, *The Atlantic*, *Entertainment Weekly*, Scholastic, Nike, IDEO, and many other distinguished editorial, advertising, publishing, and institutional clients. His illustration work has been recognized by the Society of Illustrators, Communications Arts, and American Illustration. Kyle now works closely with Adobe product teams on the development of future brushes for Adobe Creative Cloud.

To add the Kyle T. Webster brushes to Photoshop, open the Brushes panel (Window > Brushes), and choose Get More Brushes from the Brushes panel menu. After you download a brush pack and with Photoshop running, double-click the downloaded ABR file to add its brushes as a new group in the Brushes panel.

Painting with symmetry

If you're painting a design that uses symmetry, try the Paint Symmetry brush option. When a brush type that supports Paint Symmetry is selected, you'll see the Paint Symmetry icon (🦋) in the options bar. Click that icon, and select the type of symmetry axis you want; it appears as a guide object in the document. Move, scale, or rotate the guide if you want, and then press Enter or Return. As you paint with Paint Symmetry, each of your brush strokes is repeated across the axes you set up.

You might use a single axis for simple mirror symmetry, but you can also use multiple axes arranged in different ways. For example, you can use horizontal and vertical axes to design tiles, or radial axes to design mandalas.

The axes are actually paths, so you can see and edit them in the Paths panel. You can even create your own custom axis. Draw with a tool such as the Pen, Curvature Pen, or Custom Shape tool in Path mode (not Shape mode). With the path selected in the Paths panel, choose Make Symmetry Path from the Paths panel menu.

Painting gallery

The painting tools and brush tips in Photoshop let you create all kinds of painting effects.

The following pages show examples of art created with the brush tips and tools in Photoshop.

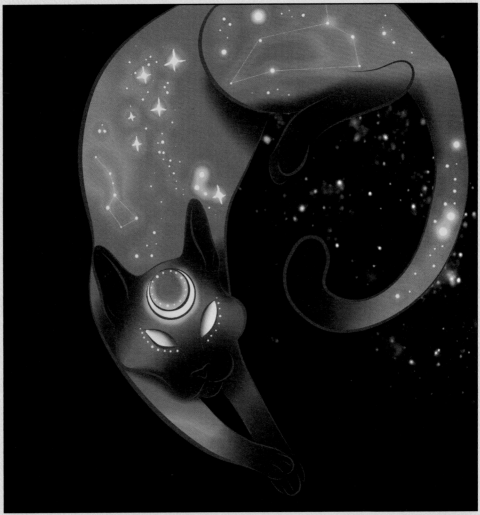

Image © Megan Lee, www.megan-lee.com

Image © Victoria Pavlov, pavlovphotography.com

Image © sholby, www.sholby.net

Image © sholby, www.sholby.net

Image © sholby, www.sholby.net

Continues on next page

Painting gallery (continued)

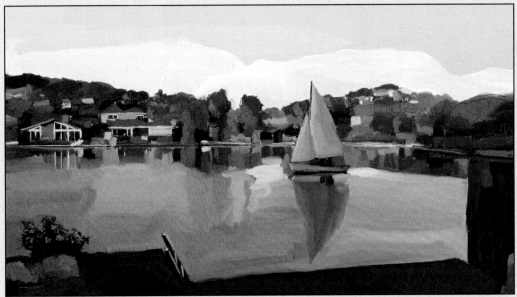

Image © Andrew Faulkner, www.andrew-faulkner.com

Image © Lynette Kent, www.LynetteKent.com

Review questions

1 What does the Mixer Brush do that other brushes don't?

2 How do you load a Mixer Brush with color?

3 How do you clean a brush?

4 What is the name of the panel that you use to customize a brush?

5 What is the name of the panel that you use to manage and select brush presets?

6 If the Mixer Brush and brush panels are not visible in the workspace, what single step makes all of them visible?

Review answers

1 The Mixer Brush mixes the current brush color with colors on a layer.

2 You can load color on a Mixer Brush by sampling a color with the Eyedropper tool or changing the Foreground color. If the brush is clean, you can choose Load Brush from the pop-up menu in the options bar to load the brush with the foreground color.

3 To clean a brush, choose Clean Brush from the pop-up menu in the options bar.

4 You customize a brush in the Brush Settings panel.

5 You manage and select brush presets in the Brushes panel.

6 Switch to the Painting workspace, using the Choose a Workspace button (or by choosing Window > Workspace > Painting).

11 EDITING VIDEO

Lesson overview

In this lesson, you'll learn how to do the following:

- Use the Timeline panel to create a video that animates a layered Photoshop document and combines it with video and audio clips.

- Sequence and trim video files in the Timeline panel.

- Add motion to still layers.

- Add transitions between video clips.

- Animate layers using keyframes.

- Add audio to a video.

- Render a finished video.

 This lesson will take about 90 minutes to complete. To get the lesson files used in this chapter, download them from the web page for this book at peachpit.com/PhotoshopCIB2024. For more information, see "Accessing the lesson files and Web Edition" in the Getting Started section at the beginning of this book.

As you work on this lesson, you'll preserve the start files. If you need to restore the start files, download them from your Account page.

PROJECT: HISTORY COURSE PROMOTIONAL VIDEO

You can edit video files in Photoshop using many of the same effects you use to edit image files. You can create a movie from video files, still images, Smart Objects, audio files, and type layers; apply transitions; and animate effects using keyframes.

About video and animation in Photoshop

A Photoshop document can contain still, animated, and video layers. In this lesson, you'll use the Timeline panel to add video clips, edit them as a sequence, overlay still layers that you animate, and add background music.

You can use Photoshop to create basic to moderately complex video projects. If you need more precision and flexibility, or better ways to work efficiently with longer videos or many layers and clips, consider using an application such as Adobe Premiere® Pro for video editing, and Adobe After Effects® for motion graphics.

Photoshop works with many commonly used video and audio formats, including video captured using smartphones and professional digital cameras. In Lesson 1, you created a still frame that announces and promotes a live video stream. In this lesson, you'll build a video version of that design that includes video and audio and animates its layers. First, look at the final video to see what you'll create.

1 Start Photoshop, and then simultaneously hold down Ctrl+Alt+Shift (Windows) or Command+Option+Shift (macOS) to restore the default preferences. (See "Restoring default preferences" on page 5.)

2 When prompted, click Yes to delete the Adobe Photoshop Settings file.

3 Choose File > Browse In Bridge.

4 In Bridge, select the Lessons folder in the Favorites panel. Then, double-click the Lesson11 folder in the Content panel, and select the 11End.mp4 file.

5 In the Preview panel, click the Play (▶) button to view the final video.

Bridge offers other ways to play a video file. You can also choose View > Full Screen Preview, or you can double-click the file to open it in the default video player on your system, such as QuickTime Player (macOS) or Movies & TV (Windows).

Note: If Bridge isn't installed, the File > Browse In Bridge command in Photoshop will start the Creative Cloud desktop app, which will download and install Bridge. After installation completes, you can start Bridge.

Tip: When a video is selected in Bridge and the Preview panel is open, press the spacebar as a shortcut for the Play button.

It's a short clip that introduces a live stream, combining multiple video clips, animated text and rectangles, and music. It's 10 seconds long.

6 Double-click the 11End.psd file to open it in Photoshop.

Using the Timeline panel

If you've used a video-editing application, you might already be familiar with a video timeline, where you can arrange video clips, still images, and audio files as a sequence. In Photoshop you do this in the Timeline panel.

1 Choose Window > Timeline to open the Timeline panel.

In the Timeline panel you see the same vertical stack of content as in the Layers panel, with the additional ability to lay out video clips, still images, and audio files horizontally (in time), and with controls specific to time and motion. Video clips are blue, and image files are purple. Audio tracks are green, appear at the bottom of the Timeline panel stack, and don't appear in the Layers panel.

Tip: If the Timeline is too short to display both video groups and the audio track all at once, make the Timeline panel taller by dragging its top border up.

A. Play button **B.** Work area start **C.** Playhead **D.** Work area end **E.** Image layer **F.** Video clip **G.** Audio track **H.** Render Video button **I.** Current time **J.** Frame rate **K.** Control Timeline Magnification slider

The timeline contents should appear visible as in the figure above. If they're collapsed against the left side so that content titles and previews aren't visible, drag the magnification slider (below the timeline) to the right to see time in more detail. If you can't see all of the tracks, drag the top edge of the Timeline panel upward to make the panel taller.

2 In the Timeline panel, click the Play button (▶) to play back the timeline.

Tip: The spacebar is a keyboard shortcut for the Play/Stop button.

The playhead moves across the time ruler, displaying each frame of the timeline. The Play button appears as a Stop button when the timeline is playing. The movie automatically stops playing when the playhead reaches the work area end marker.

3 Click the Stop button in the Timeline panel.

4 Drag the playhead to another point in the time ruler.

The playhead's time location determines what appears in the document window.

When a document is created from a video preset, Photoshop displays cyan guides across the document window. Some older televisions might crop the picture, and some video players might overlay their own graphics around the edges. To minimize

Tip: If you don't want to see the guides, choose View > Show > Guides and deselect that command.

the chance that your content near edges will be cut off or covered, keep important content within the center area marked by the guides. Guides don't appear in exported video.

5   Leave the 11End.psd file open so that you can refer to it as you work.

Getting started

In this lesson you'll start with the graphic you created in Lesson 1, because the brief for this project is to create an animated version of it.

1   Choose File > Browse In Bridge to switch back to Adobe Bridge.

2   In the Lesson11 folder, double-click the 11Start.psd file to open it in Photoshop. Close any messages that appear about new features.

Note: If Photoshop displays a dialog box telling you about the difference between saving to Cloud Documents and On Your Computer, click Save On Your Computer. You can also select Don't Show Again, but that setting will deselect after you reset Photoshop preferences.

3   Choose File > Save As, rename the file **11Working.psd**, and click Save. Click OK if you see the Photoshop Format Options dialog box.

You'll notice that the Timeline panel is empty in the start file; you'll create a video timeline soon. Also, we converted the History 301 and Live Stream type layers to shape (outline) layers (using Type > Convert to Shape) to preserve their appearance if you aren't able to install the fonts they used. There's no difference between animating type layers and other layers. However, type layers converted to shapes can no longer be edited using a type tool.

The colored rectangles that were on the same layer in Lesson 1 are now on separate layers named Rectangle A and Rectangle B. We separated them into two layers because the motion design idea is to animate each rectangle individually.

Adding video

▶ **Tip:** For your own projects, if the video must meet a specific frame rate, do this after the video timeline is created: Choose Set Timeline Frame Rate from the Timeline panel menu, enter the frame rate you need, and then click OK.

The design requires replacing the still image Arch layer with video clips fitting the same history theme. Using video requires a video timeline, so you'll create that first.

1   Choose View > Fit On Screen to show the entire canvas above the Timeline panel.

2   In the Timeline panel, click Create Video Timeline.

Layers panel content now also appears in the Timeline, as *tracks*.

Adjusting the total duration of a timeline

If you play the timeline, you'll notice that the still layers aren't animated yet, and play stops after five seconds because that's when every track ends. The 01End file shows that the total sequence length needs to be 10 seconds, so before adding more content, you'll set the *duration* (time length) of all media to 10 seconds.

1 Drag the Control Timeline Magnification slider at the bottom of the Timeline panel until the existing tracks fill about half of the Timeline panel horizontally. You want to be able to see a thumbnail of each clip and enough detail in the time ruler that you can accurately change the duration of each clip.

> **Tip:** If the Control Timeline Magnification slider is hard to control, click the magnification icons to the left and right of the slider.

Note: Dragging the left or right edge of a clip changes its duration, not its playback speed. Extending the duration of a video clip is limited by the duration of the source clip. Reducing video clip duration excludes frames at the edge you drag.

2 Drag the right edge of the first clip (Live Stream) to 10:00 (ten seconds and zero frames) on the time ruler. Because the clip starts at 0:00, ending it at 10:00 sets its duration to 10:00. As you drag, the clip End time and Duration display next to the pointer so that you can see when it's time to release the mouse button.

3 Repeat step 2 with all other tracks so that they all end at 10:00.

Adding to a video group

Tip: By default, the work area is set to the end of the track that plays the longest. For this timeline that works well, but if you want to trim the work area to a shorter duration, drag the work area end marker to the time when you want the work area to end.

In Photoshop, video exists in a special layer type called a *video group*, which makes it possible to arrange video and still content as a sequence in time. When you created this video timeline, each layer was converted into a video group. You'll add video clips to the Arch layer.

1 Click the Video menu in the Arch track, and choose New Video Group.

Video Group 1 appears above the Arch track. Video Group 1 is empty for now.

Tip: All of the clips you add in step 4 are video, but in your own projects, you can select a mix of video and still image files.

2 Click the Video menu in the Video Group 1 track, and choose Add Media.

3 Navigate to the Lesson11 folder, and open the Media folder.

4 Shift-select the video assets numbered 1–3, and click Open.

Photoshop imports all three of the assets you selected onto the Video Group 1 track, in sequence. The Timeline displays video clips with a blue background, unlike the purple background of still content. The total duration of Video Group 1 is longer than 10 seconds, but you'll change that soon. First you'll delete the still Arch layer, which is no longer needed.

5   In the Layers panel, select the Arch layer, and click the Delete Layer button (🗑) at the bottom of the panel. Click Yes to confirm the deletion.

Note: If the media appear in reverse order in the timeline, choose Edit > Undo, and when you choose Add Media again, make sure you select 1-Ship.mp4 first and then Shift-select 3-Temple.mp4. Also, it will be easiest to Shift-select the media if the files are sorted by name. It's normal for the media to appear in reverse order in the Layers panel, where the bottom layer is considered the first.

6   If the playhead isn't at the beginning of the time ruler, click the Go To First Frame button (⏮).

7   Click the Play button (▶) to see how the sequence looks so far.

In this lesson, when you're asked to play the timeline, play it from the beginning as you did in this step so that you can evaluate the entire 10 seconds.

8   Choose File > Save.

Adding audio

Before you adjust the clip durations in Video Group 1, you'll import a music clip that plays for the entire duration of the sequence. The audio needs to be added now, because you'll sync clip durations to key points in the music.

1   Click the musical-note icon at the end of the Audio Track header, and choose Add Audio.

2   In the Lesson 11/Media folder, select the file Music.mp3, and click Open.

3   Play the timeline from the beginning.

▶ **Tip:** You can also add an audio track by clicking the + sign at the far-right end of the track in the Timeline panel.

The audio file is longer than the timeline duration, so you'll shorten it to match. Playing it back revealed that it's the end of a song, so you'll edit it from its beginning.

▶ Tip: Sometimes it's more convenient to chop off part of a clip instead of shortening it. To do that, move the playhead to the time where you want to slice a clip, select the clip, and click the Split at Playhead tool (✂) in the Timeline panel. You can then delete the unwanted portion.

4 Drag the left edge of the Music clip in the Audio Track until the Duration next to the pointer says 10:00. The audio clip remains anchored to the start of the sequence, so its end now matches up with the rest of the timeline at 10 seconds.

▶ Tip: If a video clip contains audio that you don't want to hear, enable the Mute Audio option in the Audio panel for that clip.

5 Click the small triangle at the right edge of the audio clip to open the Audio panel. Then enter **0.25** seconds for Fade In and **0.5** seconds for Fade Out.

▶ Tip: You can also close the Audio panel by pressing Enter or Return.

6 Click an empty area of the Timeline panel to close the Audio panel.

Changing clip durations in a video group

● Note: All content in the same video group plays in sequence. If you want to add video clips or still images that play at the same time as others, such as B-roll clips, add them to a different video group.

The clips on Video Track 1 need to be timed to cut from one to the other at chord changes in the music. As you might have noticed when playing back to hear the audio track, they are not currently synced up with chord changes, so you'll adjust their timing.

1 Play the timeline, and notice when the music changes. The first chord change is at 02:00, and the second is at 05:00.

2 Drag the right edge of the first clip (1-Ship) until the End time is 02:00. Notice that the End time and Duration are both displayed in the preview that appears as you drag the edge.

3 Drag the right edge of the second clip (2-Shrine) until the End time is 5:00.

The last video clip extends beyond the end of the sequence, so trim its end.

4 Drag the right edge of the third clip (3-Temple) until the End time is 10:00. You may have to scroll the Timeline panel or adjust its magnification to see the end.

5 Play the timeline to check your work, and then save the file.

Animating with keyframes

Keyframes let you control animation, effects, and other changes that happen over time. A keyframe marks a point in time where you can make a layer look a certain way, such as setting its position, size, or opacity. Creating a change over time requires at least two keyframes: one for the state at the beginning of the change and one for the state at the end. Photoshop interpolates the values for the positions in between so that the change happens gradually over time. You'll use keyframes to create the layer animations you saw in the 11End.psd file.

All layers are currently in position for the last frame of the video, so for each layer you'll animate, it's easiest to begin by adding a keyframe at that time. Then you'll add another keyframe at the time that layer starts animating to set how it looks then.

Animating position (moving a layer over time)

You'll start by animating the Live Stream layer and then the colored rectangles. The Live Stream layer needs to start moving at 04:00 so that it takes one second to slide in and arrive at its final position at 5:00. To do that, you'll set two keyframes.

1 Move the playhead to 05:00, the time of the last chord change in the music.

2 Click the triangle next to the name of the Live Stream track to expand its properties, and click the stopwatch icon (⏱) next to the Vector Mask Position property to set an initial keyframe for the layer.

The keyframe appears as a yellow diamond, indicating that it's selected. A hollow keyframe indicates that it isn't selected. Now you'll add the second keyframe.

▶ **Tip:** As you adjust the duration of one clip in a video group, the clips after it shift so that there is no gap in the sequence. You can override this by dragging any clip along the timeline.

▶ **Tip:** As you work in a timeline, keep in mind that what you see on the canvas depends on where the playhead is in time.

▶ **Tip:** Photoshop displays the playhead's current time in the lower-left corner of the Timeline panel.

● **Note:** For the Live Stream track, Vector Mask Position is animated because it's a vector shape layer. For pixel layers and video clips you would animate position using the Position property instead. For editable type layers and Smart Objects, you'd animate the Transform property.

3 Move the playhead to 04:00.

▶ **Tip:** Dragging layers in this lesson may be easier if you disable Auto-Select in the options bar for the Move tool.

4 Select the Move tool (⊕), and then on the canvas, press the Shift key as you drag the Live Stream layer to the right until it's slightly beyond the canvas edge.

Photoshop creates a keyframe at the current time, recording the layer's position.

5 Play the timeline. The Live Stream layer should move into position by 05:00.

6 In the Timeline panel, click the triangle to the left of the Live Stream layer name to close its attributes, and then save your work.

▶ **Tip:** You can move to the next keyframe by clicking the right triangle next to the attribute (in this case, Transform) in the Timeline panel. Click the left triangle to move to the previous keyframe.

7 Animate the position of the two rectangles the same way: Repeat steps 1 through 6 to add their ending and starting keyframes, but use the following settings:

• For Rectangle A, set the playhead at 05:00, and click its Position property stopwatch icon to add the keyframe for its ending position. Move the playhead to 0:00, and then Shift-drag the Rectangle A layer to the right until it's slightly beyond the right canvas edge, creating the keyframe for its starting position.

- For Rectangle B, set the playhead at 05:00, and click its Position property stopwatch icon to add the keyframe for its ending position. Move the playhead to 0:00, and then Shift-drag the Rectangle B layer to the left until its left edge is aligned with the left canvas edge, creating the keyframe for its starting position.

8 Play the timeline. The two rectangles should enter the frame from opposite sides, pass each other, and end at their final positions.

Animating size

The 11End.psd file shows that the History 301 layer appears to zoom in. This is done by animating its size.

1 Move the playhead to 05:00, where all animations are planned to stop.

2 Click the triangle next to the History 301 track name to expand its properties.

You want to animate its scale (size), but no property of that type is available. One solution is to convert the layer to a Smart Object.

3 Make sure the History 301 track is selected, and then choose Layer > Smart Objects > Convert to Smart Object.

● **Note:** Different layer types (such as type layers, pixel layers, shape layers, and Smart Objects) may offer slightly different Timeline properties.

4 Expand the properties for the History 301 track, and now there is a Transform property, so click its stopwatch icon to create an initial keyframe at 05:00. The keyframe records the layer's current transform values, including its 100% scale.

5 Move the playhead to 00:00.

6 Choose Edit > Free Transform, and in the options bar, enter 1% in the W field, and then press Enter or Return twice (one to commit the value, and one to commit and exit Free Transform mode).

7 Play the timeline. The History 301 layer should grow until it reaches its final size.

Animating opacity

The final animation animates the opacity of the Paint layer. Its keyframe timing should sync with the Live Stream layer that arrives over it.

1 Move the playhead to 05:00, where all animations are planned to stop.

2 Click the triangle next to the name of the Paint track to expand its properties, and click the stopwatch icon (⏱) next to the Opacity property to set an initial keyframe for the layer. The keyframe records the current 100% Opacity value.

3 Move the playhead to 04:00, and in the Layers panel, set the Opacity value to 0%. This creates a keyframe that records the 0% Opacity value.

4 Drag the playhead between 04:00 and 05:00 to see how the animation looks.

▶ **Tip:** You can add keyframes in any order. For this sequence, it was easier to add the first keyframes to the last frame because all of the layers were already in the correct states for the end of the video.

For each animated layer in this timeline, you added one keyframe at the end time of the animation, and one keyframe at the start. In your own work, you can create more complex animations by adding keyframes between the first and last ones.

Using Motion panel animation shortcuts

If you want to apply a quick animation such as a zoom, you might not need to add keyframes. Photoshop provides pre-built effects in the Motion panel, which you open by clicking the triangle at the top-right corner of a video clip. Five animation effects are available: Pan & Zoom, Pan, Zoom, Rotate, and Rotate & Zoom.

When a Motion panel effect is applied, you can customize it using the options in the Motion panel. Applying a Motion panel effect also adds keyframes to that clip, so if you want to customize the effect further, expand that clip's properties and edit the values at each keyframe as needed.

Adding transitions

You'll add a brief cross-fade transition between the first and second clips. Adding a transition is a simple drag-and-drop step.

1 Click the Transition button (▣) near the upper-left corner of the Timeline panel. Select Cross Fade, and change the Duration value to **.25 s** (a quarter of a second).

2 Drag the Cross Fade transition and drop it where the 1-Ship and 2-Shrine clips meet. A black rectangle appears when it's OK to drop it.

Note: At low Timeline magnifications, transition icons may be condensed into small rectangles. For better visibility and control of transitions, use the Timeline magnification slider to magnify the Timeline.

Photoshop adjusts the ends of the clips to apply the transition and adds a white transition icon in the lower-left corner of the second clip.

Notice that after adding the transition, Video Group 1 is no longer 10 seconds long. That's because adding an 0.25-second cross fade means the two clips must now overlap by 0.25 seconds to allow for the transition, so the following clips were shifted earlier in time by 0.25 seconds to create that overlap. This means the sequence edits might no longer sync to the music. You'll address this by adjusting the first edit by enough frames to make the sequence 10 seconds long again.

3   Select the 1-Ship layer, and position the pointer over the out point (end) of the clip, and when the out point indicator (⊕) appears, drag to the right until the Duration in the preview reads 2:08.

Note: For more control over transitions, use a video editing application such as Adobe Premiere Pro.

You release the mouse button when the duration becomes 2:08 because the 0.25 second transition left the sequence 8 frames short of 10 seconds, so to compensate, you increased its duration from 2:00 to 2:08.

In this video group, you won't add a transition between the second and third clips because it's designed to be a straight cut synced with the dramatic last chord change in the music. In your own projects, you can drop a transition at each edit between clips. You can also fade from black at the beginning of the sequence by adding a Fade With Black transition to the start of the first clip, or fade to black using the same transition at the end of the last clip.

4   Play back the entire sequence, making sure that you're satisfied with the timing.

5   If you think any of the edit timings or animations could be improved, make those changes, and save the document.

Rendering the timeline as a finished video file

You're ready to render the timeline contents as a single file in a video format that others can play. Rendering video can involve many complex options, but Photoshop simplifies this by offering appropriate presets for different types of video delivery, such as YouTube. Just choose the right preset to set many options correctly.

1   Choose File > Export > Render Video, or click the Render Video button (↷) in the lower-left corner of the Timeline panel.

2   Name the file **11Final.mp4**.

3 Click Select Folder, navigate to the Lesson11 folder, and click OK or Choose.

4 From the Preset menu, choose YouTube HD 1080p 29.97.

5 Click Render.

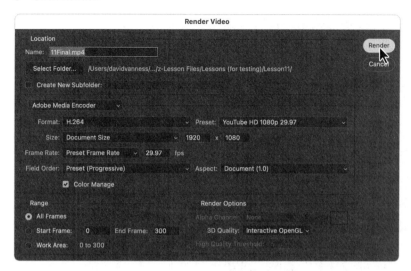

● **Note:** If the Preset menu doesn't list presets for YouTube, check the other menus in the Render Video dialog box. YouTube presets are available if the Format menu is set to H.264, and H.264 is available when the menu for that options group is set to Adobe Media Encoder (not Photoshop Image Sequence).

Photoshop displays a progress bar as it exports the video. Depending on your system, rendering the video may take several minutes.

6 Save your work.

7 Locate the 11Final.mp4 file in the Lesson11 folder in Bridge, and play back the video you made in Photoshop!

▶ **Tip:** To mark a range of frames to export, in the Timeline drag the work area start and end markers to the first and last frames to export, respectively. Then, in the Render Video dialog box, select Work Area in the Range options.

 Rendering a video is more demanding than exporting a still image, so rendering takes less time on newer or more powerful computers.

Extra credit: Frame animation

In this lesson, you use the Timeline panel in Video Timeline mode to animate using keyframes. Frame Animation mode is also available: You animate frame by frame, similar to hand-painting each frame in old film animations. One typical use is to make a looping GIF animation for a website.

1   In the Lesson11 folder, open the Frame Animation folder, open the file 11Frames_Start.psd, and save it as 11Frames_Working.psd. You'll animate this Photoshop design to match the 11Frames_End.psd and 11Frames_End.gif files in the same folder.

2   In the Timeline panel, click the arrow next to the Create Video Timeline button, choose Create Frame Animation, and then click the Create Frame Animation button. The timeline converts the document into a timeline with one frame. You'll soon add more.

3   In the Layers panel, hide the Vinyl layer. Later you'll make it appear in the last frame.

4   In the Timeline panel, click the Duplicates Selected Frame button (⊞). A copy appears.

A. Convert between video timeline and frame animation
B. Playback controls
C. Tweens Animation Frames
D. Duplicates Selected Frames
E. Deletes Selected Frames

5   With Frame 2 selected, on the canvas, use the Move tool to drag the LP Record layer group down to hide most of it.

6   In the Timeline panel menu, choose Reverse Frames. Click each frame to view it.

7   Select the second frame, and click the Tweens Animation Frames button. For Tween With, choose Previous Frame. For Frames to Add, enter **10**. Make sure All Layers is selected, and click OK. Tweening creates 10 new frames that fill in the changes to the LP Record layer group position.

8   Select the last frame in the timeline, and in the Layers panel, show the Vinyl layer.

9   Play the timeline. The animation loops too quickly. Stop playback.

10 Click the time delay menu under the last frame, and choose 5.0 seconds to hold that frame.

11 Choose File > Save a Copy, name it 11_Final.gif, and navigate to the Frame Animation folder. For Format choose GIF, click Save, and click OK in the GIF Save Options dialog box.

12 Play back 11_Final.gif using Bridge or a web browser.

Tips for working with video in Photoshop

Here are a few more ways to create the video you want by using Photoshop efficiently.

Verify the frame size. If the video must fit a specific type of screen, such as a standard high-definition television, choose Image > Canvas Size or Image > Image Size, and make sure the frame dimensions in pixels are correct before you start editing or animating a Photoshop document. In the New Document dialog box, the Film & Video presets offer standard video frame sizes.

Adjusting video clip size. If a video clip is too large or small, resize it using the same methods you use for non-video layers: Choose Edit > Free Transform, and edit using the handles or the options bar.

Adjusting video clip appearance. You can edit the tone and color of a video clip in the Layers panel using the same features you've used for non-video layers, such as adjustment layers and layer styles. To apply an effect such as a filter, you might first need to convert the video layer to a Smart Object. Photoshop can't animate adjustment layers or effects; use a video editing application to do that.

"Cropping" a video. To hide parts of a video, apply a mask of any shape to it in the Layers panel.

Creating a picture-in-picture effect. To superimpose one video over another, put the superimposed video in a separate video group higher up in the Layers panel stack. If they're the same size, then the upper clip will cover the lower clip, so either reduce the size of the upper clip or add a mask to it.

Creating a time-lapse video. On the desktop, fill a folder with images with filenames numbered in sequence. In Photoshop, choose File > Open, select the first image in the folder, and select Image Sequence, and all of the folder's images import as a single video in the Timeline.

Animation presets. You might not have to manually set up keyframes for common animations such as panning, zooming, and rotating, because presets for those effects are included in the Motion panel. See the sidebar "Using Motion panel animation shortcuts" in this lesson.

More features in menus. Although many video features are visible in the Timeline panel, you'll find more in the Timeline panel menu and in the Layer > Video Layers submenu.

Review questions

1 What are keyframes, and how do you use them to create an animation?

2 How do you add a transition between clips?

3 How do you render a video?

Review answers

1 A keyframe marks the point in time where you specify a value, such as a position, size, or style. To create a change over time, you must have at least two keyframes: one for the state at the beginning of the change and one for the state at the end. To create an initial keyframe, click the stopwatch icon next to the attribute you want to animate for the layer. When you change the value of that attribute at a different playhead time position, Photoshop creates a new keyframe to record the change at that time.

2 To add a transition, click the Transition button near the upper-left corner of the Timeline panel, and then drag a transition onto a clip.

3 To render a video, choose File > Export > Render Video, or click the Render Video button in the lower-left corner of the Timeline panel. Then select the video settings that are appropriate for the online service or device on which you'll show the video.

12 WORKING WITH CAMERA RAW

Lesson overview

In this lesson, you'll learn how to do the following:

- Open a camera raw image in Adobe Camera Raw.

- Adjust tone and color in a raw image.

- Sharpen an image in Camera Raw.

- Synchronize settings across multiple images.

- Retouch a portrait in Camera Raw using masked adjustments.

 This lesson will take about 90 minutes to complete. To get the lesson files used in this chapter, download them from the web page for this book at peachpit.com/PhotoshopCIB2024. For more information, see "Accessing the lesson files and Web Edition" in the Getting Started section at the beginning of this book.

As you work on this lesson, you'll preserve the start files. If you need to restore the start files, download them from your Account page.

PROJECT: ADVANCED PHOTO RETOUCHING

Camera raw files give you greater flexibility, especially
for adjusting color and tone, when compared to editing
JPEG format files from a camera. You can tap into that
potential by using Adobe Camera Raw, an application
integrated with Photoshop and Bridge.

Getting started

In this lesson, you'll edit several digital images using Adobe Camera Raw, a plug-in application you can use from within Photoshop or Bridge. You'll use a variety of techniques to touch up and improve the appearance of digital photographs. You'll start by viewing the before and after images in Adobe Bridge.

1 Start Photoshop, and then simultaneously hold down Ctrl+Alt+Shift (Windows) or Command+Option+Shift (macOS) to restore the default preferences. (See "Restoring default preferences" on page 5.)

2 When prompted, click Yes to delete the Adobe Photoshop Settings file.

3 Choose File > Browse In Bridge to open Adobe Bridge.

4 In the Favorites panel in Bridge, click the Lessons folder. Then, in the Content panel, double-click the Lesson12 folder to open it.

5 Adjust the thumbnail slider, if necessary, so that you can see the thumbnail previews clearly. Then look at the 12A_Start.crw and 12A_End.psd files.

Note: If Bridge isn't installed, the File > Browse In Bridge command in Photoshop will start the Creative Cloud desktop app, which will download and install Bridge. After installation completes, you can start Bridge.

Note: We used Adobe Camera Raw 16, which was the current version at the time of publication. Adobe updates Camera Raw frequently; if you're using a later version, some of the steps in this lesson may not match what you see. Also, if you have used an earlier version of Camera Raw, note that the user interface was significantly redesigned in version 12.3.

12A_Start.crw.

12A_End.psd.

The original photograph of a Spanish-style church is a camera raw file, so it doesn't have the usual .psd or .jpg file extension you've worked with so far in this book. It was shot with a Canon SLR camera, and its document uses the Canon proprietary .crw file extension. You'll process this camera raw image to make it brighter, sharper, and clearer, and then save it both as a JPEG file for the web and as a PSD file so that you can work on it further in Photoshop.

6   Compare the 12B_Start.nef and 12B_End.psd thumbnail previews.

12B_Start.nef.   12B_End.psd.

This time, the start file was taken with a Nikon camera, and the raw image has an .nef extension. You'll perform color corrections and image enhancements in Camera Raw and Photoshop to achieve the end result.

About camera raw files

Many digital cameras can save images in *camera raw* format. A camera raw file contains unprocessed picture data from a digital camera's image sensor, somewhat like undeveloped film. Raw sensor data is not yet converted to a standard multiple-channel color image file. It's still one unprocessed channel of sensor data, and in that form, it is not yet viewable as an image. You might then wonder: How can you view raw files, such as those included with this lesson, on the back of the camera and on your computer before you open them? The answer is that a camera typically saves a raw file with an embedded preview image that represents the camera's interpretation of the raw data.

Raw processing software such as Adobe Camera Raw interprets the unprocessed raw data into the multiple color channels (such as three RGB channels) that photo editing software such as Photoshop can edit. Camera raw files let you interpret the original image data in your own way, giving you more flexibility than when you edit a JPEG file saved by the camera with its interpretation of the raw data. You can use Adobe Camera Raw to make larger changes to white balance, tonal range, contrast, color saturation, noise reduction, and sharpening than you could if the raw data was already converted to RGB. You can reprocess a raw file at any time, without degrading the original image data.

To create camera raw files, set your digital camera to save files in raw format instead of JPEG format. A raw file has a manufacturer-specific filename extension such as .nef (from Nikon) or .crw (from Canon). In Bridge or Photoshop, you can process camera raw files from a myriad of supported digital cameras from Canon, Fuji, Leica, Nikon, and other makers. You can then export the proprietary camera raw files to DNG, JPEG, TIFF, or PSD file format.

Should you always capture camera raw images instead of JPEG images? If you want maximum editing flexibility, then yes. However, camera raw images require more space to store and more processing power to edit. If images from your camera don't need much editing, you can decide to capture and edit JPEG images instead.

Note: Camera raw files are typically unique to each camera model's sensor. If you have CRW files from three different Canon camera models and NEF files from three Nikon models, chances are those represent six different types of sensor data. If you buy a new camera, you might need an Adobe Camera Raw update that adds support for its specific raw data.

Processing files in Camera Raw

When you make adjustments to an image in Camera Raw, such as straightening or cropping the image, Photoshop and Bridge store your edits separately from the original file. You can edit the image as you desire, export an edited version, and keep the original intact for different or improved adjustments in the future.

Opening images in Camera Raw

Tip: You can open and edit TIFF and JPEG images in Camera Raw, if those formats are enabled in the File Handling preferences for Camera Raw. But those formats don't provide the same range of adjustments as a camera raw file.

You can open Camera Raw from either Bridge or Photoshop. You can edit multiple images in Camera Raw and apply the same edits to multiple files simultaneously. That's useful if you're working with images that were all shot in the same environment and therefore need similar adjustments.

Camera Raw provides extensive controls for adjusting white balance, exposure, contrast, sharpness, tone curves, and much more. In this exercise, you'll edit one image and then apply the settings to similar images.

1 In Bridge, open the Lessons/Lesson12/Mission folder, which contains three shots of the Spanish church you previewed earlier.

2 Shift-click to select all of the images—Mission01.crw, Mission02.crw, and Mission03.crw—and then choose File > Open In Camera Raw.

3 If a Welcome to Camera Raw 16.0 screen appears, click Get Started.

Both the Set Up Camera Raw and Welcome to Camera Raw 16.0 screens appear only the first time you start Camera Raw 16 or the first time after you reset Camera Raw preferences (which are separate from Photoshop preferences).

● Note: If a Set Up Camera Raw screen appears, make sure New ACR Default is selected, and click OK.

A. Filmstrip divider (drag to adjust)

B. Filmstrip

C. Fit and Zoom buttons, and magnification menu

D. Collapsible adjustments panels (in Edit mode; other modes display other options)

E. Histogram

F. Save a copy, with edits, of selected images

G. Camera Raw preference settings

H. Toggle Full Screen mode

I. Edit (image adjustments)

J. Crop & rotate

K. Healing

L. Masking (local) adjustments

M. Red Eye removal

N. Snapshots and Presets

O. More Image Settings menu

P. Zoom and Hand tools

Q. Toggle Sampler Overlay

R. Toggle Grid Overlay

S. Filmstrip, Sort, and Filter menus

T. Workflow preference settings

U. Rate, and mark for deletion

V. Before/After Views (click to cycle through options, click and hold for options)

W. Toggle between default and current settings

X. Exit and don't save changes

Y. Exit and save changes

Z. Exit, save changes, and open in Photoshop

4 If the photos appear in a vertical strip along the left side of the Adobe Camera Raw window, click and hold the filmstrip menu button (▦) and choose Horizontal from the menu that appears. This is so that the layout matches the figures in this lesson. If you prefer the vertical filmstrip, you may use it for your own work.

Note: If more than one image is selected in Camera Raw, in the filmstrip the thumbnails for the selected images display a gray border, and the currently previewed image displays a white border.

The Camera Raw dialog box displays a large preview of the selected image, and a filmstrip displays all open images. The histogram in the upper-right corner shows the tonal range of the selected image. The workflow options below the preview window control the selected image's color space, bit depth, size, and resolution, which you can click to change. Tools along the right side of the dialog box let you zoom, pan, crop, straighten, and make other adjustments to the image.

Note: When you first open a raw format image in Camera Raw, its appearance may seem to change. This is normal. Camera Raw renders a new preview using its settings, replacing the preview the camera generated from its settings.

In the default mode (Edit), Camera Raw displays a stack of collapsible panels under the histogram. You can expand individual panels to edit the selected image's color, tone, detail (sharpening and noise reduction); correct lens distortions; and more. You can also save settings as a preset so that you can apply them to other images.

The Camera Raw options within the Edit mode are intentionally organized so that you can get good results by using the tabbed panels from top to bottom. But it's okay to adjust the options in any order, and you don't have to adjust every option.

You will explore these controls now as you edit the first image file.

5 For this lesson it will be useful to see the filenames for each image. Click and hold the filmstrip menu button (▦), and choose Show Filenames.

Note: If the filmstrip disappears, it's because you clicked the filmstrip menu button instead of clicking and holding. Click it again to display the filmstrip.

6   Click each thumbnail in the filmstrip to preview each image before you begin. When you've seen all three, select the Mission01.crw image.

Choosing an Adobe Raw profile

An *Adobe Raw profile* affects how Camera Raw interprets the original raw data. This initial rendering is a visual starting point for the edits you make in Camera Raw. If the currently selected raw profile produces a look that's far from what you want, another raw profile may be a better starting point.

1   If the Profile panel isn't already displayed under the histogram, click the Edit button (⚞). The Profile panel is above the controls, so if it isn't visible, it might be scrolled out of view; scroll the panel stack until you can see the top.

2   Choose Adobe Landscape from the Profile menu.

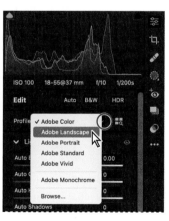

The default raw profile, Adobe Color, is good for general use. Adobe Landscape emphasizes colors in nature, like trees and skies, and is a better starting point for this image. The goal of the Adobe Portrait profile is a natural representation of skin tones, and Adobe Vivid adds punchy color contrast. Adobe Monochrome provides a high-quality conversion to black and white.

▶ **Tip:** You can also move among filmstrip images by pressing the Left Arrow or Right Arrow key. But if you clicked an option's field to edit its value, arrow keys move within the text, so add the Ctrl (Windows) or Command (macOS) key to view other images (for example, press Ctrl/Command-Right Arrow).

▶ **Tip:** If you want the image to look more like the preview generated by the camera, click the Browse Profiles icon to the right of the Profile menu, scroll down to see the list of profile categories, and try a profile from the Camera Matching category.

● **Note:** Adobe Raw profiles are different than the ICC color profiles used by your display or printer. Raw profiles affect only how camera raw data is converted to a conventional image.

▶ **Tip:** You can use Creative profiles to apply a visual style to an image. Click the Browse Profiles icon (▤) to the right of the Profile menu, scroll down to see the list of profile categories (such as Artistic, B&W, Modern, and Vintage), select one, and then click Back.

Adjusting white balance

An image's white balance represents the color conditions under which it was captured. A digital camera records the white balance at the time of exposure; this is the value that initially appears in the Camera Raw dialog box image preview.

White balance comprises two components. The first is *temperature*, which is measured in kelvins and determines the level of "coolness" or "warmth" of the image—that is, its cool blue-green tones or warm yellow-red tones. The second component is *tint*, which compensates for magenta or green color casts.

Depending on the settings you're using on your camera and the environment in which you're shooting (for example, with artificial light or mixed light sources), you may want to adjust the white balance for the image.

By default, As Shot is selected in the White Balance menu, applying the white balance settings that were in your camera at the time of exposure. If you think you could improve on the current white balance setting, Camera Raw includes other White Balance presets that you can try.

1 If you can't see White Balance options under the Profile menu, click the Color panel heading to expand it.

2 Choose Cloudy from the White Balance menu.

▶ **Tip:** Adjusting white balance is easiest when there is only one light source. When a scene is lit by multiple light sources with different color characteristics, you may have to manually choose a white balance setting and also make masked color corrections over specific areas.

Camera Raw adjusts the temperature and tint for a cloudy day. Sometimes a preset is an instant fix. In this case, though, the image still has a color cast. You'll adjust the white balance manually.

3 Select the White Balance tool (✐) to the right of the White Balance menu.

To set an accurate white balance, select an object that should be white or gray. The spot where you click becomes a reference for neutral white balance; Camera Raw shifts the image colors accordingly.

4 Click the white clouds in the image. The color balance of the image changes.

5 Click a different area of the clouds. The color balance shifts again, because that area of the clouds has slightly different color values.

To find the best color balance quickly and easily, click the White Balance tool on an area that should be neutral. Clouds are not always a neutral color, depending on the weather and time of day. In Camera Raw, clicking different areas changes color balance without altering the original image file, so you can experiment freely.

6 Click the white area of the small sign in front of the church. This removes most of the color casts.

▶ **Tip:** Clicking a known neutral area, such as the sign in step 6, applies White Balance values that result in a neutral image, with unwanted color casts removed. You are then free to use options such as White Balance expressively. For example, apply a higher Temperature value to make a scene appear shot closer to sunset, or simply to evoke a warmer mood.

Tip: To toggle between current and default settings with the keyboard, press the backslash (\) key. To cycle through the Before/After Views menu, press Q.

7   To see the changes you've made, click and hold the Before/After Views button (■.) at the bottom of the window, and choose Before/After Left/Right from the pop-up menu. (If you only click without holding, it cycles to the next option.)

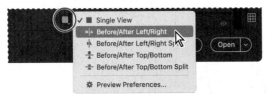

Tip: To expand Camera Raw to fill the screen, click the Toggle Full Screen Mode button (↙↗) near the top-right corner of the window, or press F.

Camera Raw displays the Before image on the left and the After image on the right so you can compare them.

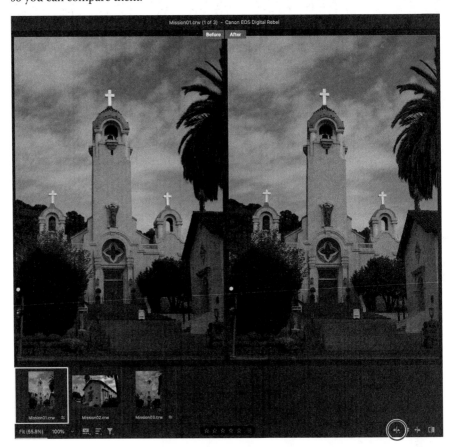

8   To see only the After image again, click and hold the Before/After Views menu and choose Single View. Or, if you prefer, you can leave both views visible so you can see how the image changes as you continue to alter it.

Making basic tonal adjustments in Camera Raw

The group of options in the Light panel affects how tones are distributed from dark to light in the image. Except for Contrast, moving a slider to the right lightens the areas of the image that it affects, and moving it to the left darkens those areas. Exposure sets the overall brightness of the image. The Highlights and Shadows options control detail in near-white and near-black tones, respectively. The Whites option defines the *white point*, or the lightest tone of the image; tones above its value are made white. Conversely, the Blacks option sets the *black point*, or the darkest tone in the image; tones above its value are made black.

Dragging the Contrast slider to the right moves darker and lighter midtones away from the midtone; dragging left moves those tones toward the midtone. In the Effects panel, you can use the Clarity and Texture sliders to apply more nuanced adjustments to local contrast, but these options are best used sparingly.

Tip: To apply Clarity properly, increase the Clarity slider until you see halos near the edge details, and then reduce the setting until the halos are not distracting.

In the Color panel, the Saturation option adjusts the intensity of all colors in the image equally. The Vibrance option is often more useful because it has a greater effect on undersaturated colors. For example, you can use Vibrance to bring life to an image without oversaturating any skin tones in it.

Now you'll try some basic adjustments to the selected image.

1 Click Auto at the top of the Edit mode panel stack.

Tip: Clicking Auto again toggles between default settings and Auto settings.

The Auto button changes several settings in the Light and Color panels, and the image is greatly improved. Auto correction may produce a useful image right away, because it's based on advanced Adobe Sensei machine learning technology, which is trained using a wide variety of professionally corrected sample images. This makes Auto a quick way to reach a good starting point for your own edits. If you like the results, you can study and learn from the adjustments made by Auto. You can choose to keep some Auto adjustments and change others. Or you can enter your own adjustments, as you are about to do.

Tip: When adjusting tones, watch out for highlight or shadow clipping (loss of detail from over-adjustment). One way to preview clipping is to hold down the Alt (Windows) or Option (macOS) key while dragging a slider for Exposure, Highlights, Shadows, Whites, or Blacks. When Alt/Option-dragging those sliders, pixels are OK if they appear black (for Exposure, Highlights, and Whites) or white (for Shadows and Blacks); otherwise, they are clipped.

2 In the Light panel, set the options as follows:

- Exposure: **+0.50**

- Contrast: **+0**

- Highlights: -**20**

- Shadows: **+70**

- Whites: **+20**

- Blacks: **−10**

3 In the Color panel set Vibrance to **+20**, and in the Effects panel, set Clarity to **+20**:

These settings brighten the image, especially the dark shadow areas, and boost color without oversaturating it. The Shadows option helps open up the dark foliage.

Tip: Expanding a panel collapses others, by default. You can keep multiple panels open simultaneously, as shown in the figure for step 3. To enable that, right-click (Windows) or Control-click (macOS) any panel heading, and choose Multiple Panel Mode. This makes better use of a large display.

About adjusting color in Adobe Camera Raw

If you capture a raw image properly in camera, in Adobe Camera Raw you may not need to do much more than apply an appropriate raw profile, White Balance setting, and Auto correction. When you need to solve more complex color issues in a camera raw file, performing major color edits in Camera Raw can be more forgiving and better preserve original image quality compared to making those edits in Photoshop. Adobe Camera Raw offers a wide range of advanced color controls:

Masked adjustment tools. To apply different color or tone settings to specific areas of an image, click the Masking icon. To save time, Camera Raw offers some automatically generated masks, such as Select Subject, Select Sky, Select Background, and Select People. For more information, see the sidebar "About Camera Raw mask types" later in this lesson.

Curve panel. Like Curves in Photoshop, you can use the Curve panel in Camera Raw to edit each color channel separately, adjusting the amount of a color channel at any level from black to white. This is one way to compensate for color casts that vary across highlights, midtones, and shadows.

Color Mixer panel. The Color Mixer panel lets you adjust specific preset colors by hue, saturation, or luminance. When you click the B&W button at the top of the Edit mode panel stack, you can use the Color Mixer to customize a color to black-and-white conversion similar to how you did in Photoshop at the end of Lesson 2.

Color Grading panel. In the Color Grading panel you can use color wheels to adjust the hue, saturation, and luminance separately for midtones, shadows, and highlights. This type of tool is familiar to video editors. Although you can use it for color correction, conventional color grading is typically a creative step applied after color correction to create an expressive color palette for a "look" or for split toning effects.

Custom raw profiles. It's possible to use Photoshop to create a custom color lookup table (color LUT or CLUT). A color LUT can be the basis for your own creative profile that you can apply with one click in the Camera Raw profile browser.

Calibration panel. The Calibration panel adjusts the fundamental color conversion from camera raw format, which affects the range of adjustment that's possible with the rest of the panel. Today, raw profiles are a more convenient way to tune that conversion, so now the Calibration panel tends to be used as a creative option for altering color relationships within an image.

Point Color panel. Point Color offers precise control over the hue, saturation, and luminance ranges of both a color you sample and your adjustments to it. You can sample and alter multiple colors per adjustment.

These tools are outside the scope of this book, but when you are in Photoshop (not Camera Raw), you can learn more about them in the Search panel (Edit > Search), which also contains interactive tutorials and help documents.

About the Camera Raw histogram

Tip: Indications of clipped shadows or highlights don't always mean you've overcorrected an image. For example, a clipped specular highlight (such as a reflection of the sun or a studio light on metal) is acceptable, because a specular highlight has no detail to lose.

The histogram in the upper-right corner of the Camera Raw dialog box simultaneously shows the red, green, and blue channels of the selected image and updates interactively as you adjust settings. As you move any tool over the preview image, the RGB values for the area under the pointer appear in the histogram. Selecting the icons at the top corners enables image overlays that indicate clipping. A red overlay marks clipped highlight detail, and blue marks clipped shadow detail.

Tip: Sharpening enhances the finest details of an image. The Clarity option in the Effects panel can help emphasize relatively large details. The Texture slider can bring out details that are between the size ranges handled by Sharpening and Clarity. Texture is typically best applied to specific areas using a masked adjustment tool to avoid emphasizing noise in broad areas.

Applying sharpening

Photoshop offers several ways to sharpen, but when an image is in raw format, it's good to apply basic sharpening in the Detail panel in Camera Raw. To see the best preview of sharpening, view the image at 100% or greater magnification.

1 Click the Zoom Levels menu (⌄) near the bottom-left corner of the window, and choose 100%. Then select the Hand tool (✋), and drag the image preview to pan (slide) it down until you see the cross at the top of the mission tower.

2 In the Edit mode panel stack under the histogram, scroll down until you see the Detail panel, and click its heading to expand it.

Tip: You can use keyboard shortcuts to go to each Edit panel directly to avoid scrolling. Press the Ctrl (Windows) or Command (macOS) key along with a number key; the panels are numbered from the Light panel down. For example, the Effects panel is the third one, so to open it press Ctrl-3 (Windows) or Command-3 (macOS).

The Sharpening option determines how much Camera Raw emphasizes fine details. One approach is to exaggerate the Sharpening value at first to more easily see the effect of other sharpening options, and after those settings are tuned, reduce the Sharpening value back down to a more realistic level.

3 Change the Sharpening value to **100**.

4 Click the disclosure triangle above the right end of the Sharpening slider to reveal more options.

Many Camera Raw features have advanced options that are hidden to save space. If you see a disclosure triangle along the right side, you know there are more options available there if you need them.

5 Change the Radius value to **0.9**.

The Radius option determines how far out from a pixel that sharpening is applied. For properly focused images without motion blur, a Radius value of 1 pixel works well to start. You might decrease the Radius value for images with fine details that are precisely focused or increase Radius to help sharpen blurred details.

6 Change the Detail value to **25**, unless it's already set that way.

The Detail option controls the balance between sharpening edges and textures for images with fine details. Lower values draw sharpening toward edges leaving broad areas smoother; higher values can bring out textures in broad areas.

7 Change the Masking value to **61**.

The Masking slider is similar to the Detail slider in that it helps keep sharpening constrained along content edges, but Masking is more generally useful because it isn't just for fine details. A higher Masking value makes it easier to increase the Sharpening value without oversharpening noise and textures in broad areas of the image that should look smooth, such as a face or the sky. Lower the Masking value when you want Sharpening to emphasize details in broad areas, such as the weave of threads in fabric.

Tip: Want to see what Masking is actually doing? Press Alt (Windows) or Option (macOS) as you drag the Masking slider. White indicates areas Camera Raw will sharpen; black areas will be left alone.

After you've adjusted the Radius, Detail, and Masking sliders, you can lower the Sharpening slider to a more reasonable final value.

8 Decrease the Sharpening slider to **70**.

Camera Raw doesn't save changes into an original raw file, because raw files are intended to be read-only. Your Camera Raw edits are saved in XMP format "sidecar" files that are stored in the same folder as the original file and have the same base filename with an .xmp filename extension. If you also added masked (local) adjustments, you may also see an .acr sidecar file with the same base filename. When you move a raw image edited in Adobe Camera Raw to another computer or storage medium, be sure to move its XMP file (and ACR file, if present) with it. Adobe Camera Raw can include edits in the same file as the raw image when exporting to the open Adobe DNG raw format.

Synchronizing settings across images

All three of the church images were shot at the same time under the same lighting conditions. Now that you've made the first one look great, you can automatically apply the same settings to the other two images using the Synchronize command.

1 Click and hold the filmstrip menu button (▣), and choose Select All to select all of the images in the filmstrip.

2 Click and hold the filmstrip menu button again, and choose Sync Settings.

The Synchronize dialog box appears, listing all the settings you can apply to the images. By default, all options except Geometry, Crop, Healing, and Masking are selected. For this project, you can accept the default selections, even though you didn't change all the settings.

3 Click OK in the Synchronize dialog box.

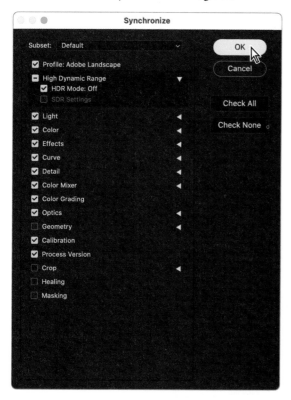

● **Note:** A yellow alert triangle may temporarily appear over a preview or thumbnail image while Camera Raw is synchronizing settings to that image. When the triangle goes away, the preview or thumbnail is up to date.

When you synchronize the settings across all of the selected images, the thumbnails update to reflect the changes you made. To review the changed images, click each thumbnail in the filmstrip.

● **Note:** It's always a good idea to review images altered by synchronizing settings. Some images may have slight variations in tone and color that may require a few more minor adjustments.

Saving Camera Raw changes as new files

Many applications don't read raw files, so before sharing them, it's typically necessary to save them in a more common image file format. First, you'll save the images with adjustments as low-resolution JPEG files that you can share on the web. Then, you'll save one image, Mission01, as a Photoshop file that you can open as a Smart Object in Photoshop. When you open an image as a Smart Object in Photoshop, you can return to Camera Raw at any time to make further adjustments.

1 In the Camera Raw dialog box, click the filmstrip menu button, and choose Select All to make sure all three images are selected.

2 Click the Convert And Save Selected Images button (⬆) near the top-right corner of the Camera Raw window.

3 In the Save Options dialog box, do the following:

- Choose Save In Same Location from the Destination menu.

- In the File Naming area, leave "Document Name" in the first box.

- Choose JPEG from the Format menu, and set the Quality level to High (8–9).

- In the Color Space area, choose sRGB IEC61966-2.1 from the Space menu.

- In the Image Sizing area, select Resize To Fit, and then choose Long Side from the Resize To Fit menu.

- In the field below Resize to Fit, enter **800** pixels. This will set the long side of an image to 800 pixels whether it's a portrait (tall) or landscape (wide) image. When you choose Long Side, the dimension of the short side will automatically be adjusted proportionally.

- Type **72** pixels/inch for the Resolution value.

These settings will save your corrected images as smaller, downsampled JPEG files, which you can share with colleagues on the web. They'll be resized so that most viewers won't need to scroll to see the entire image when it opens. Your files will be named Mission01.jpg, Mission02.jpg, and Mission03.jpg.

4 Click Save.

▶ **Tip:** If your images contain metadata that you consider private, you can restrict what metadata is included when you save copies from Camera Raw. For example, if your images contain camera information, keywords such as names of people, a copyright notice, and other metadata you entered in Bridge, choose Copyright Only from the Metadata menu to include only the copyright notice.

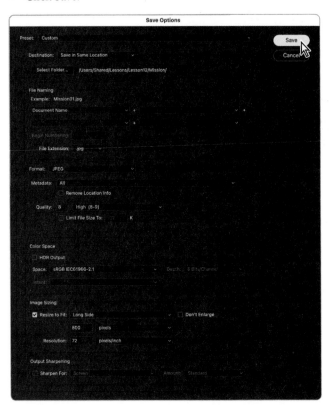

In the Camera Raw dialog box, a readout in the bottom-left corner indicates how many images have been processed until all the images have been saved. The CRW thumbnails still appear in the Camera Raw dialog box. However, in the Mission folder, you now also have JPEG versions as well as the original raw image files, which you can continue to edit or leave for another time.

Now you'll open a copy of the Mission01 image in Photoshop.

5   Select the Mission01.crw image thumbnail in the filmstrip in the Camera Raw dialog box. Then click the menu of options to the right of the Open button, and choose Open as Object. Close any messages that appear about new features.

Note: If you see a message that says "Skip loading optional and third-party plug-ins?" click No. The message appears if the Shift key is held down when Photoshop starts up.

The Open as Object button opens the image as a Smart Object layer in Photoshop: Instead of converting the camera raw file to Photoshop format, the Smart Object preserves it in camera raw format inside the Photoshop document. This lets you continue making raw-based adjustments at any time, by double-clicking the Smart Object thumbnail in the Layers panel to open Camera Raw. If, instead, you had clicked Open, the image would be permanently converted into a normal Photoshop layer, and no more raw format edits would be possible.

Tip: To change the Open button so that it's always an Open Object button, click the underlined workflow options link at the bottom of the Camera Raw dialog box, select Open In Photoshop As Smart Object, and click OK.

Note: If Photoshop displays a dialog box telling you about the difference between saving to Cloud Documents and On Your Computer, click Save On Your Computer. You can also select Don't Show Again, but that setting will deselect after you reset Photoshop preferences.

6   In Photoshop, choose File > Save As. In the Save As dialog box, choose Photoshop for the format, rename the file **Mission_Final.psd**, navigate to the Lesson12 folder, and click Save. Click OK if the Photoshop Format Options dialog box appears. Then close the file.

A photographer for more than 25 years, Jay Graham began his career designing and building custom homes. Today, Graham has clients in the advertising, architectural, editorial, and travel industries.

See Jay Graham's portfolio on the web at jaygraham.com.

Pro photo workflow

Good habits make all the difference

A sensible workflow and good work habits will keep you enthused about digital photography, help your images shine, and save you from the night terrors of losing work you never backed up. Here's an outline of the basic workflow for digital images from a professional photographer with more than 25 years' experience. To help you get the most from the images you shoot, Jay Graham offers guidelines for setting up your camera, creating a basic color workflow, selecting file formats, organizing images, and showing off your work.

Graham uses Adobe Lightroom® Classic to organize thousands of images.

"The biggest complaint from people is they've lost their image. Where is it? What does it look like?" says Graham. "So naming is important."

Start out right by setting up your camera preferences
If your camera has the option, it's generally best to shoot in its camera raw file format, which captures all the image information you need. With one camera raw photo, says Graham, "you can go from daylight to an indoor tungsten image without degradation" when it's reproduced. If it makes more sense to shoot in JPEG for your project, use fine compression and high resolution.

Start with the best material
Get all the data when you capture—at fine compression and high resolution. You can't go back later.

Organize your files
Name your images as you import them into the Lightroom catalog. "If the camera names files, eventually it resets and produces multiple files with the same name," says Graham. Use Adobe Lightroom Classic to rename, rank, and add metadata to the photos you plan to keep; cull those you don't.

Graham names his files by date (and possibly subject). He would store a series of photos taken October 18, 2017, at Stinson Beach in a folder named 171018_stinson. Within the folder, he names each image incrementally; for example, the first image would be named 171018_stinson_01. This should result in a truly unique filename for each image. "That way, it lines up on the hard drive really easily," he says. Follow Windows naming conventions to keep filenames usable on non-Macintosh platforms (32 characters maximum; only numbers, letters, underscores, and hyphens).

Convert raw images to DNG
Consider converting your camera raw images to the DNG format. Unlike many cameras' proprietary raw formats, the specifications for this format are publicly available so that software developers and device makers can more easily support it.

Keep a master image
Save your master in PSD, TIFF, or DNG format, not JPEG. Each time a JPEG is re-edited and saved, compression is reapplied, and the image quality degrades.

Show off to clients and friends
When you prepare your work for delivery, choose the appropriate color file for the destination. Convert the image to that profile, rather than assigning the profile. sRGB is generally best for viewing electronically or for printing from most online printing services. Adobe 1998 and Colormatch are the best profiles to use for RGB images destined for traditionally printed materials such as brochures. Adobe 1998 and ProPhoto RGB are best for printing with inkjet printers. Use 72 dpi for electronic viewing and 180 dpi or higher for printing.

Back up your images
You've devoted a lot of time and effort to your images: Don't lose them. To protect your photos against a range of potential disasters, it's best to have backups on multiple media such as external storage and a cloud backup service, set to back up automatically. "The question is not if your [internal] hard drive is going to crash," says Graham, reciting a common adage. "It's when."

About saving files from Camera Raw to other formats

Note: The Camera Raw dialog box doesn't have a traditional Save command (remember, its Save button actually exports a copy of each selected image). Your changes are saved when you click Done or Open, but that closes Camera Raw. The Cancel button discards all changes made during a Camera Raw session, so take care not to click the Cancel button unless you really want to start over. Avoid pressing the Esc key, a shortcut for the Cancel button.

Most websites, applications, and social media apps can't read a camera raw file or its corresponding metadata file that contains image edits, keywords, and other information you added. One way to prepare a camera raw file for other applications is to click the Open button in Adobe Camera Raw so that the image opens in Photoshop, where you can save or export the file using Photoshop commands.

If you don't need to edit the image further using Photoshop features, you can skip the step of continuing on to Photoshop. In Camera Raw you can use the Convert And Save Image button (⬆) to convert selected images to the Adobe DNG, JPEG, TIFF, or PSD format, and save those images to new files in that format.

- The **DNG (Adobe Digital Negative)** format contains raw image data from a digital camera along with metadata that defines how the image data should look. DNG is intended to be an industry-wide standard format for raw image data, helping photographers manage the variety of proprietary raw formats and providing a compatible archival format. (You can save this format only from the Camera Raw dialog box.)

- The **JPEG (Joint Photographic Experts Group)** file format is commonly used to display photographs and other continuous-tone RGB images on the web. JPEG compresses file size by selectively discarding data, starting with the visual information that our eyes are least likely to notice. The greater the compression, the lower the image quality.

- **TIFF (Tagged Image File Format)** is a flexible format supported by virtually all paint, image-editing, and page layout applications. It can save Photoshop layers. TIFF images can also be produced by most applications that control image capture hardware such as scanners.

- **PSD format** is the Photoshop native file format. Because of the tight integration between Adobe products, other Adobe applications such as Adobe Illustrator, Adobe InDesign, and Adobe After Effects can directly import PSD files and preserve many Photoshop features.

- **JPEG XL** and **AVIF (AV1 Image File Format)** can preserve the additional tonal range available when using HDR editing. See the sidebar "About HDR and panoramas in Camera Raw" on page 309.

If you click the Open button in Camera Raw to convert and open a raw file in Photoshop, you can save a copy of or export it in the additional formats that Photoshop offers, including Large Document Format (PSB), Photoshop PDF, GIF, or PNG. You may also see the Photoshop Raw format (RAW), a specialized technical file format that is not commonly used by photographers and designers—do not confuse Photoshop Raw format with camera raw files.

For more information about file formats in Camera Raw and Photoshop, see Photoshop Help.

About HDR and panoramas in Camera Raw

When you select multiple images in Camera Raw, you can choose Merge To HDR or Merge To Panorama by clicking and holding the filmstrip menu button. HDR (high dynamic range) requires darker and lighter exposures of the same composition, while a panorama requires multiple exposures as tiles of a larger scene. Photoshop also has HDR merge and panorama features, but the Camera Raw versions are simpler, provide a preview, can process in the background, and produce a DNG file that you can edit in Camera Raw with the flexibility of a raw format image.

Comparing HDR Merge and HDR Editing

Camera Raw can work with HDR images in two ways:

HDR merge. You select multiple images of different exposures and merge them into one. The original dynamic range of the images is merged and mapped down to a standard dynamic range (SDR) image. This is the method used in the Merge To HDR command in Camera Raw. You can edit an HDR merge on any supported computer or device and export a copy to a commonly used file format such as JPEG.

HDR editing. You edit an image while preserving wider dynamic range than SDR supports, particularly in the highlights. Seeing this extra dynamic range requires graphics hardware that supports full range HDR, which is less common.

In Camera Raw, you enable HDR editing by clicking the HDR button (HDR) at the top of the Edit controls. Also, enabling the HDR button reveals additional options for editing and export (not covered in this lesson) that are necessary to properly monitor and export HDR edits. In Photoshop, HDR controls and monitoring are available when an image is set to Image > Mode > 32 Bits/Channel.

To preserve the extra dynamic range outside of Adobe Camera Raw or Photoshop, for further editing save the image in Photoshop or TIFF format at 32 bits per channel. For sharing, save a copy in JPEG XL or AVIF format. At the time this book was written, relatively few applications support still image HDR formats. Also, the dynamic range of print is so low compared to an HDR display that the full tonal range of HDR editing cannot be reproduced by ink on paper. The tonal range of HDR must be mapped or compressed within the dynamic range of the printing conditions.

HDR editing is an advanced workflow that's beyond the scope of this book, but it's important to understand the difference between an HDR merge to an SDR image, and the capabilities of HDR editing on HDR-capable graphics hardware.

For more information, see the Adobe article High Dynamic Range Explained: blog.adobe.com/en/publish/2023/10/10/hdr-explained.

Retouching a portrait in Camera Raw

The image editing features in Camera Raw are deep enough that it's possible to perform most correction tasks at the raw level, using Photoshop only when you need to do more advanced retouching or masking. When you don't need to continue on to Photoshop, you can simply save finished images directly from Camera Raw. You'll use a range of Camera Raw tools to improve a raw image of a bride.

Making initial corrections

The default rendering of the raw image uses the Adobe Color profile and has a slight color cast. You'll get started by correcting both.

1 In Bridge, navigate to the Lesson12 folder. Select the 12B_Start.nef file, and choose File > Open In Camera Raw.

▶ **Tip:** You can try other profiles to see if they work better. For this image, Adobe Color produces a similar result to Adobe Portrait, but other profiles may be too garish or contrasty for skin tones.

2 In the Edit options, choose Adobe Portrait from the Profile menu to apply a more portrait-friendly initial rendering.

3 In the Color panel in Camera Raw, select the White Balance tool (🖉), and then click a white area in the model's dress to remove a green color cast.

▶ **Tip:** It may work better to click a white area of the dress that is directly lit rather than in shade. The white balance of a neutral area facing the light source is more likely to be consistent with the white balance of the light source. A neutral area in shadow might be shifted by the color of light reflected by nearby surfaces.

4   Click the filmstrip menu button (📇) to hide it. With only one file open, you don't need to use the filmstrip. Hiding it frees up more space for viewing the image.

5   In the Edit options, click Auto.

The Auto corrections improve the image; the automatic Highlights adjustment reveals more detail in the white dress and lace hair piece. However, some of the changes go too far, so you'll edit certain settings.

6   Adjust specific Light panel options:

- Double-click the slider control for Exposure to reset its value to **0**. Double-clicking is a shortcut for resetting an option to its default value.

- Set Contrast to **–20**.

7   In the Effects panel, set Clarity to **+8**.

▶ **Tip:** Be careful when applying Clarity or Texture to a portrait. Higher values may emphasize skin texture and surface characteristics such as freckles and wrinkles. Apply higher Clarity and Texture values only to specific areas, by using the masked adjustment tools covered later.

Using the Content-Aware Remove tool to correct blemishes

▶ **Tip:** In Lesson 2, you used the Spot Healing Brush and Patch tool in Photoshop. Camera Raw offers similar Healing tools when you want to make similar edits at the raw editing stage.

Now you're ready to give the model's face some focused attention. You'll use the Content-Aware Remove tool to hide blemishes and smooth the skin.

1 In the toolbar along the right edge of the Camera Raw window, click the Healing icon (✏️). Under the Histogram, Healing tools replace the Edit tools.

2 In the Healing options, select the Content-Aware Remove tool (◆).

The Content-Aware Remove tool can delete content such as skin blemishes and seamlessly fill them in with surrounding content. It's similar to the Spot Healing Brush tool you used in Photoshop in Lesson 2.

3 Set the view magnification to 100%.

4 In the Healing options, set Size to **15** and Opacity to **100**.

About Camera Raw healing tools

What are the differences between the three Healing tools in Camera Raw? They're similar to the differences among the healing tools in Photoshop.

Content-Aware Remove tool
Heal tool
Clone tool

Content-Aware Remove tool. Deletes content you brush over and intelligently replaces it with content from surrounding areas. All you have to do is brush over what you want to remove. It's possible to sample a specific content source if needed.

Heal tool. Replaces content you brush over with content sampled from another part of the image, but blended in so that it's seamlessly healed.

Clone tool. Replaces content you brush over with content sampled from another part of the image, but without blending it in. Similar to the Clone Stamp tool in Photoshop, use the Clone tool in Camera Raw when you want to paint content exactly as it is in another part of the image.

The Heal and Clone tools let you change the sampling point for filled-in content. The Content-Aware Remove tool pulls content from around the area you brushed.

5   Click one of the spots on the face. The Content-Aware Remove tool fills in the spot you clicked using the content around it.

6   Drag the Content-Aware Remove tool over the dark blemish on the neck. Dragging is useful here because the current Size setting may not be able to remove the entire blemish in one click.

▶ **Tip:** If the area filled by the Content-Aware Remove tool is not seamless because it used nearby content that's visually inconsistent, as long as that edit is selected you can Ctrl-drag (Windows) or Command-drag (macOS) somewhere else in the image to define a different source for that edit.

7   If Show Overlay is enabled in the Healing tools, click to disable it so that you can better see the results of your corrections.

When Show Overlay is enabled, you can see the locations of that tool's edits on the image, represented by icons. This lets you select and then change or delete your edits. When an edit draws from source content elsewhere in the image (more common when using the Heal or Clone tool), Show Overlay shows you where the source is and lets you drag the source to change its location.

▶ **Tip:** You can toggle Show Controls with the keyboard by pressing the V key.

8   Brush over fine lines around the eyes and mouth. You can also brush away freckles and minor blemishes on her face, neck, arms, and chest. Experiment with simply clicking, using very short strokes, and creating longer brush strokes.

Remove distracting lines and blemishes, but leave enough that the face retains its character. You can practice by removing the jewelry on the nose, but on a real job, it may be preferable to leave the jewelry visible if it's meaningful to the subject and part of their character. This might also be true for beauty spots and birthmarks. The safe thing to do is to ask the subject before removing significant identifying marks or jewelry.

You can also experiment with removing blemishes with the Heal tool instead of the Content-Aware Remove tool. In general, the Heal tool may do a better job of preserving existing textures.

Enhancing the face with masked adjustments

You'll use masked adjustments to brighten the eyes and lips. A mask constrains the adjustment to a specific area. Applying a Camera Raw masked adjustment is similar to painting white in an adjustment layer mask in Photoshop.

1 Use the Hand tool to change the view so that you can see the eyes.

2 Click the Masking icon (⚙), and then click Brush. The Masking panel appears, listing a New Mask and New Brush in italic because they have not yet been created. They will be created as soon as you use the brush.

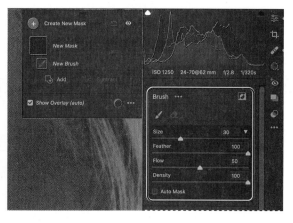

Notice that the Edit settings that were under the histogram are now under a Brush heading. When a masked adjustment is selected in the masks panel, the settings shown are for that selected adjustment—not for the entire image. You'll change Brush settings to set up what this Brush adjustment will do. You want it to increase the saturation of whatever you brush, in this case the irises of the eyes.

3 In the Brush options, change settings as follows:

- Size: **2**

- Feather: **100**

- Flow: **50**

- Density: **100**

- Auto Mask: **Off**

4 Scroll the Brush settings until you see the Color panel, and set Saturation to **+70**.

5 Drag the Brush tool over the irises in the eyes to increase their saturation.

6 If you think the irises are oversaturated, make sure Brush 1 is still selected in the masks panel, and then reduce the Saturation value until it looks reasonable.

Mask 1 no longer appears in italics because the mask was created after you brushed. If you make many masks, naming them helps you identify them later.

7 In the masks panel, double-click Mask 1, rename it **Eye Irises**, and click OK.

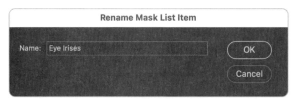

8 In the masks panel, select the Show Overlay option to enable it.

A red overlay appears, showing you where you brushed. If you see areas you did not intend to brush with the current adjustment, as long as the brush mask is selected in the masks panel you can subtract areas from the mask by holding down the Alt (Windows) or Option (macOS) key as you brush.

Now you'll create another brush mask to desaturate the red corners of the eye.

▶ Tip: When you hold down the Alt or Option key to use the Brush adjustment in Erase mode, the Brush settings may change. That's because Erase mode can have different Brush settings.

● **Note:** You may
notice the Add button
within the Eye Irises
mask. The reason you do
not click Add in step 8
is that Add creates
another submask within
Eye Irises. Eye Irises
adds Saturation, and
all submasks within
Eye Irises would do
the same. But now you
want to desaturate, so
you need to create a
different mask, not a
submask of Eye Irises.
Add is useful when you
want to control multiple
submasks using the
same settings.

9 In the masks panel, click the blue Create New Mask button, and choose Brush.

10 In the Color panel, set Saturation to −50, and brush the red corners of the eyes.

11 In the masks panel, double-click Mask 1, rename it **Eye Corners**, and click OK.

Now you'll use another brush adjustment to brighten other areas around the eyes.

12 In the masks panel, click the blue Create New Mask button, and choose Brush.

13 Scroll the Brush settings until you see the Light panel, and set Exposure to **+.50**.

14 Brush over the white areas of the eyes, the irises, and the shadows above the eye.

15 In the masks panel, double-click Mask 1, rename it **Eye Brighten**, and click OK.

Now step back and review your work.

16 In the masks panel, click the eye icon for the Eye Brighten mask to hide it; then click it again to show it. Evaluate whether you need to adjust anything, and make any needed adjustments to that mask while it is selected.

Tip: To save clicks, you can do a simpler before/after: Position the pointer over a mask's eye icon and hold down (instead of clicking) the mouse button. The mask is temporarily hidden only as long as you hold down the mouse button; when you release the mouse button, the mask is permanently restored.

For example, if Exposure is too strong, make sure the Eye Brighten mask is selected in the masks panel and reduce the Exposure value. You can experiment with how other Light settings affect this mask, such as Shadows and Whites, to find the right combination. Or create more brush masks with different settings for each area.

Using Camera Raw as a filter

In this lesson, Camera Raw is used to preprocess a camera raw file before saving a converted copy in a standard file format, or opening the camera raw file in Photoshop after converting it to a Photoshop document.

Some features in Camera Raw, such as Texture and Clarity, are not available in Photoshop. But you can use those features in Photoshop by using Camera Raw as a filter on a selected Photoshop layer. For example, if you're working on a document in Photoshop and you want to use the Texture or Clarity options on a layer, select that layer in the Layers panel, and choose Filter > Camera Raw Filter. That opens the layer in Camera Raw, where you can apply Texture or Clarity. When you click OK to close Camera Raw, the Photoshop layer is updated with the Camera Raw changes.

Some Camera Raw features, such as the Crop tool and Save option, are not available when you use Camera Raw as a filter. It's usually because the missing features are intended to work with an entire document, but when used as a filter, Camera Raw is operating only on a layer within a Photoshop document.

Tip: As with other filters, if you want to be able to edit Camera Raw Filter changes at any time in the future, first convert the Photoshop layer to a Smart Object (such as by choosing Filter > Convert for Smart Filters) and apply the Camera Raw Filter to that Smart Object.

Smoothing skin texture

▶ **Tip:** You can also select a color range and skin tones when an image is open in Photoshop. Choose Select > Color Range, and in the Color Range dialog box, choose Skin Tones from the Select pop-up menu.

In Camera Raw you can use a masked adjustment that automatically recognizes skin on people so that it's easier to retouch skin without affecting the entire raw image.

1 Set the view magnification to Fit In View.

2 In the masks panel, click the Create New Mask button, and choose Select People.

Camera Raw searches for people in the image, which may take a few moments. Then, under Person Mask Options, a list of identified people appears. In this image, there is only one person. Mask 1 appears in the masks panel; this is the current mask. A red overlay for Mask 1 appears over the image.

3 In Person Mask Options, if options are not active, click the circular Person thumbnail to select it.

4 Make sure that Facial Skin and Body Skin are selected and that all the other options are deselected, and click Create.

Camera Raw automatically isolates face and body skin areas and creates masks for those areas—you didn't have to do any manual masking. It creates a new Mask 1 with separate Body Skin and Facial Skin submasks for the person (named Person 1).

5   Make sure Mask 1 is selected.

6   You'll need to see skin details, so set the view magnification to 100%.

7   In the options for Mask 1, scroll until you see the Effects panel, and set the Texture value to −**30**.

You should see the skin texture become smoother, because a negative Texture value de-emphasizes detail. (If you didn't notice the change, toggle the eye icon for Mask 1 in the masks panel.) Again, if you think the adjustment is too much or too little, go ahead and adjust the Texture value while Mask 1 is selected in the masks panel.

While the skin mask is selected, it's a good time to also make any other skin tone or color adjustments you think are needed. For example, if there is a color cast to remove from the skin, try adjusting options in Mask 1 panels such as Color and Curve. (If you want to correct a color cast across the entire image, after step 8 click the Edit button to exit masking; then adjust options in the general Edit panels.)

8   In the masks panel, double-click Mask 1, rename it **Skin**, and click OK.

9   Click the Edit button (⌘) to close the masks panel, and set the view magnification to Fit In View so that you can review the entire image.

You opened an image from Bridge into Camera Raw and performed portrait retouching, without opening Photoshop. If you need a finished copy to distribute, you can click the Save icon as you did with the mission buildings earlier in this lesson. If you want to apply more advanced retouching techniques that Camera Raw can't do, you can click Open to convert the image into a Photoshop document and continue editing in Photoshop. But for now, let's make sure all of the work you did in Camera Raw is saved.

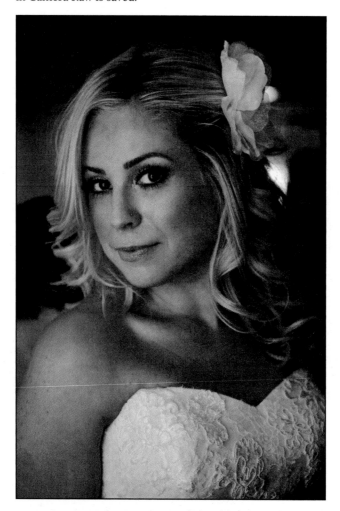

10 Click Done. Great work! The Done button saves your changes and closes Camera Raw, returning you to Bridge.

Secrets of the More Image Settings menu

In Adobe Camera Raw, the More Image Settings menu is not always noticed, but it offers powerful features, some of which aren't visible in the Camera Raw window. To open this menu, click the More Image Settings button (…), the last button in the button group at the upper-right corner of the Camera Raw window.

Here are some of the more useful commands in the More Image Settings menu. For more information about them, see Camera Raw online help.

Reset to Open and Reset to Default. These discard edits so you can start over. Reset to Open reverts an image to its state at the time you opened it in Camera Raw, and Reset to Default reverts to default Camera Raw settings, which you can customize (see Set Raw Defaults below).

Commands for managing snapshots and presets. These work with the Snapshots and Presets panels; their buttons are above the More Image Settings menu.

Commands for copying and pasting settings. Use these to transfer edits to other images in the filmstrip, similar to the Sync Settings command shown in this lesson.

Load Settings and Save Settings. Normally, Camera Raw reads edits from and writes edits to an XMP metadata file in the same folder as the current camera raw file. These commands let you load edits from or save them as an XMP file in another folder, or using a different filename.

Save Image. This is the same as the Save button (⬇) near the upper-right corner of the Camera Raw window. Its submenu applies Save presets, skipping the dialog box.

Enhance. This opens the Enhance dialog box, which uses machine learning to apply **AI Denoise** noise reduction, **Raw Details** detail improvement, and **Super Resolution** upscaling, producing an enhanced DNG copy of the image file.

Set Raw Defaults. If you wish Camera Raw options had different starting values, use this command to customize Camera Raw default settings.

Many of these commands are also available on the Camera Raw filmstrip menu, or in the context menu that appears when you right-click (Windows) or Control-click (macOS) an image or its filmstrip thumbnail.

▶ **Tip:** Try AI Denoise when the Manual Noise Reduction options in the Detail panel are not effective enough. Try Super Resolution when the Resample options in Image > Image Size are not effective enough.

● **Note:** Enhance options run fastest on recent powerful graphics hardware, especially graphics hardware that supports machine learning. On older or less powerful graphics hardware, AI Denoise in particular may take many minutes to process one image.

About Camera Raw mask types

Masking corrections in Camera Raw can potentially save you a trip to Photoshop. Camera Raw offers more mask types than the ones you used in this lesson.

Subject, Sky, Background, and People. Camera Raw uses machine learning to recognize specific types of content and create a mask for them, similar to the Select > Sky and Select > Subject commands and Object Selection tool in Photoshop.

The difference between Subject and People is that Subject can also identify and mask objects that are not people.

Objects. When Select Subject doesn't select what you want, drag the Select Objects masking tool around a specific object to select it more precisely.

Linear Gradient and Radial Gradient. These create a mask that fades out gradually from one end to the other (for a Linear Gradient) or from the center of an ellipse outward (for a Radial Gradient). A Linear Gradient can be useful for equalizing tone or color differences on different sides of an image. A Radial Gradient is useful for emphasizing a spot within an image or creating an off-center vignette.

Color Range, Luminance Range, and Depth Range. A range mask is defined by a range of colors (Color Range), tones (Luminance Range), or distances (Depth Range) that you specify. For example, if you specify a Luminance Range mask that targets just the shadow tones in an image, you can then increase Exposure and reduce Noise across that range of tones only. Or you can create a Color Range mask that targets skin tones.

The Depth Range mask is available only if a camera embedded depth metadata into the image, as some smartphone cameras do.

Review questions

1 How is editing a camera raw image different than editing a photo in a format such as JPEG or Photoshop file format?

2 What is the advantage of the Adobe Digital Negative (DNG) file format?

3 How can you apply the same settings to multiple images in Camera Raw?

4 How do you apply a Camera Raw edit to specific areas of an image?

Review answers

1 A camera raw file contains unprocessed picture data from a digital camera's image sensor. Camera raw files give photographers control over interpreting the image data, rather than letting the camera apply an initial conversion and adjustments. When you edit the image in Camera Raw, it stores the edits separately so that the original raw file is not altered. This way, you can edit the image the way you want, export it, and keep the original intact for future re-interpretation or for other adjustments.

2 The Adobe Digital Negative (DNG) file format contains the raw image data from a digital camera as well as metadata that defines what the image data means. DNG is an industry-wide standard for camera raw image data. DNG can help photographers manage proprietary camera raw file formats using an openly available standard, and it provides a compatible archival format that includes edits.

3 To apply the same settings to multiple images in Camera Raw, select the images in the filmstrip, click the filmstrip menu button, and choose Sync Settings. Then select the settings you want to apply, and click OK.

4 To apply a Camera Raw edit to specific areas of an image, click the Masking icon, and create a new mask that isolates the areas you want to edit.

13 PREPARING FILES FOR THE WEB

Lesson overview

In this lesson, you'll learn how to do the following:

- Use the Frame tool to create a placeholder for a layout.
- Create and stylize a button for a website.
- Use layer groups and artboards.
- Optimize design assets for the web.
- Record an action to automate a series of steps.
- Play an action to affect multiple images.
- Save entire layouts and individual assets using Export As.
- Design for multiple screen sizes with multiple artboards.

 This lesson will take about an hour to complete. To get the lesson files used in this chapter, download them from the web page for this book at peachpit.com/PhotoshopCIB2024. For more information, see "Accessing the lesson files and Web Edition" in the Getting Started section at the beginning of this book.

As you work on this lesson, you'll preserve the start files. If you need to restore the start files, download them from your Account page.

PROJECT: MUSEUM WEBSITE

Artboards let you create multiple designs in a single Photoshop document. For example, you can consistently design both the mobile and desktop versions of a website. When it's ready, the Export As workflow makes it easy to save layers, layer groups, and artboards as separate image assets that you can deliver to a web developer, or for review.

Getting started

In this lesson, you will build buttons for the home page of an art museum's website and then generate appropriate graphics files for each button. You'll use layer groups to assemble the buttons and then create actions to prepare a set of images for use as a second group of buttons. First, you'll view the final web design.

1 Start Photoshop, and then simultaneously hold down Ctrl+Alt+Shift (Windows) or Command+Option+Shift (macOS) to restore the default preferences. (See "Restoring default preferences" on page 5.)

2 When prompted, click Yes to delete the Adobe Photoshop Settings file.

3 Choose File > Browse In Bridge.

● **Note:** If Bridge isn't installed, the File > Browse In Bridge command in Photoshop will start the Creative Cloud desktop app, which will download and install Bridge. After installation completes, you can start Bridge. For more information, see page 3.

4 In Bridge, click Lessons in the Favorites panel. Double-click the Lesson13 folder in the Content panel.

5 View the 13End.psd file in Bridge.

There are eight buttons at the bottom of the page, arranged in two rows. You'll transform images into buttons for the top row and use an action to prepare the buttons for the second row.

6 Double-click the 13Start.psd thumbnail to open the file in Photoshop. Click OK if you see the Missing Profile dialog box, and close any messages that appear about new features.

● **Note:** If Photoshop displays a dialog box telling you about the difference between saving to Cloud Documents and On Your Computer, click Save On Your Computer. You can also select Don't Show Again, but that setting will deselect after you reset Photoshop preferences.

13Start.psd.

13End.psd.

7 Choose File > Save As, rename the file **13Working.psd**, and click Save. Click OK in the Photoshop Format Options dialog box.

Creating placeholders with the Frame tool

When you create a print, web, or mobile device project, it's common to design the layout before you have the final graphics for it. You could add temporary graphics that you plan to replace later with final graphics, but then you must manage more files. One way to simplify the design process is to create placeholder shapes, called *frames*, during the early stages of design. As you refine the design and as final graphics become available, it's easy to place the final graphics directly into placeholder frames. Designing with placeholder frames is common in page layout applications such as Adobe InDesign.

You create frames using the Frame tool. A frame can contain an imported graphic, a Smart Object, or a pixel layer. When you create a frame, it appears in the Layers panel, because a frame is like a layer group with a vector mask.

The document 13Working.psd contains empty gray boxes. The gray boxes exist only to help you position new frames that you'll create for this lesson. When you create your own designs, you can design using the Frame tool alone.

1 Choose Edit > Preferences > Units & Rulers (Windows) or Photoshop > Settings > Units & Rulers (macOS). In the Units area of the dialog box, make sure Pixels is selected in the Rulers menu, and then click OK.

Note: If you're using macOS 12 or earlier, the Settings command is named Preferences.

You want to work in pixels because this document is intended to be a web page.

2 Choose Window > Info to open the Info panel.

The Info panel displays information dynamically as you move the pointer or make selections. Which information it displays depends on the tool that is selected. You'll use it to determine the position of the ruler guide (based on the Y coordinate) and the size of an area you select (based on the width and height). It's also handy for seeing the values of colors under the pointer.

3 If the rulers aren't visible, choose View > Rulers.

Tip: A quick way to change the unit of measure is to right-click (Windows) or Control-click (macOS) the rulers.

Tip: To customize the Info panel display of the color values under the pointer, click an eyedropper or crosshair icon in the Info panel, and then choose the display option you want.

Tip: The keyboard shortcut for showing or hiding rulers is Ctrl+R (Windows) or Command+R (macOS).

Adding a frame

A frame is easy to add, because you create one the same way you'd create a shape such as a rectangle or circle.

▶ **Tip:** You can create an elliptical or circular frame by selecting the Elliptical Frame icon in the options bar for the Frame tool.

1 In the Tools panel, select the Frame tool (⊠).

2 Drag to create a rectangular frame over the large gray rectangle at the top of the document.

▶ **Tip:** To create a frame of any shape, such as a star, first draw the shape using a Pen tool or a shape tool. Then, with the shape layer selected in the Layers panel, choose Layer > New > Convert To Frame.

The frame appears as a rectangle with an X inside it. The X indicates that it's not just a vector shape, but also a placeholder frame. As a placeholder, it's ready to contain a graphic at any time.

Adding a graphic to a frame

When you finalize the images and other graphics that go into a document, you can add them to the placeholder frames you've created.

1 In the Layers panel, make sure the Frame 1 layer is still selected.

2 Choose File > Place Linked.

3 Navigate to the Lesson13/Art folder, select the NorthShore.jpg file, and click Place.

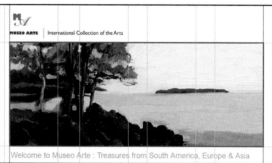

The image appears inside the selected frame and automatically resizes to fill the frame.

You can also drag an image from Bridge or the desktop and drop it into a frame in a Photoshop document window. This embeds the image—it makes a complete copy of it inside the Photoshop document. To have the frame link instead, so that it always loads the current version of the image from outside the Photoshop document, hold down Alt or Option as you drag.

Editing frame attributes with the Properties panel

When a frame is selected in the Layers panel, you can see and edit frame attributes in the Properties panel so that you can change a frame after you create it.

1 With the Frame tool, draw a rectangle frame between the row of four gray squares and the bottom of the document. The exact size and position aren't important, because you're about to edit them.

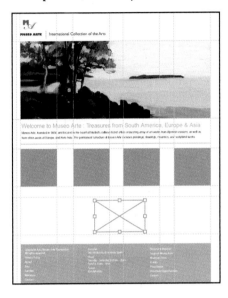

2 With the frame selected, enter the following values in the Properties panel (if it isn't already open, choose Window > Properties):

- Width: **180**
- Height: **180**
- X: **40**
- Y: **648**

▶ **Tip:** As in the options bar, you can change the unit of measure in a Properties panel field by right-clicking (Windows) or Control-clicking (macOS) the field. Or you can override a field's unit of measure by typing the unit after the value, for example, **4 in**.

After you apply all of the values, the size and position of the frame should now match the first gray square.

Duplicating frames

The other three squares in the row are the same size, so instead of drawing all four squares manually, you can simply duplicate them. Duplicating a frame is similar to duplicating a layer, because frames appear in the Layers panel.

1 In the Layers panel, drag the Frame 1 layer, and drop it on the Create A New Layer button (⊞). The duplicate layer, Frame 1 Copy, appears in the Layers panel.

2 With the Frame 1 Copy layer selected, in the Properties panel change the X value to **300**. This makes the duplicate square frame line up with the second gray square.

▶ **Tip:** It's always your choice to size and position a selected layer by dragging or by precisely editing values in the Properties panel or options bar.

3 Repeat step 1 to create two more duplicate frames. In the Properties panel, change the X value of the third frame to **550** and the X value of the fourth frame to **800**.

You've created a complete row of four placeholder frames.

Adding images to frames

When graphics become available to use in the layout, you can quickly add them to each frame. One convenient way is by using the Properties panel.

1 Make sure the first square frame (Frame 1) is selected.

2 In the Properties panel, click the Inset Image menu, and choose Place From Local Disk - Linked.

3 Navigate to the Lesson13/Art folder, select the Beach.jpg file, and click Place.

The Beach.jpg file is scaled to fit the frame, the name of the frame changes to Beach Frame, and the Properties panel displays the folder path to the linked document that's placed in the frame.

4 Repeat step 2 for the other three square frames, placing the files NorthShore.jpg, DeYoung.jpg, and MaineOne.jpg. Remember that you can also add a linked image to a frame by Alt-dragging (Windows) or Option-dragging (macOS) an image from the desktop or Bridge and dropping it into a frame.

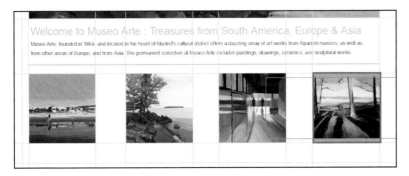

5   In the Layers panel, click to select the frame layer thumbnail (the right thumbnail with the link icon) of the MaineOne Frame layer. This selects just the contents of the frame. (Clicking the left thumbnail would select the frame.)

6   Choose Edit > Free Transform, drag the image or any of its edge handles to improve the composition of the image within the frame, and press Enter or Return when you're done.

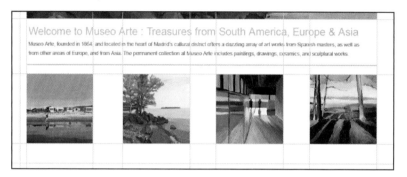

After adding graphics to frames, it's always a good idea to inspect all of the frames to make sure the graphics are well-composed within them. Feel free to adjust any of the other images within their frames.

Using layer groups to create button graphics

Layer groups make it easier to organize and work with layers in complex images, especially when there are sets of layers that work together. You'll use layer groups to assemble the layers that make up each button, and this organization will make things easier later, when you export them as website assets.

The four frames you created now serve as the basis for buttons. You'll add a label to each, identifying the gallery it represents, and then add a drop shadow and a stroke.

1   If the Info panel isn't already open, choose Window > Info to open it.

2   Position the Move tool pointer over the horizontal ruler, and drag a ruler guide down until the Y value in the Info panel is 795 pixels.

You'll use this guide to draw a band across the bottom of the image for the label.

3   Zoom in on the first square image, of the man on the beach. Then select Beach Frame in the Layers panel.

You'll use this image to design the first button.

4   Select the Rectangle tool (□) in the Tools panel. Then, drag to create a rectangle shape across the bottom of the image, aligned with the guides and image edges. The shape should be 180 pixels wide and 33 pixels high. Press Enter or Return to commit the new shape, which is named Rectangle 1. Rename it **Band**.

5   With the Band layer selected, click the Fill swatch in the options bar, click the Color Picker icon, and then select a dark blue; we entered the hex color **194879**. Click OK to close the Color Picker, and then press Enter or Return to close the Fill options.

6   Click the Stroke swatch in the options bar, click No Color (☑), and close the Stroke options.

The new shape appears as a dark blue band at the bottom of the first image. You'll add text to it next.

7   Select the Horizontal Type tool, and select the following settings in the options bar:

- Font Family: Myriad Pro

- Font Style: Regular

- Font Size: **18** pt

- Anti-aliasing: Strong

- Alignment: Center

- Color: White

▶ **Tip:** As you position the text layer, if it snaps to a vertical magenta Smart Guide that appears in the middle of the Beach Frame and Blue Band layers, that means the text layer is centered in front of those layers.

8   Click in the center of the blue band, and type **GALLERY ONE**. Use the Move tool to adjust the position of the type layer if necessary.

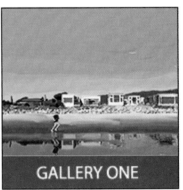

▶ **Tip:** When multiple layers are selected in the Layers panel, you can also create a layer group from them by clicking the New Group button or by pressing the keyboard shortcut Ctrl+G (Windows) or Command+G (macOS).

9   Select both the GALLERY ONE and Band layers in the Layers panel, and choose Layer > Group Layers.

Photoshop creates a group named Group 1.

10 Double-click the Group 1 layer group, and rename it **Gallery 1**. Then expand the group. The layers you selected are indented, indicating they're part of that group.

11 Drag the Gallery 1 layer group up so that it's above all of the frame layers.

12 Choose File > Save.

Duplicating button bands and text

You've designed the label for one button. You could go through all those steps again to create the band and text for each of the other buttons, but it's faster to duplicate the layer group you created for the first band and text and then edit the copies.

1 In the Layers panel, make sure the Gallery 1 layer group is selected.

2 With the Move tool selected, make sure Auto-Select is not selected in the options bar.

3 With the Move tool, hold down the Alt (Windows) or Option (macOS) key as you drag the Gallery One button to the right, and drop it when it snaps into alignment with the second square frame and its guides.

Note: In the Layers panel, moving a selected layer group moves all layers in it, even if the group's individual layers don't appear selected in the Layers panel. What's important is that the group is selected.

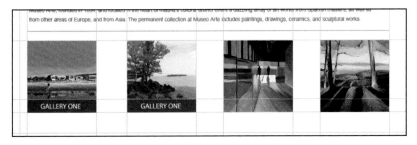

Holding down Alt or Option creates a copy of the selected layer group as you drag it with the Move tool. When you release the mouse button, the copy (Gallery 1 copy) should be selected in the Layers panel.

4 Repeat step 3 by Alt-dragging (Windows) or Option-dragging (macOS) a copy of the second button over the third square frame, and then do it one more time to copy the third button over the fourth square frame, completing the row.

Now edit the text in the three copies to match their images.

5   With the Horizontal Text tool, select the ONE text in the second button, and change ONE so that it now says **GALLERY TWO**.

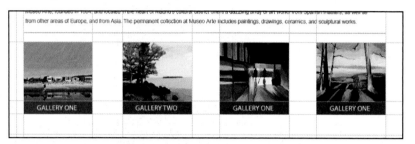

6   Repeat step 5 for the third and fourth buttons so that they say **GALLERY THREE** and **GALLERY FOUR**, respectively.

7   After you finish editing the GALLERY FOUR text, commit the last text edit by selecting the Move tool.

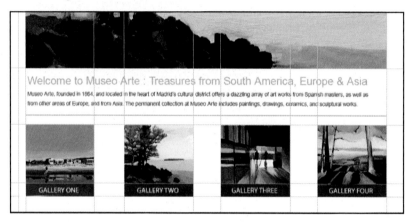

8   In the Layers panel, rename the layer groups to be consistent with their contents:

▶ **Tip:** These steps are easier if you make the Layers panel taller so that you can see multiple expanded layer groups at once.

*   Double-click the name of the "Gallery 1 copy" layer group, and name it **Gallery 2**.

*   Double-click the name of the "Gallery 1 copy 2" layer group, and name it **Gallery 3**.

*   Double-click the name of the "Gallery 1 copy 3" layer group, and name it **Gallery 4**.

Now move each button image into its layer group.

9 In the Layers panel, do the following:

● **Note:** When dragging layers in step 9, position the pointer over the layer name, not the thumbnails, before dragging.

- Drag the Beach Frame layer into the Gallery 1 layer group, below the GALLERY ONE and Band layers.

- Drag the upper NorthShore Frame layer into the Gallery 2 layer group, below the GALLERY TWO and Band layers.

- Drag the DeYoung Frame layer into the Gallery 3 layer group, below the GALLERY THREE and Band layers.

- Drag the MaineOne Frame layer into the Gallery 4 layer group, below the GALLERY FOUR and Band layers.

10 Click the arrow next to each of the Gallery layer group icons to collapse them, simplifying the Layers panel display.

Now you'll add a drop shadow and stroke to improve the appearance of the button.

11 Select the Gallery 1 layer group in the Layers panel. Then, click the Add A Layer Style button (*fx*) at the bottom of the Layers panel, and choose Drop Shadow.

► Tip: When you apply a layer style to a group, it applies to all layers in that group. In this book you have now tried applying a layer style to one layer and also to a layer group.

12 In the Layer Style dialog box, change the following settings in the Structure area:

- Opacity: **27**%

- Distance: **9** px

- Spread: **19**%

- Size: **18** px

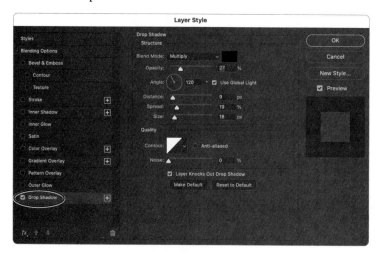

● Note: Be sure to click the word "Stroke." If you click only the checkbox, Photoshop applies the layer style with its default settings, but you won't see the options.

13 With the Layer Style dialog box still open, select Stroke on the left, making sure that it's enabled, and apply the following settings:

- Size: **1** px

- Position: Inside

- Color: Click the color swatch to open the Color Picker. Then click the blue band to sample its color, and click OK to select it.

14 Click OK to apply both layer styles.

The drop shadow and stroke appear on the button's layer group in the document and also in the Layers panel.

15 In the Layers panel, position the pointer over the fx icon next to the Gallery 1 layer group. Then hold down the Alt (Windows) or Option (macOS) key as you drag the fx icon and drop it on the Gallery 2 layer group. This is a quick way to copy layer effects to another layer or layer group.

▶ **Tip:** Another way to transfer the effects of one layer or layer group to another is to drag its Effects header. That does the same thing as dragging the fx icon.

16 Repeat step 15 to copy the layer effects to the Gallery 3 and Gallery 4 layer groups.

17 In the Layers panel, expand the Button Art layer group, and then click the eye icon for the Navigation layer to make it visible. Then collapse the Button Art layer group.

This layer represents the navigation among sections of the museum website.

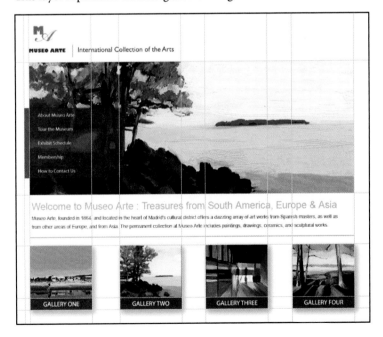

18 Save the file, and then close it.

Automating a multistep task

You can record a set of one or more commands and play it back to apply to a single file or a batch of files. In Photoshop this feature is called an *action*. (Some applications call this kind of feature a *macro*.) In this exercise, you'll create an action that prepares a set of images to serve as buttons for additional galleries on the web page you're designing.

Recording an action

▶ **Tip:** Actions are easy to use, but limited in scope. To automate Photoshop with more control, you can write a script. Photoshop can run scripts written in VBScript (Windows), AppleScript (macOS), or JavaScript (Windows and macOS).

You'll start by recording an action that resizes an image, changes its canvas size, and adds layer styles so that the additional buttons match the ones you've already created. You use the Actions panel to record, play, edit, and delete individual actions. You also use the Actions panel to save and load action files.

There are four images in the Buttons folder that will serve as the basis for new gallery buttons on your website. The images are large, so the first thing you'll need to do is resize them to match the existing buttons. You'll perform each of the steps on the Gallery5.jpg file as you record the action. You'll then play the action to make the same changes on the other images in the folder automatically.

1 Choose File > Open, and navigate to the Lesson13/Buttons folder. Double-click the Gallery5.jpg file to open it in Photoshop.

2 Choose Window > Actions to open the Actions panel. Close the Default Actions set (folder); you'll create and use your own set for this lesson.

3 Click the Create New Set button (▢) at the bottom of the Actions panel. In the New Set dialog box, name the set **Buttons**, and click OK.

The Default Actions set includes prerecorded sample actions that you can use and study. As you build your own actions, you can organize them by creating action sets.

4 Click the Create New Action button (⊞) at the bottom of the Actions panel. Name the action **Resizing and Styling Images**, and click Record.

It's a good idea to name actions in a way that makes it clear what the actions do so you can find them easily later.

At the bottom of the Actions panel, the Begin
Recording button turns red to let you know that
recording is in progress.

Even though you're recording, there's no need to rush. Take all the time you need
to perform the procedure accurately. Actions don't record in real time; they record
steps as you complete them, but they play them back as quickly as possible.

You'll start by resizing and sharpening the image.

5   Choose Image > Image Size, and do the following:

- Make sure Resample is selected.

- For Width, choose Pixels from the units menu, and then change the Width to
  180.

- Confirm that the Height has changed to **180** pixels. It should, because
  original proportions are preserved using the Constrain Aspect Ratio link icon
  to the left of the Width and Height values, which is selected by default.

6   Click OK.

7   Choose Filter > Sharpen > Smart Sharpen, apply the following settings, and
    click OK:

- Amount: **100**%

- Radius: **1.0** px

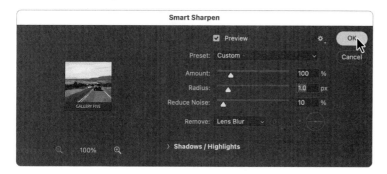

You need to make some additional changes to the image that you can't make as long as the Background layer is locked. You'll convert it to a regular layer.

8 Double-click the Background layer name in the Layers panel. In the New Layer dialog box, name the layer **Button**, and click OK.

▶ **Tip:** If you want to convert a background layer to a regular layer and you don't need to name it, simply click the Background layer's lock icon in the Layers panel.

When you rename a Background layer, you're converting it to a regular layer, so Photoshop displays the New Layer dialog box. But no layers are added; the Background layer becomes the new layer.

Now that you've converted the Background layer, you can change the canvas size and add layer styles.

▶ **Tip:** Use Canvas Size when you want to add area to or remove area from a document; use Image Size when you want to resample, change the physical dimensions, or change the resolution of a document.

9 Choose Image > Canvas Size, and do the following:

- Make sure the unit of measure is set to Pixels.

- Change the Width to **220** pixels and the Height to **220** pixels.

- Click the center square in the anchor area to ensure the canvas is extended evenly on all sides.

- Click OK.

10 Choose Layer > Layer Style > Drop Shadow.

11 In the Layer Style dialog box, apply the following settings:

- Opacity: **27**%

- Angle: **120**°

- Distance: **9** px

- Spread: **19**%

- Size: **18** px

▶ **Tip:** Stay on task while the Actions panel is recording. It records any Photoshop image edits, so if you record unwanted steps, you'll have to edit them out later. The Actions panel doesn't record view changes such as scrolling and zooming.

12 With the Layer Style dialog box still open, select Stroke on the left, and apply the following settings:

- Size: **1** px

- Position: Inside

- Color: If the color swatch doesn't already match the other blue band you made, click the color swatch and sample the blue band as you did earlier.

13 Click OK to apply both layer styles.

● **Note:** Be sure to click the word "Stroke." If you click only the checkbox, Photoshop applies the layer style with its default settings, but you won't see the options.

14 Choose File > Save As, choose Photoshop for the Format, and click Save. Click OK if the Photoshop Format Options dialog box appears.

15 Close the file. The Home screen appears, so click the Photoshop icon so that you can see the Actions panel again.

16 Click the Stop Playing/Recording button at the bottom of the Actions panel.

 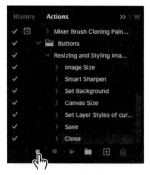

Tip: As you review an action, you can edit the sequence by dragging steps, edit steps by double-clicking them (if applicable), or remove unneeded steps by deleting them.

The action you just recorded (Resizing and Styling Images) is now saved in the Buttons set in the Actions panel. Click the arrows to expand different sets of steps. You can examine each recorded step and the specific selections you made.

Batch-playing an action

Applying actions is a timesaving process for performing routine tasks on files, but you can streamline your work even further by applying actions to multiple files at once. You'll apply the action you've created to the three remaining images.

1 Choose File > Open, and navigate to the Lesson13/Buttons folder. Ctrl-select (Windows) or Command-select (macOS) the Gallery6.jpg, Gallery7.jpg, and Gallery8.jpg files, and click Open. They open as tabs in the document window.

2 Choose File > Automate > Batch.

Tip: You can create conditional actions that change their behavior based on criteria you define. To do this, choose Insert Conditional from the Actions panel menu.

3 In the Batch dialog box, do the following:

- Confirm that Buttons is chosen in the Set menu and that Resizing and Styling Images—the action you just created—is chosen in the Action menu.

- Choose Opened Files from the Source menu.

- Make sure None is chosen for the Destination.

- Click OK.

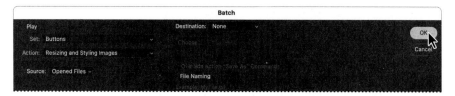

Photoshop plays the action, applying its steps to all the files that are open. You can also apply an action to an entire folder of images without opening them.

Note: If you get an error when running an action, click Stop. There may be a problem with the action that was recorded, especially if you had to correct a mistake while recording. Try troubleshooting or re-recording the action.

Because you saved the file and closed it while you were recording the action, Photoshop saves each of the images as a PSD file in its original folder and then closes the file. After Photoshop closes the last file, the Home screen appears.

Placing files in Photoshop

The four additional button images are ready to be placed into the design. You probably noticed that each already has a blue band with its gallery name included in the image, so you don't need to perform those steps. They're ready to go.

1 If the file 13Working.psd is in the Recent list in the Home screen, click its name to reopen it. If not, choose File > Open to open it.

2 In the Layers panel, select the Gallery 4 layer group name. This ensures that the files about to be placed are not added inside any layer groups, because new layers are added above the selected layer.

3 Choose File > Place Embedded.

You'll place these files as embedded Smart Objects. Because they're embedded, the entire image is copied into the Photoshop file.

4 In the Place Embedded dialog box, navigate to the Lesson13/Buttons folder, and double-click the Gallery5.psd file.

Photoshop places the Gallery5.psd file in the center of the 13Working.psd file. But that's not where you want it to go, so you'll move it.

5 Drag the image into position below the Gallery One button. Use the guides to align the image with the one above. When it's in position, commit the change by pressing Enter or Return.

Note: The bounding box of the placed image is larger than the button, because the bounding box includes the complete extent of the drop shadow.

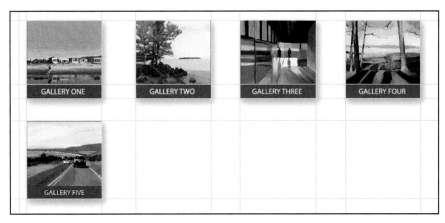

Tip: You can also place embedded files by dragging them into the Photoshop document from the desktop or from other applications. You can drag multiple images to place at once; after you commit one image, the next will be placed.

6   Repeat steps 3–5 to place the Gallery6.psd, Gallery7.psd, and Gallery8.psd files, aligning them below the Gallery Two, Gallery Three, and Gallery Four buttons.

7   You've completed the web page! Save your work and close the file.

Designing with artboards

Tip: If you want automatic export of layers for web and mobile user interfaces, you might try Adobe Generator. When Adobe Generator is on, Photoshop exports layers to image assets as you work. A layer naming convention controls the specs of the exported assets.

When you're designing websites or user interfaces for mobile devices, you may need to create separate image files for buttons and other content. In Photoshop, you can use the Export As feature to export an entire document or individual layers to web- and mobile-friendly formats including PNG, JPEG, or GIF. In addition to being able to export multiple layers to individual files at once, Export As makes it possible to export to multiple sizes at once if you need to produce sets of images for low- and high-resolution displays.

You may need to coordinate different ideas for a single design, or design variations for different display sizes. This is easier when you use artboards, which are like multiple canvases in a single Photoshop document. You can also use Export As to export entire artboards.

Tip: You may notice or have been taught to use the older Save For Web command in Photoshop. Although that command is still available under File > Export > Save For Web (Legacy), Save For Web can't export multiple layers, artboards, or scaling factors, while Export As can.

With Export As, you control what exports by selecting artboards or layers in the Layers panel.

Duplicating an artboard

You'll use artboards to adapt the design of the museum website for a different screen size. Later, you'll export both designs at once.

1   In the Photoshop Home screen, click Open. Navigate to the Lesson13 folder, and open the file 13Museo.psd.

2   Choose File > Save As, rename the file **13Museo_Working.psd**, and click Save. Click OK in the Photoshop Format Options dialog box.

This is a web page that's being adapted for a responsive web design so that it will work well on display sizes from desktops to smartphones.

3   Choose Select > All Layers.

● **Note:** Select > All Layers doesn't select the Background layer, because it's locked by default. However, you will find that step 4 converts the Background layer to Layer 0.

4 Choose Layer > New > Artboard From Layers, name the new artboard **Desktop**, and click OK. The artboard name appears above the new artboard and also on its new artboard group in the Layers panel.

5 Make sure the Artboard tool (⌐) is selected; it's grouped with the Move tool in the Tools panel. Then Alt/Option-click the Add Artboard button to the right of the artboard to duplicate both the Desktop artboard and its contents.

6 In the Layers panel, double-click the name of the duplicate Desktop Copy artboard, and name it **iPhone**.

7 In the Properties panel, click the Set Artboard to Preset menu, and choose **iPhone 8/7/6**. That artboard preset applies the pixel dimensions of an iPhone 8, iPhone 7, and iPhone 6 (750 pixels wide by 1334 pixels tall). Now you can develop a design for that iPhone size, using the elements of the Desktop design. It will also be easier to maintain design consistency, because both the desktop and mobile designs are in the same document.

8 Save your work.

▶ **Tip:** You can choose artboard presets from the Size menu in the options bar when the Artboard tool is selected. If none of the artboard presets matches the display you're designing for, such as a newer model, you can enter your own values for Width and Height in the options bar or Properties panel.

Creating a design variation with artboards

You now have different artboards for desktop and smartphone display sizes; the next task is to fit the desktop-sized objects within the width of the smartphone display's pixel dimensions.

1 In the Layers panel, expand the iPhone artboard, and Shift-select the first and last layers in that artboard only. Don't select the artboard name itself.

2 Choose Edit > Free Transform.

3 In the options bar, do the following:

- Click the Toggle Reference Point checkbox to select it; this makes the reference point visible in the transformation bounding box and makes it possible for you to reposition the reference point.

- Select the top-left square of the reference point location option. Scaling, rotating, or other transformations will now be performed from the top-left corner of the bounding box (instead of the center) until the transformation is committed.

- Make sure the Maintain Aspect Ratio button (the link icon) is selected so that the selected layers will scale proportionally.

- Enter **726px** for W (Width).

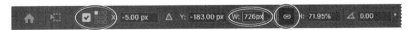

4 Press Enter or Return to apply the new settings to all selected layers as a unit. (Press Enter or Return only once to apply the value in the options bar. If you press Enter or Return a second time, it will commit the transformation.)

Tip: You can position the reference point anywhere inside or outside the transformation bounding box by dragging it.

Those settings proportionally scale the selected layers to 726 pixels wide, from the top-left corner of the selection, to better fit the artboard.

5   Position the pointer inside the Free Transform bounding box, and then Shift-drag the selected layers down until you can see the entire Museo Arts logo at the top of the page.

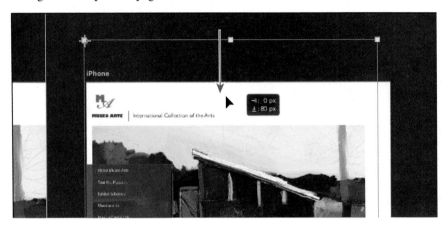

6   Press Enter or Return to exit Free Transform mode, and choose Select > Deselect Layers.

7   In the Layers panel, select the Logo layer, and choose Edit > Free Transform.

8   Drag the bottom-right handle on the Free Transform bounding box until the transformation values next to the pointer indicate that the logo is 672 pixels wide, matching the width of the other elements. Then press Enter or Return. Enlarging the logo makes it more readable on a smartphone screen.

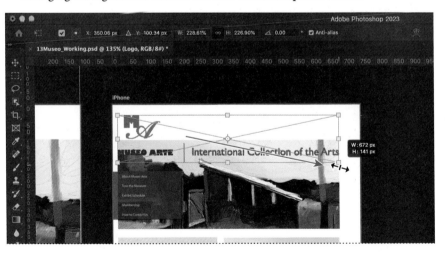

9 In the Layers panel, select the Banner Art, Left Column, and Right Column layers.

10 With the Move tool, Shift-drag the selected layers down until the top is even with the top of the blue button stack on the left.

▶ **Tip:** Remember that you can also nudge selected layers using the arrow keys if that makes it easier to precisely align them with the top of the blue button stack.

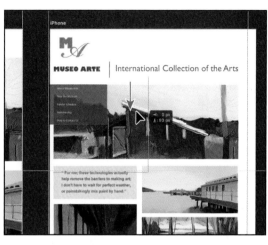

Now you'll take the two-column layout and make each column fill the width of the artboard. But first you'll need to accommodate them by making the artboard taller.

11 Select the iPhone artboard in the Layers panel, and then, with the Artboard tool, drag the bottom handle of the iPhone artboard until the transformation values next to the pointer indicate that it's 2800 px tall.

▶ **Tip:** You can also change the height of an artboard by entering a new Height in the Properties panel when an artboard is selected.

● **Note:** If a document uses artboards, resize them using only the Artboard tool. The Image > Image Size and Image > Canvas Size commands work best with a Photoshop document that doesn't use artboards.

12 Select the Right Column layer group in the Layers panel, and then choose Edit > Free Transform.

13 In the options bar, do the following:

- Make sure the Toggle Reference Point checkbox is selected, and then select the top-right square of the reference point location option.

- Make sure the Maintain Aspect Ratio (link) button is selected, and enter **672px** for Width.

- Press Enter or Return to apply the new width.

14 Position the pointer inside the Free Transform bounding box, and then Shift-drag the selected layer group down until the transformation values next to the pointer indicate a vertical move of 1200 px (the Y value in the options bar should say about 1680 px when the top-right square of the reference point locator is selected). Press Enter or Return to commit and exit the transformation.

15 Select the Left Column layer group in the Layers panel, and then choose Edit > Free Transform.

16 In the options bar, do the following:

- Make sure the Toggle Reference Point checkbox is selected, and then select the top-left square of the reference point location option.

- Make sure the Maintain Aspect Ratio (link) button is selected, and enter **672px** for Width.

- Press Enter or Return to apply the new width.

- Then press Enter or Return to commit and exit the transformation.

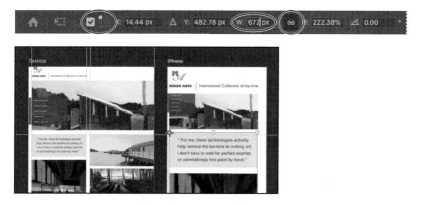

Feel free to adjust the positioning and the vertical spacing among the layer groups and layers.

17 Choose View > Fit On Screen to see both artboards at once, and then save your work.

▶ **Tip:** To nudge selected layers or layer groups when the Move tool is active, press the arrow keys. When Free Transform is active, you can also nudge by clicking in a number field and pressing the up arrow or down arrow key.

You've adapted a desktop-sized, multicolumn web page layout for a single-column smartphone layout. Both layouts exist on two artboards in the same document.

Exporting artboards with Export As (File menu)

When it's time to have a client review your designs, you can use the Export As command to easily export any artboard, layer, or layer group into its own file. You'll export the complete desktop and smartphone artboards, and then you'll export the layers of each artboard to their own folder.

1 Choose File > Export > Export As. This command exports each whole artboard so you see each artboard in the list on the left side of the Export As dialog box.

Note: The Export As dialog box doesn't preview multiple Scale All options. Artboards are previewed at 1x.

You can preview the exported dimensions and file size of each item; the preview is determined by the settings on the right side of the Export As dialog box.

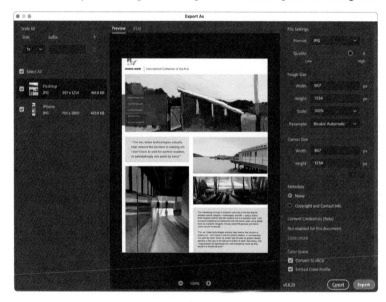

Tip: Not sure about the best combination of format, compression, and visual quality? Click the 2-up tab at the top of the Export As dialog box to see two views. Select one view and change the settings; then select the other view and change its settings. Now you can compare their quality, and you can see the resulting file size below each preview.

2 In the list on the left, click the Desktop artboard to highlight it, and then set the Export As options to the following:

- In the Scale All section, make sure Size is set to 1x and Suffix is empty.

- In the File Settings section, choose JPG from the Format menu, and make sure Quality is set to **6**.

- In the Color Space section, make sure Convert To sRGB is selected.

- Other settings can be left at the defaults.

3 In the list on the left, click the iPhone artboard to highlight it, and apply the same settings as in step 2.

4   Make sure Select All is selected, click Export, navigate to the Lesson13 folder, double-click the Assets folder, and then click Save or Open.

Tip: If you often use the Export As command with the same settings, choose File > Export > Export Preferences, and specify the settings you use the most. Now you can export to those settings in one step by choosing File > Export > Quick Export As or choosing Quick Export As (*Format*) from the Layers panel menu.

5   Switch to the desktop or Bridge, and open the Assets folder in the Lesson13 folder to see the Desktop.jpg and iPhone.jpg files representing each artboard. The filenames are based on the artboard names. You can send those files for review by a client or web development team.

6   Switch back to Photoshop.

Exporting layers as assets with Export As (Layer menu)

If the reviewers approve the design, you can then use Export As to create separate files for each layer on each artboard, such as images or buttons. Those assets can be used by a web or application developer who executes the design in code.

1   In the Layers panel, Shift-select all layers of the Desktop artboard.

2   Choose Layer > Export As. (Do not choose File > Export As.)

Notice that in the Export As dialog box, each layer is listed separately, because they will export separately.

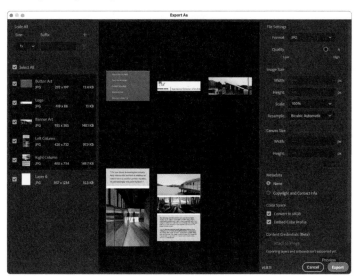

3   Click Button Art to highlight it; then hold down Shift and click Right Column to highlight the five top layers. Now when you adjust settings in the following steps, those changes will affect all highlighted layers.

4   In the Export As dialog box, enter the same settings as you did in step 2 of the previous section (on page 354).

5   Deselect the checkbox for Layer 0 so that it will not export. It's a solid white background that should be implemented through the web page code itself.

6   Click Export, navigate to the Assets_Desktop folder in the Lesson13 folder, and click Open or Save.

You have exported all assets for the Desktop artboard into a single folder.

7   Repeat steps 1–4 for the iPhone artboard.

8   Click Export, navigate to the Assets_iPhone folder in the Lesson13 folder, and click Open or Save.

9   In Photoshop, choose File > Browse In Bridge.

10 Navigate to the Assets_Desktop folder in the Lesson13 folder, and inspect the images by browsing each file with the Preview panel open. If you want, you can also inspect the assets you exported to the Assets_iPhone folder.

▶ **Tip:** If a developer asks for assets at multiple scale factors (for Retina/HiDPI display resolutions), in the Export As dialog box click the plus button in the Scale All section to add and specify additional scale factors (Size) such as 2x or 3x. Those will be exported at the same time. Be sure to specify the proper option in the Suffix field for each scale factor.

Each layer you exported is in its own file. You were able to quickly produce two different sets of files for two different screen sizes:

- By using the file-based Export As command (File > Export > Export As), you created JPG images of the complete desktop and iPhone artboards.

- By using the layer-based Export As command (on the Layers panel menu or Layer > Export As), you created assets from the individual layers of each artboard.

11 In Photoshop, save your changes, and close the document.

Review questions

1 What is a layer group?

2 What is an action? How do you create one?

3 How can you create assets from layers and layer groups in Photoshop?

Review answers

1 A layer group is a set of layers organized as a unit in the Layers panel. Layer groups make it easier to work with layers in complex images, especially when there are sets of layers that need to stay together when moved or scaled.

2 An action is a set of one or more commands that you record and then play back to apply to a single file or a batch of files. To create one, click the Create New Action button in the Actions panel, name the action, and click Record. Then perform the tasks you want to include in your action. When you've finished, click the Stop Recording button at the bottom of the Actions panel.

3 Use the Export As command to create assets from artboards, layers, and layer groups in Photoshop. To create images of each whole artboard, choose the Export As command on the File menu (File > Export > Export As). To create assets from selected layers and layer groups, choose the Export As on the Layers panel menu or Layer menu (Layer > Export As).

14 PRODUCING AND PRINTING CONSISTENT COLOR

Lesson overview

In this lesson, you'll learn how to do the following:

- Understand how images are prepared for printing on presses.

- Closely examine an image before final output.

- Define RGB, grayscale, and CMYK color spaces for displaying, editing, and printing images.

- Proof an image for printing.

- Prepare an image to print on a color printer.

- Save an image as a Photoshop PDF file.

 This lesson will take less than an hour to complete. To get the lesson files used in this chapter, download them from the web page for this book at peachpit.com/PhotoshopCIB2024. For more information, see "Accessing the lesson files and Web Edition" in the Getting Started section at the beginning of this book.

As you work on this lesson, you'll preserve the start files. If you need to restore the start files, download them from your Account page.

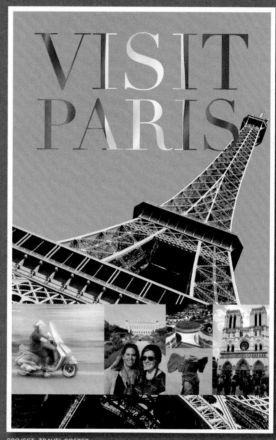

PROJECT: TRAVEL POSTER

To produce consistent color, you define the color space in which to edit and display RGB images and the color space in which to edit, display, and proof CMYK images. This helps ensure a close match between onscreen and printed colors.

Preparing files for printing

Whether you'll print the document on your own printer or send it to a printing service, you should perform the following tasks before printing. (Some of these tasks are covered in detail later in this lesson.)

Note: One exercise in this lesson requires that your computer be connected to a printer that supports Adobe PostScript. If you don't have access to one, you can do most of the exercises. PostScript is not required to print photo-quality images. PostScript is more commonly used in prepress workflows (preparing jobs for printing on a press).

- Understand how the printing conditions affect how you prepare your image, ideally before the work is complete. If you're going to send your work to a print service provider, ask in advance about their technical requirements, such as any color limitations and what file format they prefer. In some cases, they may request a file exported to a specific Adobe Portable Document Format (PDF) standard or preset.

- Verify that the image resolution is appropriate. For professional printing, a good guideline is 300 ppi at an image's final printed dimensions. This value can be different depending on factors such as the screening method used for the press, or the grade of paper. To determine the best print resolution for your project, consult your production team, print service provider, or printer user manual.

- Do a "zoom test": Zoom into the image to check and correct sharpness, color correction, noise, and other issues that can affect the final printed image quality.

- If you want any part of a design to print all the way to the edge of the page, set up a *bleed* (extending the artwork past the page edge) for the document. A bleed ensures that there isn't an unprinted gap at the page edge if the page is trimmed a little wide of the crop marks. You may need to extend the canvas and the design on all sides, typically by ¼ inch. For files you send out, your print service provider can recommend the bleed amount that works best on their equipment. When printing on a desktop printer that offers a "borderless" option, the printer driver software typically creates the bleed by slightly enlarging the print to extend it beyond the edges of the selected paper size.

- Keep images in their original color space, such as Adobe RGB (see "About Color Management" on page 366), unless your print service provider instructs you to convert them. If you do, convert copies of the images, not the originals. Today, many prepress workflows keep content in its original color space throughout editing to preserve color flexibility as long as possible, converting images and documents to CMYK automatically during printing.

- Before flattening Photoshop documents, always ask your production team first. Some workflows may depend on preserving, not flattening, Photoshop layers so that other applications, such as Adobe InDesign, can control the visibility of imported Photoshop layers from within their documents.

- Soft-proof the image to simulate onscreen how the colors will print.

Getting started

You'll prepare a travel poster for printing on a CMYK press. The Photoshop file size is relatively large, because it contains several layers at document dimensions of 11×17 inches at 300 ppi resolution.

First, start Photoshop, and restore its default preferences.

1 Start Photoshop, and then simultaneously hold down Ctrl+Alt+Shift (Windows) or Command+Option+Shift (Mac) to restore the default preferences. (See "Restoring default preferences" on page 5.)

2 When prompted, click Yes to delete the Adobe Photoshop Settings file.

3 Choose File > Open, navigate to the Lesson14 folder, and double-click the 14Start.psd file. Close any messages that appear about new features.

4 Choose File > Save As, navigate to the Lesson14 folder, and save the file as **14Working.psd**. Click OK if the Photoshop Format Options dialog box appears.

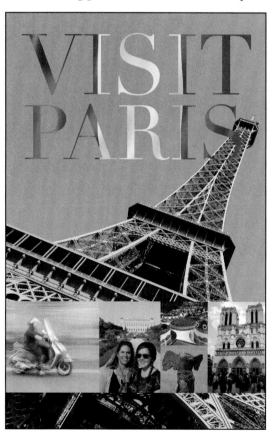

● Note: If Photoshop displays a dialog box telling you about the difference between saving to Cloud Documents and On Your Computer, click Save On Your Computer. You can also select Don't Show Again, but that setting will deselect after you reset Photoshop preferences.

Performing a "zoom test"

Note: If you consider changing the print size, remember that for photos, ppi resolution is tied to the print size—the same number of pixels is spread across more or less area. If this document (300 ppi at 11×17-inches) was printed at 50% size (8.5 inches tall), it would be 600 ppi. Printed at 200% size, it would be 150 ppi.

It's expensive to redo a big print job, so before you send out an image, take a few minutes to make sure everything is appropriate for your output device and that you haven't overlooked any potential problems. Start with the image resolution.

1 Choose Image > Image Size.

2 Verify that the width and height are the final output size in inches and that the resolution is appropriate.

This image has a width of 11" and a height of 17", which is the final size of the poster. Its resolution is 300 ppi. The size and resolution are appropriate for press printing.

3 Click OK to close the dialog box.

Tip: If your keyboard has Page Up, Page Down, Home, and End keys, you can use them to inspect a magnified Photoshop document. Home goes to the top-left corner, and End goes to the bottom-right corner. Add the Ctrl key (Windows) or the Command key (Mac) to make Page Up/Page Down keys navigate horizontally, and add the Shift key to scroll in smaller increments.

Next, you'll look closely at the image and correct any problems. When you prepare your own images for printing, zoom in and scroll to view the entire image closely.

4 Select the Zoom tool in the Tools panel, and zoom in on the photos in the lower third of the poster.

The photo of tourists is flat and a little muddy-looking.

5 Select the Tourists layer in the Layers panel, and then in the Adjustments panel, scroll down to the Single Adjustments list and click the Curves icon.

A new Curves adjustment layer appears above the Tourists layer.

6 Click the Clip To Layer button (⌐□) at the bottom of the Properties panel to create a clipping mask. In the list, the layer indents with a small arrow.

The clipping mask ensures that the adjustment layer affects only the layer it's associated with in the Layers panel. If the new adjustment layer was not made into a clipping mask, it would affect all of the layers below it.

▶ **Tip:** It's best to click the White Point eyedropper tool on a spot that is the lightest neutral area of an image that contains detail, not a specular highlight.

7   In the Properties panel, select the White Point eyedropper tool, and then click the white shirt of the person behind the tourists to define that point as the brightest neutral part of the image. (Zoom in as needed to click precisely.) Because the white shirt was darker than it would normally be, clicking it as a white point reference brightens it and the rest of the tones in the rest of the image and rebalances the colors in the image.

▶ **Tip:** After you click the White Point eyedropper, notice that the curves for the red, green, and blue channels have shifted to define the point you clicked as a neutral color, setting the color balance for the image. That's why it's important to click a spot that should be neutral.

The image of tourists looks better. But the image of the statue appears flat and lacks contrast. You'll fix that with a Levels adjustment layer.

8   Select the Statue layer in the Layers panel, and then in the Adjustments panel, scroll down to the Single Adjustments list and click the Levels icon.

9 Click the Clip To Layer button at the bottom of the Properties panel to create a clipping mask so that the adjustment layer affects only the Statue layer.

10 In the Properties panel, click the Calculate A More Accurate Histogram icon () to refresh the histogram display.

The alert icon next to the initial Calculate A More Accurate Histogram icon indicates that the histogram is based on cached image data. Photoshop first displays the histogram based on cached data because it displays more quickly, but it's often less accurate. Refreshing the histogram ensures that it's accurate and up to date before you make edits based on it.

11 Move the input level sliders to punch up the image. We used the values 31, 1.60, 235. Remember that to increase contrast, drag the black point (left) and white point (right) input sliders toward the center, making sure that highlight and shadow detail is still visible, not clipped (excluded).

Note: In the example for step 11, the levels are adjusted manually instead of using an eyedropper. The result of using an eyedropper wouldn't look right because the image doesn't contain a truly neutral highlight, midtone, or shadow. It should retain a slightly warm color cast.

12 Save the file. The whole poster looks better after your improvements to the photos of the tourists and statue.

About color management

Because the RGB and CMYK color models use different methods to display colors, each reproduces a different color *gamut* (color range). RGB creates color using transmitted light (such as a backlit digital display), and CMYK creates color using reflected and absorbed light (using inks). These differences determine the gamut each color model can reproduce. In general, RGB can reproduce more colors than CMYK (for example, CMYK is not large enough to reproduce highly saturated blue or neon green), although both can reproduce certain color ranges that the other cannot.

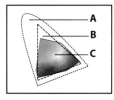

A. *Natural color gamut*
B. *RGB color gamut*
C. *CMYK color gamut*

RGB color model.

CMYK color model.

▶ **Tip:** Some color spaces represent a device, such as a display or a printer. Other color spaces, such as Adobe RGB, are intended for maintaining color flexibility when editing originals that might be delivered in print and onscreen.

But there are differences even within RGB and CMYK. Each monitor and printer model is built differently, so each reproduces a slightly different gamut. For example, one brand of monitor may produce slightly brighter blues than another. The *color space* for a device is defined by the gamut it can reproduce.

The color management system in Photoshop uses International Color Consortium (ICC) color profiles that work like translators, helping to maintain color appearance when converting colors from one color space to another. An *ICC color profile* is a description of a color space, such as the CMYK color space of a press standard. You can use Photoshop to embed a profile into an image file so that Photoshop and other applications can consistently interpret the colors of your images.

● **Note:** Your monitor may have been factory-calibrated, but you may not know how precisely and to what standard. For example, if your print service provider recommends that your monitor use the common prepress standard of a D65 white point, how do you know how well your monitor meets that standard? To make sure, calibrate and profile your monitor with D65 set as the target standard.

About calibration and profiling

Calibration means adjusting a device to meet a standard, like making sure a monitor displays neutral gray when neutral gray color values are sent to it. A *profile* describes whether the device meets a standard and, if not, how far off it is so that a color management system can correct for the difference and show image colors accurately.

To get the most out of color management, calibrate and profile your monitor so that you evaluate color on a screen using an accurate display profile. You can use calibration/profiling software that drives a color profiling device. The software uses the device to measure the colors produced by your screen and corrects for inaccuracies by creating a customized ICC display profile of your monitor. Your system uses this display profile to show colors accurately in any software that is color-managed, such as Photoshop and most other Adobe graphics software.

RGB color model

Much of the visible color spectrum can be represented by mixing red, green, and blue (RGB) colored light in various proportions and intensities. Where the colors overlap, they create cyan, magenta, yellow, and white.

Because the RGB colors combine to create white, they are also called *additive* colors. Adding all colors together creates white—that is, all light is transmitted back to the eye. Additive colors are used for lighting, video, and monitors. For example, an LCD monitor creates color by emitting its backlight through red, green, and blue filters.

CMYK color model

The CMYK model is based on the light-absorbing quality of ink printed on a substrate (surface) such as paper or packaging. As white light strikes translucent inks, part of the spectrum is absorbed, while other parts are reflected back to your eyes.

In theory, pure cyan (C), magenta (M), and yellow (Y) pigments should combine to absorb all color and produce black. For this reason, these colors are called *subtractive* colors. But because all printing inks contain some impurities, these three inks actually produce a muddy brown and must be combined with black (K) ink to produce a denser black. (K is used instead of B to avoid confusion with blue.) These are called *process colors* because they are used in four-color process printing.

Setting up color management defaults

By default, the Color Settings dialog box is set up for color gamuts typically used in an RGB-based workflow. If you're preparing artwork for printing on a press, as in the document used in this lesson, you may want to change the settings to be more appropriate for CMYK-based prepress production rather than screen display.

Many of the options in Color Settings are defaults you can override as needed, such as when preparing images for different media. When a document already has a color profile, Photoshop uses that instead of Color Settings defaults.

You'll customize the default settings for interpreting color.

1   Choose Edit > Color Settings to open the Color Settings dialog box.

2   Without clicking (don't change settings), hover the pointer over each part of the dialog box, including the names of sections (such as Working Spaces), the menu names, and the menu options. As you move the pointer, Photoshop displays information about each item in the Description area at the bottom of the Color Settings dialog box.

3 Choose the North America Prepress 2 preset from the Settings menu. The working spaces and color-management policy options change.

Tip: The Color Settings dialog box can seem complex, so remember that the only thing you usually need to do is pick the Settings preset that matches your workflow most closely. Each Settings preset changes the rest of the options for you. If you're working with a print service provider, they might recommend specific settings that work best with their equipment.

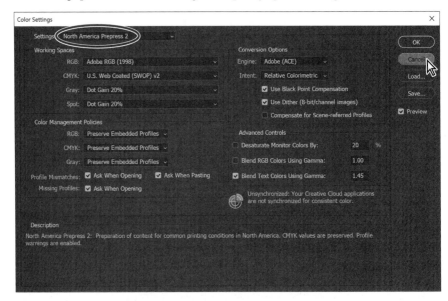

You won't save this change, because leaving it set to North America Prepress 2 may display warnings you aren't expecting if you don't normally use that workflow.

4 Click Cancel so that the settings aren't changed.

Identifying out-of-gamut colors

The color range covered by typical CMYK printing can reproduce many, but usually not all, of the colors in an RGB image from a digital camera or scanner. For example, colored LED lights or vivid flowers may produce colors that are outside a printer's CMYK gamut. Those colors may print with less detail and saturation than expected. Some intense blue colors in RGB can shift toward purple in CMYK.

Before you convert an image from RGB to CMYK, you can preview which RGB color values are outside the gamut of CMYK.

1 Choose View > Fit On Screen.

2 Choose View > Gamut Warning. Photoshop compares the document colors to the current CMYK color space and displays a neutral gray in the document window to indicate where document colors are outside the CMYK color gamut.

The gray gamut warning covers much of the image, especially the blue areas. A typical CMYK press can reproduce a relatively narrow range of blue compared to most RGB gamuts, so it's not unusual for an image to have RGB blue values that are outside a CMYK printing gamut. In out-of-gamut areas, the printer would end up printing the closest shade of blue its inks can reproduce on a given paper.

Because the gray indicator color can be hard to distinguish in the image, you'll change it to a more visible color.

3   Choose Edit > Preferences > Transparency & Gamut (Windows) or Photoshop > Settings > Transparency & Gamut (Mac).

● **Note:** If you're using macOS 12 or earlier, the Settings command is named Preferences.

4   Click the color sample in the Gamut Warning area at the bottom of the dialog box. Select a vivid color, such as purple or bright green, and click OK.

5   Click OK to close the Preferences dialog box.

▶ **Tip:** If your gamut warning area looks different, you may be using different settings in the View > Proof Setup > Custom dialog box (see page 370).

The bright new color you chose appears instead of the neutral gray as the gamut warning color; it should be much more obvious which areas are out of gamut. If this was a real job, you might consult your prepress service provider to discuss how their press will reproduce that blue color and whether it's worth editing the color.

6   Choose View > Gamut Warning to turn off the preview of out-of-gamut colors.

Next, you'll simulate onscreen how the document colors might print, and then you'll bring those colors into the printing gamut.

▶ **Tip:** When you have concerns about how a color will reproduce on press, you can ask your prepress service provider about seeing a *hard proof* (test print).

Proofing document colors on a monitor

You'll select a proof profile so that you can view an onscreen simulation of what document colors will look like when printed. An accurate proof profile lets you proof on the screen (*soft-proof*) for printed output.

That onscreen simulation is based on a *proof setup*, which defines the printing conditions. Photoshop provides a variety of settings that can help you proof images for different uses, including for different printers and devices. For this lesson, you'll create a custom proof setup. You can then save the settings for use on other images that will be output the same way.

1 Choose View > Proof Setup > Custom. The Customize Proof Condition dialog box opens. Make sure Preview is selected.

Tip: A printer profile represents not only the output device but also a specific combination of settings, ink, and paper. Changing any of those components can change the color gamut being simulated by the onscreen proof, so choose a profile that's as close as possible to the final printing conditions.

2 From the Device To Simulate menu, choose a color profile that represents the final output device, such as that for the printer you'll use to print the image. If you don't have a specific printer, use the profile Working CMYK–U.S. Web Coated (SWOP) v2, the current default.

3 If you've chosen a different profile, make sure Preserve Numbers is *not* selected.

The Preserve Numbers option simulates how colors will appear if they're not converted to the output device color space. This option may be named Preserve CMYK Numbers when you select a CMYK output profile.

4 Make sure Relative Colorimetric is selected for the Rendering Intent.

A rendering intent determines how the color is converted from one color space to another. Relative Colorimetric preserves color relationships without sacrificing color accuracy and is the standard rendering intent for printing in North America and Europe.

5 Select Simulate Black Ink if it's available for the profile you chose. Then deselect it and select Simulate Paper Color; notice that selecting this option automatically selects Simulate Black Ink.

Tip: When the Customize Proof Condition dialog box isn't open, you can view the document with or without the current proof settings by selecting or deselecting the View > Proof Colors command.

Notice that the image appears to lose contrast. Most paper is not pure white; Paper Color simulates that. Most black ink is not perfectly solid or neutral black, so Black Ink simulates the actual ink. Both get that information from the output profile, if available.

Don't be alarmed by the loss of contrast and saturation that you may see when you turn on the Display Options. While the image might look worse, the soft-proofing simulation is just being honest about how the image will actually print; paper and ink simply cannot reproduce the same range of tones and colors as a monitor. Choosing higher-quality paper stock and inks can help a printed image match the screen more closely.

6   Toggle the Preview option to see the difference between the image as it is displayed onscreen and as it will print, based on the profile you selected. Then click OK.

Tip: If you want to check the print color simulation as you work, you can quickly toggle Proof Colors on or off by using the keyboard shortcut for View > Proof Colors: Press Ctrl-Y (Windows) or Command-Y (macOS).

Normal image.

Image with Simulate Paper Color and Simulate Black Ink options selected.

7   Click the View menu, and if Proof Colors is enabled, choose Proof Colors to disable it. You can use this command to enable or disable the soft-proof settings that you set up in the Customize Proof Condition dialog box.

Bringing colors into the output gamut

The next step in preparing an image for output is to make any necessary color and tonal adjustments based on what you see in the proofs. In this exercise, you'll add some tonal and color adjustments to correct an off-color scan of the original poster.

So that you can compare the image before and after making corrections, you'll start by making a copy.

1   Choose Image > Duplicate, and click OK to duplicate the image.

2   Choose Window > Arrange > 2 Up Vertical so you can compare the images as you work.

You'll adjust the hue and saturation of the image to move all colors into gamut.

3   Select 14Working.psd (the original image) to make it active, and then select the Visit Paris layer in the Layers panel.

Tip: You might not need to adjust colors that are indicated as out of gamut. You should definitely inspect them, but if those areas look acceptable and don't lose detail when proofing, you may not need to spend time editing them. Some would leave the blue sky alone because it's a flat area, so there are no details to lose after converting the file to the printer color gamut.

4 Choose Select > Color Range.

5 In the Color Range dialog box, choose Out of Gamut from the Select menu, and then click OK.

● **Note:** In the Color Range dialog box, the color range marked as Out of Gamut is calculated using the profile selected for the CMYK Working Space in the Edit > Color Settings dialog box. Make sure the correct profile is selected for the printer or press for your job.

The areas that were marked as out of gamut earlier are now selected, so you can make changes that affect only those areas.

6 In the Adjustments panel, scroll down to the Single Adjustments list and click Hue/Saturation to create a Hue/Saturation adjustment layer. (Choose Window > Adjustments if the panel isn't open.) The Hue/Saturation adjustment layer was created with a layer mask based on your selection.

7 Choose View > Gamut Warning to enable it, and in the Properties panel, adjust the Hue/Saturation value to bring out-of-gamut colors into the printer color gamut so that the gamut warning mostly disappears. We used the following settings:

- Leave the Hue setting at 0.

- Drag the Saturation slider to reduce the value (we used –14). Reducing Saturation is one way to bring colors into a target gamut.

- Drag the Lightness to the left (we used –2).

8   Close the duplicate image file (the 14Working copy tab) without saving it.

In this exercise, you shifted out-of-gamut colors into the printing gamut mostly by desaturating them. While desaturating is quick and easy, it's considered a basic technique. Skilled image editors use more advanced techniques to preserve color detail while maintaining color relationships as much as possible.

Converting an image to CMYK

It's generally a good idea to work in RGB mode as long as possible so that your edits can take place within the larger color gamut of RGB. Also, converting between modes can cause color value rounding errors that may result in unwanted color changes, especially over multiple conversions.

If your printing workflow requires final images to be in CMYK, save CMYK copies after completing final corrections. If you also want to output the image to an inkjet printer or distribute it digitally later, keep the original document in RGB mode.

1   Click the Channels tab to bring the Channels panel to the front.

The image is currently in RGB mode, so there are three channels listed: red, green, and blue. The RGB channel is not actually a channel, but a composite of all three. You also see a channel named Hue/Saturation 1 Mask; this channel contains the mask information for the layer currently selected in the Layers panel.

2   Choose Image > Mode > CMYK Color.

3   Click Merge in the message that warns you that you might lose some adjustment layers. Merging the layers helps preserve the appearance of colors.

Another message appears, saying: "You are about to convert to CMYK using the 'U.S. Web Coated (SWOP) v2' profile. This may not be what you intend. To choose a

Tip: If you aren't sure if or when you should convert images to CMYK, ask the print service provider that will output your job. They can recommend the image preparation steps that work best with their prepress equipment.

different profile, use Edit > Convert To Profile." This message lets you know that the active CMYK profile is U.S. Web Coated (SWOP) v2, the Photoshop default profile for CMYK color. That profile might not represent the actual prepress specification or proofing standard that will be used.

In a real job, you would ask the print service provider which CMYK profile to use for color conversions; they may be able to provide a custom profile that accurately represents how their equipment reproduces tones and colors. You would then load that custom CMYK profile into your operating system's standard location for ICC profiles so that you can select it as the CMYK Working Space in the Edit > Color Settings dialog box or so you can select it when converting the image to CMYK using the more advanced and precise Edit > Convert To Profile command.

4 Click OK in the message about the color profile used in the conversion.

The Channels panel now displays four channels: cyan, magenta, yellow, and black. On top, it lists the composite view of all CMYK channels together. The layers were merged during conversion, so there is only one layer in the Layers panel.

About CMYK color separations

When a document is sent to a CMYK press, each of the CMYK channels becomes *color separated*—sent to its own printing plate. As the paper moves through the press, each of the four plates prints its ink on the paper. Your eyes combine the four inks and see a full color image.

In Photoshop, the Print dialog box includes options that let you print separations for a CMYK document. However, this is usually not useful for previewing a job. A desktop printer's resolution, precision, and *screen* method (how it uses ink dots to build colors) are different than a prepress platesetter. The color separation options in the Photoshop print dialog box are intended to be used by those operating prepress equipment.

If you just want to know on which plate certain elements of your document will print, you can view each CMYK channel in the Channels panel.

5   In the Channels panel, see what will print in each channel by clicking each of the channels in turn: Cyan, Magenta, Yellow, and Black. When you're done, click CMYK to once again see the composite view of all channels together.

Saving the image as Photoshop PDF

When print jobs are submitted in various document formats, components such as type, fonts, and transparency might not be included or might be handled in different ways. To solve this problem, some print service providers may request that you submit a print job in PDF format, which is popular because it can consistently preserve many document attributes that are important for high-quality printing on press.

1   Choose File > Save A Copy.

2   In the Save A Copy dialog box, navigate to the Lesson14 folder, choose Photoshop PDF from the Format menu, name the file **14Print.pdf**, and then click Save.

3   Click OK if a message appears about Save Adobe PDF settings.

4   In the Save Adobe PDF dialog box, choose [PDF/X-4:2008] from the Adobe PDF Preset menu. How do you know which preset to choose? Ask your print service provider which preset best matches their printing workflow.

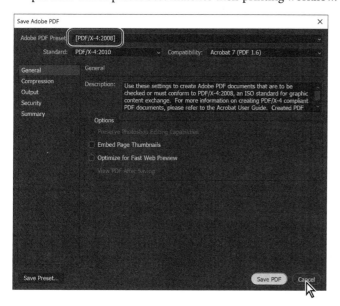

Tip: PDF/X is an industry standard for storing printing information for high-quality reproduction on press. Newer PDF/X standards support more printing features.

The five panels along the left side of the bottom of the Save Adobe PDF dialog box (General, Compression, etc.) contain many PDF options. Fortunately, if you know or have been told which Adobe PDF Preset to choose, you don't have to think about any of those options, because choosing a preset sets those options for you.

5 Click Save PDF. Photoshop saves the PDF version in the Lesson14 folder.

If you want, you can open the Lesson14 folder in Adobe Bridge or on the desktop and double-click the 14Print.pdf file. It opens in the default PDF application on your computer. If Adobe Acrobat is installed, it may open in that application.

Printing to a desktop color printer

● **Note:** This exercise requires a printer connected to your computer, and driver software for that printer installed on your computer.

Many color inkjet printers make high-quality prints of photographs and other image files. However, they reproduce color differently than a press. You'll get the best results if you do the following:

• Make sure the printer's driver software is installed and up to date.

• Use the appropriate paper for your intended use, such as coated paper for photographs, high-quality matte for graphic design, or textured for digital paintings. Plain paper and inexpensive office-grade paper may not reproduce color and detail with the quality you want for photographs and graphic art.

• Don't convert an RGB image to CMYK to print on a desktop color printer. Most desktop printers are designed to receive RGB color data. The printer driver software converts from RGB to the specific ink set used in that printer. For example, a pro inkjet printer that uses eight inks to reproduce a wider color gamut needs to convert RGB to its own eight-ink colors, not the four CMYK ink colors.

▶ **Tip:** Want to see more print settings at once? Resize the Photoshop Print Settings window by dragging a corner or edge.

1 Choose File > Print.

2 In the Printer Setup section, select a printer from the Printer menu.

3 Click Print Settings, set the appropriate paper size and any other options needed for the print job, and click Save to return to Photoshop Print Settings.

It's not possible to cover the Print Settings button in more detail, because the settings and layout differ depending on whether you are using macOS or Windows, and which printer you're using. The driver software for each printer adds options specific to that printer brand and model. Typically, it's important to set the paper/media type, paper size, and color management settings here. For more information, consult the help files for your operating system and your printer.

● **Note:** If you set Color Handling to Photoshop Manages Colors, you typically want to disable color management in the printer driver settings to avoid double color management. Either the printer or Photoshop should control print colors, but not both.

4 In the Color Management section, for general-purpose color printers set Color Handling to Printer Manages Colors. For professional photo or fine art printers, you may get better results by setting Color Handling to Photoshop Manages Colors; selecting a color profile for your combination of printer, ink, and paper from the Printer Profile menu; and making sure color management is disabled in the printer driver settings.

5   Check the preview on the left to see if the document print size and position is correct relative to the paper size. If not, change options in the Position and Size section, or change the paper size by clicking the Print Settings button at the top.

6   If you need any marks printed outside the image area, such as crop marks or print information, set them up in the Printing Marks and Functions sections. For marks to have room to print outside the image, the paper size must be larger than the image size.

7   If you want to print, click Print. If you don't want to print now and you want to save the changes you made for when you print later, click Done.

▶ **Tip:** If Scale to Fit Media isn't selected, you can enter dimensions in the Scale section, and position and scale the image in the print preview on the left.

● **Note:** The PostScript Options section is not covered here because it's typically used by print service providers, not with common desktop printers.

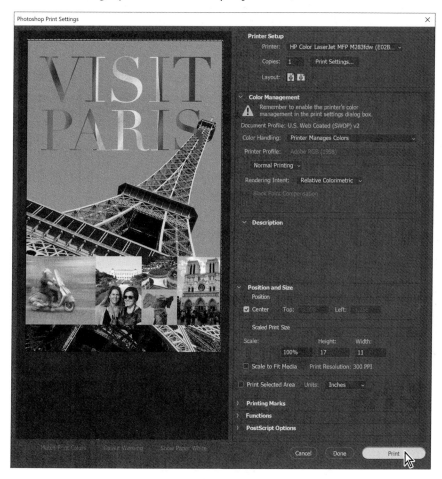

Congratulations…you've learned a lot about preparing a document to be printed!

Extra credit

Sharing your work on Adobe Portfolio

Integrated into Adobe Creative Cloud is Adobe Portfolio, which you can use to quickly create a well-designed and functional website that showcases your creations, with one-click connections to your social media presence (such as your Instagram, Facebook, and Twitter feeds) and a prebuilt contact form that makes it easy for potential clients and customers to get in touch with you. To test it, you'll first prepare this lesson's image for viewing in a web browser.

1   Open the 14Start.psd file in Photoshop, if it isn't already open. Click OK if the Embedded Profile Mismatch dialog box appears.

    As the original RGB version of the image in this lesson, 14Start.psd contains a wider color gamut than the later version that was converted to CMYK for prepress.

2   Choose File > Export > Export As to prepare the image for display on a website. It's a large, print-resolution image, so it may take a while to display in the Export As dialog box.

3   Choose JPG from the Format menu, and set Quality to **6**.

4   In the Image Size section, enter a Height in pixels to proportionally resize the exported image. We entered **1000** pixels, enough to show the image with a good amount of detail on many displays.

5   In the Color Space section, select Convert To sRGB and Embed Color Profile to help ensure consistent color in web browsers where color profile support is enabled.

6   Click Export. Navigate to the Lesson14 folder, and click Export or Save.

Now you can start making your website. The Portfolio user interface you see may vary as Adobe updates the service. Some of the following steps may appear only when creating a Portfolio website for the first time.

1 In a web browser, go to myportfolio.com, the web address for Adobe Portfolio.

2 At the top of the Adobe Portfolio home page, click Sign In, enter your Adobe ID email address and password, and click Sign In.

3 On the next screen, click to select the type of site you want to create: Full Portfolio or Welcome Page. We clicked Welcome Page to make a quick one-page website and scrolled down to pick the Cover Left - Light theme.

4 After the site is created, click the Click To Upload An Image/Video button. Navigate to the Lesson14 folder, select 14Start.jpg, and then click Choose, Open, or Upload (the button name depends on the web browser you use). Adobe Portfolio processes the image and replaces the left-side placeholder with it.

5 Now edit the text on the splash page. On the right side of the page, double-click in any text object to edit its text. You can add a brief description of you and your work.

6 Click Preview. The buttons at the bottom of the preview show you how the page will look on different device displays and orientations, such as a smartphone held vertically or horizontally.

7 Click Back To Edit.

Continues on next page

Extra credit (continued)

As you move the pointer over different page elements, icons appear over them. If you see an edit icon (a blue rectangle with a pencil), click it to edit that object. If you see an add icon (a circle containing a plus sign), click it to add new content to a page, such as photos, video, or embedded media.

8   Position the pointer over the button labeled Edit This Button, click the edit icon that appears on the left side of its containing object, and in the menu that appears, click Edit Button. In the Options tab that appears on the left, you can change options such as the button text or the button font, and you can add a link. Other tabs offer options for other button states, such as how it looks when you hover the pointer over it. To exit click the back button (<) at the top-left corner of the Edit Button panel. If you want, edit other sections, such as the social media icons.

9   Use the options along the left side of the Portfolio editor to add or organize pages, customize the design (including the theme, fonts, and page backgrounds), or set options for the entire website, such as password protection. You can also create and manage multiple websites.

If your site looks good and you want the world to see it, click Publish Site. It's live!

If you have your own Internet domain name, you can easily connect it to Adobe Portfolio so that your website's address is fully consistent with your brand. To do this, click Settings, and then edit settings in the Domain Name panel.

If you don't use a custom domain name, your website address is a subdomain of myportfolio.com. For example, if you name the site "parisvisitor," then parisvisitor.myportfolio.com is the default web address.

Review questions

1 What steps should you follow to reproduce color consistently?

2 What is a gamut?

3 What is a color profile?

4 What are color separations?

5 What are two reasons it is typically not necessary to convert an RGB image to CMYK before printing it?

Review answers

1 To reproduce color consistently, first calibrate and profile your monitor, and then use the Color Settings dialog box to specify which color spaces to use by default. For example, you can specify which RGB color space to use for online images and which CMYK color space to use for images that will be printed. You can then proof the image, check for out-of-gamut colors, and adjust colors as needed.

2 A gamut is the range of colors that can be reproduced by a color model or real-world device. For example, the RGB and CMYK color models have different gamuts. Within each color model, various printers, printing standards, and device displays reproduce different gamuts.

3 A color profile is a description of a color space, such as the CMYK color space of a particular printer. Applications such as Photoshop can read the color profiles representing different applications, platforms, and devices, to maintain consistent color across them.

4 Color separations are separate plates for each ink used in a document being reproduced on press, such as the four color separations required to print the cyan, magenta, yellow, and black process colors on a press.

5 For prepress jobs, many workflows now convert RGB to CMYK in the equipment at the print service provider. For desktop color printing, RGB is converted to CMYK by the printer driver software because the ink or toner colors used by many desktop printers do not exactly match the inks used on press.

15

EXPLORING NEURAL FILTERS

Lesson overview

In this lesson, you'll learn how to do the following:

- Understand how Neural Filters are different than other filters and effects in Photoshop.

- Explore the Neural Filters workspace.

- Apply a Neural Filter to an image.

- Combine multiple Neural Filters in a single layer or document.

This lesson will take about 30 minutes to complete. To get the lesson files used in this chapter, download them from the web page for this book at peachpit.com/PhotoshopCIB2024. For more information, see "Accessing the lesson files and Web Edition" in the Getting Started section at the beginning of this book.

As you work on this lesson, you'll preserve the start files. If you need to restore the start files, download them from your Account page.

PROJECT: COMPOSITING WITH NEURAL FILTERS

Landscape: © Jurik Peter, Shutterstock; superhero: © sunlight19, Shutterstock

Neural Filters are advanced filters trained using machine learning. You can explore ideas that would be more labor-intensive, or sometimes impossible, with conventional digital photo filters and effects.

Understanding Neural Filters

If you worked through the earlier lessons in this book, you've used Photoshop filters such as Surface Blur, Smart Sharpen, Clouds, and Liquify. Those are conventional filters that produce their results with algorithms—procedural programs where the code itself determines the result.

The newer Neural Filters produce results in a different way, combining traditional algorithms with *machine learning* and other advanced techniques. Machine learning means that a filter in Neural Filters can be trained using many examples of desirable and undesirable results, potentially creating better images than what could be achieved with procedural computer code alone.

Neural Filters are different from other Photoshop effects in the following ways:

● **Note:** You can use Neural Filters if your computer meets the system requirements for Photoshop, but performance is better with a more powerful CPU, more powerful graphics hardware, and in some cases a faster Internet connection.

- Neural Filters are trained using machine learning techniques.

- Some filters need to be downloaded before the first time you use them. This is partly to save space on your computer, because some Neural Filters and their machine-learning models can be large. If you need to download a Neural Filter, you can do it with one click in the Neural Filters workspace.

- Some filters display a message saying that they process image data in the cloud (on Adobe Creative Cloud servers). They may need more power than a desktop computer has, or a machine-learning model may be too large to download.

It's possible to use some Neural Filters without an Internet connection, but you get the most options when your computer is connected to the Internet.

Getting started

● **Note:** If Bridge isn't installed, the File > Browse In Bridge command in Photoshop will start the Creative Cloud desktop app, which will download and install Bridge. After installation completes, you can start Bridge. For more information, see page 3.

Neural Filters offer many possibilities to explore. Let's first take a look at the files you'll work with.

1 Start Photoshop, and then simultaneously hold down Ctrl+Alt+Shift (Windows) or Command+Option+Shift (macOS) to restore the default preferences. (See "Restoring default preferences" on page 5.)

2 When prompted, click Yes to delete the Adobe Photoshop Settings file.

3 Choose File > Browse In Bridge to open Adobe Bridge.

4 In Bridge, click Lessons in the Favorites panel. Double-click the Lesson15 folder in the Content panel.

5 Compare the files 15Restore.psd and 15Restore_End.psd, 15Colorize.psd and 15Colorize_End.psd, and 15Composite.psd and 15Composite_End.psd. Using Neural Filters, you'll create the finished files in just a few clicks.

Exploring the Neural Filters workspace

1   In Bridge, double-click the 15Restore.psd file to open it in Photoshop. If the Embedded Profile Mismatch dialog box appears, click OK.

2   Save the document as **15Restore_Working.psd** in the Lesson15 folder.

3   Choose Filter > Neural Filters.

In the Neural Filters workspace, the image appears in a large preview area on the left, and the Neural Filters panel is on the right:

•   When you select a filter, its options appear in the Neural Filters panel.

•   To use a filter, it must be enabled. A filter is enabled when its toggle switch is moved to the right position and in color. You can enable multiple filters.

•   If the selected filter recognizes faces in the image, they're listed in the thumbnail preview menu at the top of the options. In the document, a blue rectangle indicates the selected face; gray rectangles indicate other detected faces. Select a face in the face menu or in the document.

•   To compare the current filter results with the original image, click the Show Original icon at the bottom of the workspace to select it and display the original layer. Click again to deselect it and preview the filter results again.

•   When a document has multiple layers, the Layer Preview button controls whether the preview displays one layer or the entire document.

•   Along the left side, the top two tools let you paint a mask to hide filter effects from some areas, similar to the layer masks you edited in Lessons 6 and 8.

Note: If Photoshop displays a dialog box telling you about the difference between saving to Cloud Documents and On Your Computer, click Save On Your Computer. You can also select Don't Show Again, but that setting will deselect after you reset Photoshop preferences.

Note: If the Neural Filters command is not available, make sure a visible layer is selected.

A. Add To Selection and Subtract From Selection tools

B. Hand tool

C. Zoom tool

D. Selected face

E. Filter lists

F. Filter toggle, enabled

G. Use Graphics Processor (GPU) option

H. Thumbnail menu for selecting a detected subject, such as a face

I. Reset filter options to default settings

J. Options for the selected Neural Filter

K. Show Original/Preview Changes button

L. Show current layer or all layers (Layer Preview)

M. Output options

Restoring an antique portrait photo

To learn more about Neural Filters, let's see how they can help restore old photos.

Note: Adobe may update Neural Filters after this book is published, so the list of categories and filters you see may depend on the version of Photoshop you are using. Also, if Adobe updates how Neural Filters effects are trained, you may see different results than those in this lesson.

1 In the filters list, scroll down to the Restoration category, and click the toggle switch next to the Photo Restoration filter to enable and apply it. (If options are not available and a Download button appears instead, click the Download button because it means the filter is not yet installed. When the download completes, the filter will install itself and be ready for you to use.)

A. *Photo Enhancement*

B. *Enhance Face*

C. *Scratch Reduction*

Note: Some Neural Filters may be labeled Beta, which means they function but are still under development. You can use them, but when the finished version is released, those filters may produce different results or some options may be different.

2 To compare the changes with the original, click the Show Original button at the bottom of the workspace. Click once to hide the changes and see the original, and click again to preview the changes again. If you don't notice a change, zoom in to 100% or higher magnification.

3 As needed, adjust the first two Photo Restoration options, and then repeat step 2 to check your work:

- We left Photo Enhancement at its default value of 50.

- We reduced Enhance Face to 15 to preserve more of the original film texture.

4 Scroll up or zoom out as needed until you can see the top of the image. That part of the photo print is scratched and torn.

5   Adjust Scratch Reduction to about 20. A progress bar at the bottom of the image may indicate that it will take a little while. When it's done, the scratch is intelligently removed, which you can verify using the Show Original button.

▶ **Tip:** If you increase the value of a Neural Filter option, watch out for negative side effects on some parts of the image. It's typically better to leave minor spots and wrinkles, cleaning them up quickly using the retouching techniques you learned in Lesson 2.

6   You greatly improved this image using the Restoration Neural Filter. For Output, choose Smart Filter, and then click OK to exit Neural Filters. Close the document, saving your changes.

Adding color and depth blur

You can use Neural Filters to colorize black-and-white images and add depth blur.

1   In Bridge, double-click the 15Colorize.psd file to open it in Photoshop. If the Embedded Profile Mismatch dialog box appears, click OK.

2   Save the document as **15Colorize_Working.psd** in the Lesson15 folder.

3   Choose Filter > Neural Filters.

4   In the filters list, scroll down to the Color category, and click the toggle switch next to the Colorize filter to enable it. Make sure Auto Color Image is selected.

● **Note:** If the Colorize options aren't available because the filter needs to be downloaded, download it.

The Colorize filter applies assumed colors to objects and regions it recognizes, such as the leaves on the tree and the boy's skin and clothing. If you disagree with a color choice Colorize made (for example, if the shirt is not all the same color), you can apply custom colors to specific areas.

▶ **Tip:** For a different look, expand the Adjustments section in Colorize and select a Profile. If the result is too strong, reduce the Profile Strength, and make any other changes you like using the other Adjustments options.

Tip: If the results of the Colorize filter aren't perfect, you can combine it with manual Photoshop techniques. For example, after closing Neural Filters, add a new layer that uses the Color blending mode, and paint on that layer to colorize the image under it.

5   In the preview image on the right, click to add a new color focal point over an area you want to change, and set its color using the color picker below the image. Repeat for other areas where you want to change the color.

6   In the Photography category in the filters list, click the toggle switch next to the Depth Blur filter to enable it (download it if needed).

7   Adjust filter options as needed until you like the result. We disabled the Focus Subject option because it included part of the tree, and we set our Focal Range to 40 so that more of the bicycle remains in focus.

8   You've brought this image back to life! For Output, choose Smart Filter, and then click OK to exit Neural Filters. Close the document, saving your changes.

About Output options in Neural Filters

A Neural Filter may provide several options for applying filter results to the document, in the Output menu. The number of options you see may be different than in the figure below, depending on which filter and filter options are selected. Your choice affects the amount of editing flexibility you have later.

Current Layer applies the result to the selected layer. This permanently alters the original layer. The only way to back out of it is to undo it before you close and save the document. We recommend using one of the following options instead, because they leave the current layer intact.

New Layer applies the result to a full copy of the selected layer, leaving that original unchanged.

New Layer Masked applies the result to a copy of the selected layer with the changed areas showing through a layer mask. This helps ensure that areas of the image that were not supposed to be changed remain as they are on the original layer.

Smart Filter applies the result to a Smart Object created from the selected layer. You can edit the filter settings later by double-clicking that layer's Neural Filters instance in the Layers panel.

New Document applies the result to a duplicate document containing the filter results on one layer.

The choice you make can depend on the balance you want between flexibility and file size. Additional layers and Smart Objects provide more editing freedom, but tend to create larger file sizes.

When you make multiple edits within a filter, such as changing multiple faces differently in a group portrait, all changes are included in the output. For example, if you apply Smart Portrait and Style Transfer to the same layer, all of those results are applied to a single layer or Smart Filter.

Neural Filters might not produce perfect results right away. By applying Neural Filters results as a separate masked layer, you can freely blend them with the original layer to achieve a more convincing result, while still saving many steps compared to traditional, more labor-intensive methods.

Creating a more convincing composite

When compositing multiple images, the images may not be consistent in tone and color. Some Neural Filters can help resolve this.

1 In Bridge, double-click the 15Composite.psd to open it in Photoshop. If the Embedded Profile Mismatch dialog box appears, click OK.

2 Save the document as **15Composite_Working.psd** in the Lesson15 folder. Click OK in the Photoshop Format Options dialog. This image will become a thumbnail image for a video, but the color palette and subject need to be closer to the look of the art director's concept.

3 In the Layers panel, make sure the Planet layer is selected, and then choose Filter > Neural Filters.

4 In the filters list, scroll down to the Creative category, and click to enable the toggle switch next to the Landscape Mixer filter (if needed, download it first). The Landscape Mixer filter can apply the look of one landscape image to another. Depending on the landscape images you mix, you can even change a scene from summer to winter or fill a desert image with green foliage.

> **Tip:** You can use your own image to drive the style applied by Landscape Mixer. Click Custom, click Select An Image, and open an image from your computer. Also, Landscape Mixer options let you adjust attributes such as the amount of Day or Night and the time of year. For example, you can add snow by increasing the Winter value.

5 In the Landscape Mixer options, click different Presets to experiment with how each of them alters the landscape attributes of the layer.

6 Click the fourth preset. That's the one to use for this project.

7 For Output, choose Smart Filter, and then click OK to apply the changes.

8 In the Layers panel, click the eye icon for the Heroine layer to make it visible. Its tone and color doesn't quite match up with the landscape, so let's improve that.

9 With the Heroine layer selected, choose Filter > Neural Filters, and in the Color category in the filters list, click to enable the toggle switch next to the Harmonization filter (if needed, download it first). The Harmonization filter helps match the color and tone of a layer to another layer in the document.

10 In the Reference Image section, click Select A Layer, and select Planet.

The color and tone of the Heroine layer change to better match the color and light of the Planet layer, but it could be improved.

11 In the Harmonization options, drag the Cyan/Red slider about halfway toward Red, drag Saturation to about +15, and reduce Brightness to about –30. Make any other adjustments that make the composite more convincing. Remember to use the Show Original button to check your work.

▶ **Tip:** The best thing you can do to make your composite images the most convincing is to make sure all of your original images are consistent in as many ways as possible—not only color and tone, but other visual details such as the quality of lighting (including sources, angles, and shadows), lens focal length, and camera distance from the ground.

12 For Output, choose Smart Filter, and then click OK to apply the changes.

ADOBE PHOTOSHOP CLASSROOM IN A BOOK 2024 RELEASE **391**

13 In the Layers panel, click the eye icon for the Guardian type layer to make it visible.

You've completed the video thumbnail…nice work! You used Neural Filters to transform the look of both images in just a few steps, making them work together to match the mood and the look of the production.

14 Save your work, and close the document.

You've learned the basics of using Neural Filters. The results created in this lesson required only a few steps each; for example, retouching the old images was almost no work compared to the steps you learned in Lesson 2 and Lesson 5.

You're ready to explore the possibilities of the Neural Filters with your own images!

Finding the filter or effect you want

It can be a challenge to find the right filter or effect, because Photoshop offers them in multiple places in the workspace and menus, and some filters are similar to others. Here is a quick guide to the places to find filters and effects in Photoshop:

General filters are on the Filter menu and its submenus. Not every filter is visible on the submenus, so also remember to look inside the next two filter galleries.

Filter Gallery (Filter > Filter Gallery) offers many conventional (algorithmic) filters, such as Diffuse Glow and Mosaic Tiles. These are mostly intended for creative effects.

Neural Filters (Filter > Neural Filters) offer filters trained by machine learning. They can produce results that are better than, or not possible with, conventional filters.

To explore all your options, keep those multiple filter locations in mind. For example, if you want to improve skin complexion, you can use the more traditional multistep technique in Lesson 12 that uses the Surface Blur filter, compare that to the results you get from using the one-step Skin Smoothing filter in Neural Filters, and choose the result you think is better for a specific image.

Layer styles are nondestructive, easy ways to apply drop shadows, glows, and other effects you have tried in this book. You can find them by clicking the fx button at the bottom of the Layers panel or on the Layer > Layer Style submenu.

As you have practiced in this book, even a destructive filter (permanently altering layer pixels) can be applied nondestructively (allowing edits or removal later) if the layer is a Smart Object. You can prepare a selected layer for nondestructive filtering by first choosing Filter > Convert For Smart Filters.

To combine filters on a layer, you can typically apply each filter in turn. In a filter gallery dialog box or workspace (Filter Gallery, Neural Filters, and Blur Gallery), you can combine multiple filters before you exit the dialog box or workspace.

Neural Filters gallery

In addition to the Neural Filters you try in the lesson, this gallery shows examples of other Neural Filters included with Photoshop. Some are useful for restoring and correcting images; others are fun ways to explore creatively. Adobe may update or change the available Neural Filters, so the exact list of Neural Filters in Photoshop may depend on the version installed on your computer.

Before. *After.*

Smart Portrait lets you tune details of portraits such as emotions, facial expressions, facial age, and gestures such as which way the eyes are looking. In this example, the head was turned slightly forward.

Before. *After.*

Skin Smoothing can reduce acne, blemishes, and other skin irregularities, while preserving the overall character of the skin and maintaining the sharpness of facial features such as eyes.

Super Zoom, 3x.

Super Zoom is a convenient way to enlarge part of a photo to use as a portrait. For example, you can pick out one person in a group photo and create an enhanced, sharpened enlargement for a profile picture. Or, if a person's face is too small in the middle of a smartphone photo, you can fill more of the frame with their face. Unlike many scaling methods, Super Zoom offers detail enhancement, noise reduction, and JPEG artifact removal powered by machine learning. Super Zoom is optimized for portraits, but you can try it with other types of subjects.

Image © mangostock. Shutterstock

Before.   After.

JPEG Artifacts Removal helps reduce unsightly side effects produced by applying JPEG image compression at a low quality setting. JPEG artifacts are typically seen as banding or blocks in areas that should be smooth. Although it's always better to use the highest quality version of an image, JPEG Artifacts Removal might save the day when a low-quality JPEG image is all that's available to you.

Before.   After.

Style Transfer lets you apply the artistic style of one image to another image. You can choose from a range of Artist Styles presets and then customize the look further using the filter's options. You can even apply your own style by clicking the Custom tab and selecting an image from your computer.

Improving Photoshop with your usage data and images

An important way that software developers improve features based on machine learning is to train them using examples of good results and bad results. Any company that uses machine learning needs a way to train the models that their software uses, ideally using examples that represent the interests of the customers of the software. But many software developers don't have very large data sets of actual customer files, and even if they store customer files in the cloud, they typically do not have customers' permission to use their files to train software.

To make it easier to improve Photoshop, Adobe added a Product Improvement pane to the Preferences dialog box in Photoshop. The purpose of the Photoshop Improvement Program is to request permission to use your images and usage data to help improve Photoshop features; this is not necessarily limited to machine learning. The "Yes, I'd like to participate" option is disabled by default, but if you want to participate, you can enable it. When it's enabled, Adobe researchers may collect usage data, cloud documents, and other images you edit in Photoshop.

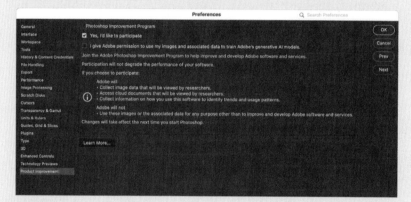

Whether or not you participate in the Photoshop Improvement Program is partly a personal decision. You may want to participate if you think your usage data might help improve how well Photoshop handles the kinds of image editing that you do.

However, if you work for a company or organization that handles confidential documents, if you need to protect the privacy or proprietary data of your clients, or if you are legally bound by nondisclosure agreements, you should be aware of the potential consequences of participating in the Photoshop Improvement Program.

For more information about how your usage information is handled, see the Adobe Product Improvement Program web page at adobe.com/privacy/apip.html.

Review questions

1 How does a filter in Neural Filters differ from other filters in Photoshop?

2 How does an Internet connection affect how you use Neural Filters?

3 Why is it typically best to choose any Neural Filters output option except Current Layer?

4 How can Neural Filters help restore digitized images of old prints and slides?

5 How can Neural Filters help with compositing multiple images?

Review answers

1 Neural Filters are trained using machine learning, so they are capable of results that are not attainable using conventional algorithmic filters.

2 If you are connected to the Internet, you can download Neural Filters and use Neural Filters that process image data in the cloud. If you choose to participate in the Photoshop Improvement Program, an Internet connection allows your usage data and images to be sent to Adobe for use by researchers.

3 The Current Layer option applies the results of Neural Filters to the selected layer, permanently changing it (destructive editing). The other Output options apply the results of Neural Filters to a separate layer or as a Smart Filter, preserving a layer's original state, so that you can start over at any time (nondestructive editing).

4 The Photo Restoration Neural Filters (and possibly Super Zoom) can help improve the quality of digitized images of old prints and slides. The Colorize Neural Filter can re-create colors for a black-and-white photo. JPEG Artifacts Removal can improve images that were saved at a low-quality JPEG compression setting. Depth Blur can help focus attention on the subject of a photo.

5 Neural Filters such as Landscape Mixer, Harmonization, and Color Transfer can help unify a composite by making its layers more visually consistent with each other.

INDEX

SYMBOLS
32 Bits/Channel mode 309

A
actions
    playing 344
    recording 340–345
    sets 340
Actions panel 340
Add Artboard button 348
Add Audio option 274
Add Layer Mask button 120
Add Media button 272
Add Noise filter 241
adjustment layers
    about 114–115
    Black & White 62
    Brightness/Contrast 238
    Channel Mixer 238
    Curves 126–127
    Exposure 239
    Hue/Saturation 114, 212
    Levels 136
Adobe After Effects 308
Adobe Bridge
    installing 3
    Load Files into Photoshop Layers
        command 225
    opening files in Camera Raw from 290
    opening files in Photoshop from 44
    previewing a file 134, 268
Adobe Camera Raw
    about 289
    adjusting white balance in 294
    AI Denoise 321
    Before/After Views button 291, 296
    cameras supported by 290
    Clone tool 312
    Content-Aware Remove tool 312
    Enhance command 321

    file formats for saving changes 308
    filmstrip 311
    filter 317
    gradient masks 322
    Heal tool 312
    histogram 300
    masks panel 291, 314
    Open as Object button 305
    opening images in 290
    profiles 293
    Raw Details 321
    saving files from 303–304
    Select Background 299, 322
    Select Objects 322
    Select People 299, 318, 322
    Select Sky 299, 322
    Select Subject 299, 322
    Super Resolution 321
    synchronizing settings across images 302
    version 288
    workspace 292
Adobe Capture 216
Adobe Creative Cloud
    installing applications 3
    mobile apps 216
    portfolio online 378
Adobe Creative Cloud desktop application 3, 7
Adobe DNG (Digital Negative) file format 290,
    307, 308, 309, 323
Adobe Firefly 40
Adobe Fonts 4, 26, 182, 193, 196
Adobe Generator 346
Adobe Illustrator 202, 308
Adobe InDesign 185, 308
Adobe Lightroom 11
Adobe Lightroom Classic 306–307
Adobe PDF (Portable Document Format)
    Photoshop PDF format 193
    printing on press 360

Adobe Photoshop
  installing 3
  new features 2
  resetting default preferences 10
  starting 4, 10
  work area 10–41
Adobe Photoshop Classroom in a Book
    2024 Release
  about 1
  lesson files and Web Edition 5
  prerequisites 2
Adobe Portfolio 378–380
Adobe PostScript 360
Adobe Raw profile 293
Adobe Stock 12
  designing with 120
  Libraries panel import 103
  licensing 120
  Search Adobe Stock command 94
AI Denoise, in Adobe Camera Raw 321
alpha channels 157
anchor points 203, 206
animating
  Pan & Zoom effect 279
  position 275
  text 275–278
animation, frame 282
anti-aliasing 76
applying an edit 15
arrow keys, nudging with 75–76
artboards
  about 346
  adding 348
  duplicating 346
  exporting 354
  mobile devices and 349
  presets for sizes 348
  resizing 351
Artboard tool 348, 351
audio, in a video timeline
  adding 273
  fading 274
  muting 274–275
Audio track 274
Auto-Align Layers 146
automating tasks 340–346
Auto-Select option 116
AVIF file format 308, 309

B
background layer
  about 90, 92
  converting to a regular layer 92, 342
  erasing 95
background, removing 157
barrel distortion, correcting 141
batch processing. See actions
bitmap images
  overview 10
  vector graphics vs. 200–201
black and white, converting color images
  in Adobe Camera Raw 293
  in Photoshop 62
black point 297
Black & White adjustment layer 62
Blend Images Together option 135
blending modes
  applying to layers 99
  deciding which to use 100
  definition 98
  previewing 99, 100
Bloat tool in the Liquify filter 233
blog, Photoshop tips and info 7
blur
  Field Blur 132
  Iris Blur 130–131, 132, 238
  Path Blur 132, 133
  restore noise 133
  Spin Blur 132
  Tilt-Shift 132
Blur Effects panel 133
Blur Gallery 130–133
borders, adding 95, 116
Bridge. See Adobe Bridge
brightening an image 126–127, 136
Brightness/Contrast adjustment
    layer 238
bristle tips, for brushes 248
Browse In Bridge command 44
brushes
  loading with color 253
  presets. See brush presets
  rotation angle 257
  settings 249
Brushes panel 255
brush presets
  exporting 256
  loading 255–258
  painting with 258–260
  Brush Settings panel 249

Brush tool
  about 32
  Paint Symmetry 261
buttons, as web graphics
  creating 327–346
  duplicating 335

C
calibration, monitor 366
Calibration panel, in Adobe Camera
    Raw 299
Camera Raw. See Adobe Camera Raw
Canvas Size command 342
center, selecting from 80
Channel Mixer adjustment layer 238
channels. See color channels
Character panel 105, 195
character styles 185
checkerboard transparency indicator 95
chromatic aberration 141
Clarity, in Adobe Camera Raw 311, 317
Classroom in a Book. See Adobe
    Photoshop Classroom in a Book
    2024 Release
Clean Brush After Every Stroke
    icon 252
Clean Brush option 253
clipping masks
  about 157, 179
  creating 115, 182–184, 363
  indicator 183
  shortcut 183
Clone Stamp tool 60
closing a Photoshop file 12
Cloud Documents
  about 67
  opening 11, 68
  saving 68
Clouds filter 103
CMYK color mode, converting to 368
CMYK color model 366, 367
collaborating
  libraries and 216
  sharing an image 16
color
  additive 367
  adjusting overall 51
  changing foreground 31
  channels. See color channels
  converting to black and white 62

color (continued)
    default text 182
    fonts 195
    foreground and background 31
    management. See color management
    mixing with the Mixer Brush 252
    out-of-gamut 368
    previewing gamut clipping 368
    sampling 31, 249
    softening edge transitions 76
Color blending mode 100, 234
Color Burn blending mode 100
color casts, removing 51
color channels 157, 290, 364, 373–375
Color Dodge blending mode 100
color gamut. See gamut
Color Grading panel, in Adobe Camera
    Raw 299
Colorize Neural Filter 387
color management 366–369, 367, 376
Color Mixer panel, in Adobe Camera
    Raw 299
color profile. See profiles, color
Color Range command 84, 318
color samplers, in Adobe Camera
    Raw 291
color separations 374
Color Settings dialog box 367–368
color settings, saving and restoring 6
color space 366
combining images
    using Adobe Bridge 225
    by dragging layers 93–96
    into an HDR merge 309
    into a panorama 134–137, 309
    using Place Embedded/Linked
        commands 14
    with different perspectives 147–151
Commit button 86, 101
committing (applying) an edit 15
compositing. See combining images
Content Authenticity Initiative 40
Content-Aware Crop 138
Content-Aware Fill for panoramas 135
Content-Aware Move tool 60, 152
Content-Aware Remove tool, in Adobe
    Camera Raw 312
Content Credentials 40
Content panel, in Bridge 45
context menus 91, 98, 119, 184, 193
Contextual Task Bar 15

Contrast slider in Camera Raw 297
Control Timeline Magnification
    slider 272
Copy command 93
copying
    anti-aliasing edges 76
    commands 83
    images 119, 371
    layers 93, 93–95
    selected pixels 82, 83
    settings in Camera Raw 302
Copy Merged command 83
corner points 203
Create Video Animation 282
Create Video Timeline 270
Creative Cloud. See Adobe
    Creative Cloud
Crop and Straighten Photos
    command 53
Crop tool 47–50, 86–87
    in Adobe Camera Raw 291
    clearing settings 50
    crop shield 50
    leveling 50
Cross Fade transition 280
Curvature Pen tool 201, 202, 205
curved paths 203
Curve panel, in Adobe Camera Raw 299
Curves adjustment layer 51, 126

D
Darken blending mode 100
Darker Color blending mode 100
Decontaminate Colors option 167
defaults
    in Adobe Camera Raw 321
    resetting Photoshop 5, 10
Define Custom Shape command 217
Define Pattern command 173
Delete Cropped Pixels option 50
deleting documents
    from Adobe Camera Raw 291
    from Cloud Documents 69
depth map 131
depth of field, extending 144
Deselect command 72
Detail panel, in Adobe Camera Raw 300
Difference blending mode 100
Difference Clouds filter 237
Direct Selection tool 203, 211
Discover panel 6

discretionary ligatures 195
distortions, correcting 147
DNG. See Adobe DNG (Digital Negative)
    file format
docking panels 30
document size, displaying 16, 118
document window
    fitting image to 81
    scrolling 20
    Status Bar 18
dots per inch (dpi) 49
drag-and-drop importing 103
Drop Shadow layer style 337, 342
drop shadows 110–111, 112
duplicating
    buttons 335–339
    images 119, 371
    layers 335
duration of video clips, changing 274

E
educators, resources for 7
Elliptical Marquee tool
    centering selection 80
    circular selection 74
    in Tools panel 66
emoji fonts 195
Enhance command, in Adobe Camera
    Raw 321
Enhance Edge option 71
enlargement 394
Exclusion blending mode 100
Expand command 73
Export As command 354, 355
exporting
    Adobe Camera Raw edited version
        290, 303–309, 321
    artboards 354
    brushes 256
    layers as separate files 355
    video 281
Exposure adjustment layer 239
Extras command 76
Eyedropper tool 31, 32, 249
eye icon, in the Layers panel 91

F
face adjustments
    with healing tools 312
    with Liquify filter 128, 228
    with Smart Portrait filter 394

Face-Aware Liquify filter 128
fading audio 274
Farrer, Lisa 408
Faulkner, Andrew 264
Feather command 76
feathering 76
Field Blur 132
file formats. *See name of format*
file size 49
fills
    foreground color 117
    gradient 106
    pattern 173
    shape layer 201
filmstrip, Adobe Camera Raw 291
filtering lists
    filmstrip in Camera Raw 291
    Layers panel 99
filters 393
    adding clouds with 102
    Add Noise 241
    Adobe Camera Raw 317
    Difference Clouds 237
    Liquify 228–229
    Neural Filters 384
    Smart Filters. *See Smart Filters*
    Smart Sharpen 61, 341
    where to find different 393
Find. *See Search command*
Fit On Screen command 81
    Hand tool shortcut 80
Flatten Image command. *See flattening*
flattening 52, 118, 360
fonts
    alternates 195
    changing in the options bar 26
    color 195
    emoji 195
    Font Similarity 193
    formats 178
    installing 4
    OpenType 195
    PostScript 195
    previewing in context 181
    selecting 180
    special characters 194
    variable 195
Font Similarity option 193
Foreground and Background
    colors 31, 108
forum, Photoshop community 7

four-color printing (CMYK) 367
fractions 195
frames 327
Frame tool 327
Freeform Pen tool 201
freehand selections 77–78
Free Transform command 226, 228
    moving with 231
    options bar settings 349
    resizing with 101
    rotating with 187
Free Transform Path command 171

G

gamut, color
    colors outside of 368–369
    defined 366
Gamut Warning 368–369
Generative Credits 40
Generative Expand 138
Generative Fill 36–38, 40, 57–59
Generator. *See Adobe Generator*
GIF animation 282
GIF format 90, 282, 346
Global Light option 110
Glyphs panel 194, 195
Go To First Frame button 273
GPU. *See graphics hardware*
GPU acceleration 3
gradients
    editing 109
    listing by name 107
    masks in Adobe Camera Raw 322
Gradients panel 108
Gradient tool 108
Graham, Jay 306, 408
graphics hardware 3
grid
    in Adobe Camera Raw 291
    in Lens Correction filter 142
guides
    adding 179
    ruler 332
    Smart Guides 220

H

Hand tool 80
Hard Light blending mode 100
Hard Mix blending mode 100
Harmonization Neural Filter 391

HDR, in Adobe Camera Raw
    HDR editing 303, 308, 309
    HDR merge 309
Healing Brush tool 56, 60
Heal tool, in Adobe Camera Raw
    291, 312
HEIF format 131
Help, Photoshop 7
hiding
    layers 94
    selection edges 76–77
HiDPI 49, 356
histogram
    Camera Raw 291, 300
    in Curves and Levels adjustment
        layers 52, 365
History panel 237–242
Home screen 11
Horizontal Type tool 26, 105, 180
hue, adjusting for printing 371
Hue blending mode 100
Hue/Saturation adjustment layers 212

I

Illustrator. *See Adobe Illustrator*
importing. *See also Place Embedded*
        command, Place Linked command
    audio 273
    embedded Smart Objects 345
    multiple files from Bridge 225
InDesign. *See Adobe InDesign*
Info panel 327, 332
inkjet printers 376
Inner Shadow layer style 183
installing the software 3
integrated graphics 3
interface. *See user interface*
International Color Consortium
    (ICC) 366
iPad, Apple 67
iPhone, designing for 348
Iris Blur 130–131, 132, 238
Isolate Layers command 99

J

JPEG Artifacts Removal Neural
    Filter 395
JPEG file format
    Camera Raw and 290, 303, 308
    compared to other formats 308
    compression artifacts 395

JPEG file format *(continued)*
    Export As 354
    image quality degradation 307
    type quality 193
    web design 346
JPEG XL file format 308, 309

K
Kent, Lynette 264
keyboard shortcuts
    customizing 254
    duplicating 82
keyframes
    animating with 275
    appearance of 275
    moving to the next or previous 276
Kost, Julieanne 7, 162, 184, 201, 254, 408

L
Landscape Mixer Neural Filter 390
Large Document Format 308
Lasso tools 66, 77–78
layer comps 118
layer effects
    adding 110–115
    updating 116
layers
    about 90
    adding 102–103
    Background 92
    blending modes 98–99
    converting Background 92, 342
    copying 93–95
    copying and centering 93, 97
    copying and merging 83
    copying and pasting 93
    copying to other 93
    duplicating 98, 335
    effects. *See* layer effects; *See
        also* layer styles
    exporting individually 355
    flattening 118, 119
    generating images from 346
    groups 332
    hiding and showing 91, 94, 95
    linking 101–103
    locking 91
    masks 157
    merging visible 118
    opacity 98
    overview 90

    painting 234
    rearranging 96–98
    renaming 93
    resizing 101–103
    rotating 101
    saving in GIF or JPEG formats 90
    showing and hiding 94
    styles. *See* layer styles
    thumbnail icons 91
    transforming 101
    transparency 98–99
    type 105
Layers panel
    filtering 99
    overview 91–92
layer styles 393
    adding to type 183
    applying 106–109, 110–113
    in Creative Cloud Libraries 111
    Drop Shadow 110, 113, 337, 342
    overview 106, 110
    presets 219
    Satin 113
    Stroke 112, 338
leading 192
learning resources for Adobe
        Photoshop 6
Learn tutorials 12
Lee, Megan 262
Lens Correction filter 141–143
lens flaws, correcting 141–143
lesson files, accessing 5
Levels adjustment layers 52–53, 136
Libraries, Creative Cloud
    Adobe Stock 103
    color swatches 103
    images 103
    layer styles 111
    linked Smart Objects 216
    mobile apps 216
Libraries panel 120
licensing, Adobe Stock 120
ligatures 195
Lighten blending mode 100
lightening an image 126–127, 136
Lighter Color blending mode 100
Light panel, in Adobe Camera Raw 297
Lightroom. *See* Adobe Lightroom Classic
Lightroom photos online storage 41
Linear Burn blending mode 100
Linear Dodge blending mode 100

linear gradients 102–104
Linear Light blending mode 100
Liquify, Face-Aware filter 128
Liquify filter 228–229
Load Files Into Photoshop Layers
    command 225
low resolution images, upscaling
    243, 394
luminance mask 84, 322
Luminosity blending mode 100

M
machine learning 57, 66, 84, 159, 196,
    243, 297, 321, 322, 384, 396
macros. *See* actions
Magic Wand tool 66, 70–71
Magnetic Lasso tool 66, 79–80
magnification. *See* Zoom tool
    document 18–20
    Timeline panel 272
magnifying glass. *See* Zoom tool
mandalas, painting 261
marching ants. *See* selection marquee
marquee tools 66
masks 156
    in Adobe Camera Raw 299, 314
    channel 157
    creating 157–160
    luminance 84
    overview 156
    refining 162–167
    compared to selections 156
    terminology 157
    vector 157
Match Font command 196
megapixels 48
memory (hardware) 3
Merge Visible command 119
merging
    images 144
    images into a panorama 134
    images with different
        perspectives 147–151
    layers 118
mistakes, correcting 34–41
Mixer Brush tool
    about 248
    cleaning the brush 253
mixing colors
    with a photograph 255
    with Mixer Brush tool 252

mobile devices
    designing for, with artboards 349
    using with libraries 216
monitor calibration 366
More Image Settings button in Adobe
    Camera Raw
    321
motion blur effects 133
Motion panel 279
Move tool
    Auto-Select option 116
    moving selections 72
    scissors icon 81
moving
    layers. *See* Move tool
    panels 30
    selections 72–73
Multiply blending mode 100
muting audio 274–275

N

navigating
    in Adobe Camera Raw 291
    keyboard shortcuts 362
    using the Navigator panel 20
Navigator panel 20
Neural Filters 129, 384, 393
    compared to other filters 393
    downloading filters 386
    Output options 389
    previewing changes 386
    using 385
nondestructive filters 228
notes. *See* Note tool
    deleting 193
    Notes panel 191
Note tool 191
nudging layers 353
nudging selected pixels 75

O

Object Selection tool 73–74, 120
on-image adjustment tool. *See* targeted
    adjustment tool
opacity, changing 98–99
opening images in Camera Raw 290
Open Object button (in Camera
    Raw) 305
OpenType font format 178, 195
OpenType SVG 195

options bar 15
    reference point icon 349
    setting type options in 26
organizing photos 306–307
out-of-gamut color 368–369
output options, Neural Filters 389
output resolution, determining 49
Overlay blending mode 99, 100

P

painting
    layers 234
    wetness options 250
    with the Mixer Brush tool 246–260
painting gallery 262
Paint Symmetry option 261
panels
    adding to another group 30
    defined 15
    docking 30
    floating 30–31
    resizing 30
    undocking 30
panning with the Navigator panel 20
panoramas
    in Adobe Camera Raw 309
    in Photoshop 134–137
Pan & Zoom option 279
Paper Color option 370
paper, simulating white 370
paper size, print 376
paragraph styles 185
paragraph type 180
Paste command 93
Paste in Place command 83
Paste Into command 83, 244
Paste Outside command 83
Paste Profile Mismatch dialog box 242
Paste Without Formatting
    command 83, 191
pasting layers 93
Patch tool 60
Path Blur 132–133, 133
paths
    about 201
    adding type to 185–186
    closing 203
    compared to shapes 209
    converting to/from selection 212
    drawing 202–207
    drawing curved segments 203

    drawing straight segments 203
    editing 211
    moving 211
    saving 203
    work path 203
Path Selection tool 211
Paths panel 204
patterns
    Pattern command 173
    Pattern Preview command 171
    Patterns panel 219
patterns, creating 170
Pavlov, Victoria 263
PDF. *See* Photoshop PDF file format
Pen tool. *See also* paths
    drawing paths 202–206
    keyboard shortcut 201
    overview 201–202, 203
    as selection tool 202
    setting options 204–205
people masks, in Adobe Camera
    Raw 318
Perspective Warp command 147
Photomerge 134–137
photo restoration, manual 54–55
Photo Restoration Neural Filter 386
Photoshop PDF file format 193, 308, 375
Photoshop Raw format (not camera raw
    format) 308
pincushion distortion 141
Pin Light blending mode 100
pixel dimensions 48
pixels
    compared to vector graphics 200
    defined 10
    path tools option 209
    resolution and 48
pixels per inch 48
Placed Linked command 328
Place Embedded command 182,
    345, 346
placeholders 327
PNG (Portable Network Graphics) file
    format 308, 346
Point Color panel, in Adobe Camera
    Raw 299
point type
    defined 180
    distorting 188–189
Polygonal Lasso tool 66
Polygon tool 170

portfolio. *See* Adobe Portfolio
position, animating in video 275
PostScript fonts 195
ppi (pixels per inch) 48
preferences
    Adobe Camera Raw 291
    Export 355
    gamut-warning color 369
    History States 242
    opening 22
    Product Improvement 40, 396
    restoring defaults 5, 10
    searching 22
    Units & Rulers 22, 327
Preserve Details (Enlargement)
    option 243
Preserve Numbers option 370
presets
    in Adobe Camera Raw 291, 294, 321
    artboard 348
    brush 255–258
    Curves panel 126
    Gradients panel 108
    overview 35–36
    shapes 215
    Styles panel 219
previewing
    colors for printing 369
    edits in dialog boxes 61
    files in Adobe Bridge 45
    fonts in context 181
printing
    CMYK model and 366–367
    on a desktop printer 376
    for press 359–381
    identifying out-of-gamut
        color 368–369
    for inkjet printers 376
    preparing images for 360
    proofing images onscreen 369–372
printing inks, simulating onscreen 370
privacy 396
process colors 367
profiles, Adobe Raw 293, 310
profiles, color
    CMYK 374
    display (monitor) 366
    ICC 366
    printer 370
proofing images 369–372

Properties panel 15–16, 108
    artboard editing 348
    clipping masks 363
    Curves adjustment 51
    targeted adjustment tool 62
    type settings 181
proxy icon 349
PSB (Large Document Format) 308
PSD (Photoshop) format 290, 308
public domain 40
Pucker tool in the Liquify filter 233
Puppet Warp command 168

Q

Quick Mask mode 84, 157
Quick Selection tool 66, 71, 159

R

radial symmetry 261
RAM. *See* memory (hardware)
range masks, in Adobe Camera Raw 322
raster images, overview 200
rate images, in Adobe Camera Raw 291
Raw Details, in Adobe Camera Raw 321
raw profiles 299
recording actions 340–344
Rectangular Marquee tool 66, 333
red eye, correcting 124–126
Red Eye Removal, Adobe Camera
    Raw 291
Red Eye tool 125–126
Redo command 34
reference point 349
Refine Edge. *See* Select and Mask
Refine Edge Brush tool 162
Remove tool 40, 53–54, 60
rendering video 281
repositioning selections 74
resampling 47
Reselect command 75
Reset, in Adobe Camera Raw 321
resizing. *See also* scaling
    from center 231
    layers 101
    panels 30
    proportionally 82
resolution
    about 48–49
    Adobe Stock images 94, 120
    best practices 307

bitmap images vs. vector
    graphics 200
Camera Raw 292, 304
Crop tool option 47
    increasing 243
    professional printing 360, 362
    screens of high and low 346, 356
    text 197
resolution, Retina/HiDPI scale
    factors 356
responsive design 347
Retina resolution 49, 356
retouching a portrait, in Adobe Camera
    Raw 310
retouching/repairing
    removing blemishes 53–54
    with the Remove tool 53
Return To Adobe Photoshop
    command 130
RGB color model 366, 367
rotating
    constraining 78
    layers 101
    paths 187
    in Puppet Warp 169
    selections 78
    stylus 257
rounded corners, creating 172
ruler guides 179, 332
rulers 22, 180

S

sampling colors 31, 249
Satin layer style 113
Saturation blending mode 100
saturation in Camera Raw 297
Save for Web (Legacy) command 346.
    See also Export As command
saving documents. *See also* exporting
    as Cloud Documents 68
    flattening and 118–121
    as Photoshop PDF format 193
    as Photoshop PDF 375
Scale to Fit Media print option 377
scaling
    animating 277
    using Crop tool 50
    document (Image Size command) 48
    using Free Transform command 101
    in Lens Correction filter 142

low resolution image 243
pattern fills 174
when printing 377
proportionally 82
raster (bitmap) images vs. vector
graphics 200
using Scale command 82
in Sky Replacement 140
using Free Transform command 349
Screen blending mode 100
screening, print 374
scrubbing numeric values 27
Search command 6
search icon 16
Search icon 11, 12
searching
Adobe Stock 120
Preferences 22
within Photoshop 11
Select and Mask command 157
selecting. See also selections
about 66
adding to selection 72
center point, from 80–81
by color 66
creating from a path 212
high-contrast edges 79–80
intersecting with existing 72
modifier keys 72, 75
new selection 72
non-transparent pixels 84
skin tones 318
a subject automatically 159
subtracting from 72
text 116
selection marquee 76
selections. See also selecting
circular 81
converting between pixels and
paths 85, 212
copying 83
duplicating 82
elliptical 73–81
feathering 76
freehand 66
geometric 66
hiding edges of 76
in Adobe Camera Raw 322
moving 72–73, 75, 81–82, 82
rotating 78–79

showing edges of 76
softening 76
selection tools 66–67
separations. See color separations
shapes
creating your own 217
defined 209
editing 217
presets 213–216
Share button 16
Share for Review command 191
sharpening
in Adobe Camera Raw 300–301
in Adobe Photoshop 61
sholby (artist) 263
shortcuts. See keyboard shortcuts
shortening video clips 274
Show/Hide Visibility column 95
side by side documents 93
sidecar XMP files 302
Single Column Marquee tool 66
Single Row Marquee tool 66
Skin Smoothing Neural Filter 394
skin tones, selecting 318
Sky Replacement command 140
Smart Filters 130, 149, 228–231, 233,
245, 389
Smart Guides 28, 82, 217, 220, 227
Smart Objects
converting layers to 228
editing 131, 230
embedded 345
icon badge 228
linked 216
Smart Filters and 228
Smart Portrait Neural Filter 394
Smart Sharpen filter 61, 341
smooth points 203
snapshots, in Adobe Camera Raw
291, 321
Soft Light blending mode 100
soft-proofing 369–372
sort, in Camera Raw 291
special characters 194
spell checking 184
Spin Blur 132
Spot Healing Brush tool 60
stacking order, changing 96–98
star, creating a 170
starting Photoshop 10

Status Bar 16, 18
Stop Recording button 344
stopwatch icon in Timeline panel 275
Straighten button 47, 138
strobe effect 133
Stroke layer style 112, 338
strokes 201
Structure option 152
Styles panel 219
Style Transfer 395
Super Resolution, in Adobe Camera
Raw 321
Super Zoom Neural Filter 394
SVG (Scalable Vector Graphics) file
format 195
swashes 195
symmetry, painting with 261
synchronizing Camera Raw settings 302
system requirements 3

T
tablet, graphics 249
tabs, document 15
targeted adjustment tool 62
teachers, resources for 7
temperature, image color 294
text. See also type
adding 180
applying edits 181
centering 105
creating 26, 105–106
default color 182
moving 106
selecting 116, 181
Texture, in Adobe Camera Raw 311,
317, 319
thumbnail icons, layer 91
TIFF (Tagged Image File Format)
camera raw images and 290–291, 308
compared to other formats 307, 308
type quality 193
Tilt-Shift Blur 132
timeline, creating 270
Timeline panel 269
changing the magnification 272
returning to the first frame 273
Tint
in Black & White adjustment
layers 62
in white balance (Camera Raw) 294

Toggle Last State command 237
Toggle Reference Point option 349
Tolerance option for Magic Wand
    tool 70
tone, adjusting 51–52
tools
    Brush tool 32
    Clone Stamp tool 60
    Content-Aware Move 152
    Content-Aware Move tool 60
    Crop tool 47
    Elliptical Marquee 244
    Eyedropper 31, 249
    Healing Brush tool 56, 60
    Horizontal Type tool 26
    keyboard shortcuts 201
    Lasso tool 77
    Magic Wand tool 70, 73
    Magnetic Lasso tool 77, 79
    Object Selection tool 58, 66, 73
    Patch tool 60
    Polygonal Lasso tool 77
    Quick Selection tool 71, 159
    Rectangle tool 333
    Remove tool 53, 60
    selection 66–67
    Spot Healing Brush tool 60
    using 17–23
Tools panel. See also tools
    selecting and using tools from 18–24
tool tips, displaying 18
tracing a photo 208
tracks, in a timeline 270
transforming 101. See also Free
    Transform command
Transform Selection command 74
transitions, video 280
transparency
    adjusting 98–99
    blending modes and 100
    recognizing (checkerboard) 95
Transparency & Gamut preference 369
TrueType fonts 195
tutorials built into Photoshop 11
type. See also text
    aligning 180
    clipping mask 179, 182–184
    creating 180–181
    on a path 185–186
    overview 178
    resizing 178

    setting options 180
    swashes 195
    tricks 184
    true fractions 195
    warping 188–189
typefaces. See fonts
Typekit. See Adobe Fonts
type layers
    creating new 105, 184
    selecting contents 184
Type tool 26–27

U

undocking panels 30
undoing steps
    with commands 34–35
    with the History panel 237–242
unit of measure 22
Units & Rulers command 22
Units & Rulers preferences 327
upscaling images 243, 394
Use Global Light command 110
user interface
    Adobe Camera Raw 292
    overview 10–12

V

Variable Fonts 195
vector graphics
    bitmap images vs. 200
    defined 10
    overview 200
vector masks 157
version, Photoshop 2
Vibrance, in Adobe Camera Raw
    297
video
    adding audio to 273
    adding pan and zoom
        effects 279–280
    adding transitions 280–281
    clip duration, changing 274
    exporting 281
    groups 273
    overview 268
    rendering 281
video card. See graphics hardware
vignetting 141
visibility icon. See eye icon
Vivid Light blending mode 100

W

warping
    images with the Liquify filter 228
    perspective 147–151
    Puppet Warp 168–169
    type 188–195
watermark, Adobe Stock 120
Weaver, Gawain 54, 408
web assets, exporting from layers 355
web design
    HiDPI 356
    responsive 347
    Retina 356
    workflow 324
Web Edition 5
Webster, Kyle T. 261
wetness options, in painting 250
White Balance tool (in Camera
    Raw) 294–296
white point 297
White Point eyedropper tool 364
work area 10–41
workflow preferences, Adobe Camera
    Raw 291
workflows
    color-managed 367–369
    compositing 90
    frame animation 282
    prepress 360
    professional photography 306–307
    video 266
    web design 325
work path 203
workspaces
    Graphics and Web 179
    Painting 249
    Workspaces menu 16
Workspaces menu 16

X

XMP files 302

Y

YouTube 281

Z

Zoom option in video 279
Zoom tool. See also magnification
    in Adobe Camera Raw 291
    shortcuts 162

Pearson's Commitment to Diversity, Equity, and Inclusion

Pearson is dedicated to creating bias-free content that reflects the diversity of all learners. We embrace the many dimensions of diversity, including but not limited to race, ethnicity, gender, socioeconomic status, ability, age, sexual orientation, and religious or political beliefs.

Education is a powerful force for equity and change in our world. It has the potential to deliver opportunities that improve lives and enable economic mobility. As we work with authors to create content for every product and service, we acknowledge our responsibility to demonstrate inclusivity and incorporate diverse scholarship so that everyone can achieve their potential through learning. As the world's leading learning company, we have a duty to help drive change and live up to our purpose to help more people create a better life for themselves and to create a better world.

Our ambition is to purposefully contribute to a world where:

- Everyone has an equitable and lifelong opportunity to succeed through learning.
- Our educational products and services are inclusive and represent the rich diversity of learners.
- Our educational content accurately reflects the histories and experiences of the learners we serve.
- Our educational content prompts deeper discussions with learners and motivates them to expand their own learning (and worldview).

While we work hard to present unbiased content, we want to hear from you about any concerns or needs with this Pearson product so that we can investigate and address them.

- Please contact us with concerns about any potential bias at pearson.com/report-bias.html.

Production Notes

Adobe Photoshop Classroom in a Book 2024 Release was created electronically using Adobe InDesign. Art was produced using Adobe InDesign, Adobe Illustrator, and Adobe Photoshop. The Myriad Pro and Warnock Pro OpenType families of typefaces were used throughout this book. For information about OpenType and Adobe fonts, visit adobe.com/type/opentype/.

References to company names in the lessons are for demonstration purposes only and are not intended to refer to any actual organization or person.

Images

Photographic images and illustrations are intended for use with this book's lessons only.

Lesson 1 arch image: © Styve Reineck, Shutterstock

Lesson 2 autumn image: © gillmar, Shutterstock

Lesson 4 ukulele image from Adobe Stock, stock.adobe.com

Lesson 11: Sailboat video © Openfinal, Shutterstock; Fushimi Inari Shrine video © Guitar photographer / Shutterstock; Vitala temple video © Krothapalli Ravindra Babu / 123RF; trailer music © Vladislav Litvinenko / 123RF; arch image: © Styve Reineck, Shutterstock

Lesson 15 head shots: © Djomas, Shutterstock; photo of pair in fabric shop: © mangostock, Shutterstock; restoring an antique photo: © Oleksandra Vasylenko, Shutterstock; Martian landscape with craters: © Jurik Peter, Shutterstock; photo of boy with bicycle: © Elzbieta Sekowska, Shutterstock; Red cape superhero: © sunlight19, Shutterstock

Team credits

The following individuals contributed to the development of *Adobe Photoshop Classroom in a Book 2024 Release*:

Writer and Designer: Conrad Chavez

Illustrator and Compositor: David Van Ness

Project Manager: Anne-Marie Praetzel

Copyeditor and Proofreader: Kim Wimpsett

Keystroke Reviewer: Megan Ahearn

Indexer: Conrad Chavez

Technical Reviewer: David Van Ness

Production Assistant: Giacomo Di Domenico

Interior Design: Mimi Heft

Art Director: Conrad Chavez

Adobe Press Executive Editor: Laura Norman

Adobe Press Production Editor: Tracey Croom

Adobe Press Associate Editor: Anshul Sharma

Contributors

Jay Graham began his career designing and building custom homes. He has been a professional photographer for more than 25 years, with clients in the advertising, architectural, editorial, and travel industries. He contributed the "Pro photo workflow" tips in Lesson 12. www.jaygraham.com

Lisa Farrer is a photographer based in Marin County, CA. She contributed photography for Lesson 12.

Julieanne Kost is a veteran Adobe product evangelist.

Gawain Weaver has conserved and restored original works by artists ranging from Eadweard Muybridge to Man Ray, and from Ansel Adams to Cindy Sherman. He contributed to "Real-world photo restoration" in Lesson 2. www.gawainweaver.com

Special Thanks

We offer our sincere thanks to Stephen Nielson, Joel Baer, Russell Brown, Rikk Flohr, Steve Guilhamet, Meredith Payne Stotzner, Jeff Tranberry, and Pete Green for their support and help with this project. We couldn't have done it without you!